The IDEA MAGAZINE FOR TEACHERS.
MAILBOX.

2004–2005 YEARBOOK

The Education Center, Inc.
Greensboro, North Carolina

The Mailbox® 2004–2005 Kindergarten–Grade 1 Yearbook

Managing Editor, *The Mailbox* Magazine: Amy Erickson

Editorial Team: Becky S. Andrews, Kimberley Bruck, Karen P. Shelton, Diane Badden, Sharon Murphy, Karen A. Brudnak, Sarah Hamblet, Hope Rodgers, Dorothy C. McKinney

Production Team: Lisa K. Pitts, Margaret Freed (COVER ARTIST), Pam Crane, Rebecca Saunders, Jennifer Tipton Cappoen, Chris Curry, Sarah Foreman, Theresa Lewis Goode, Ivy L. Koonce, Clint Moore, Greg D. Rieves, Barry Slate, Donna K. Teal, Zane Williard, Tazmen Carlisle, Irene Harvley-Felder, Amy Kirtley-Hill, Kristy Parton, Cathy Edwards Simrell, Lynette Dickerson, Mark Rainey

ISBN 1-56234-662-8
ISSN 1088-5528

The Education Center, Inc.
P.O. Box 9753
Greensboro, NC 27429-0753   # a5105647   SA040

Look for *The Mailbox® 2005–2006 Kindergarten–Grade 1 Yearbook* in the summer of 2006. The Education Center, Inc., is the publisher of *The Mailbox®, Teacher's Helper®, The Mailbox® BOOKBAG®*, and *Learning®* magazines, as well as other fine products. Look for these wherever quality teacher materials are sold, or call 1-800-714-7991.

Contents

Arts & Crafts

Arts & Crafts

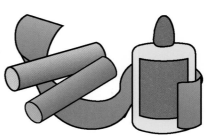

Desktop Apples

These nifty three-dimensional apples make great open house decorations! For best results, work with students in small groups to help each youngster complete his project.

Materials for one apple:
three 1" x 9" red, green, or yellow construction paper strips, each with a hole punched at either end and in the middle
4" brown chenille stem
2" x 3" piece of green construction paper
leaf template (approximately 1½" x 2½")
brad
scissors
access to a hole puncher

Steps:
1. Stack the strips. Insert the brad in the middle hole of each strip. Open the brad.
2. Place the strips on a work surface and fan them out as shown.
3. Trace the leaf on the green paper. Cut out the tracing.
4. Hole-punch one end of the leaf. Fold the leaf in half lengthwise and then unfold it.
5. Poke one end of the chenille stem through the hole in the leaf. Fold the stem in half.
6. Lift the end of one paper strip and curve it over so that the side that was on the work surface is facing up; insert both ends of the chenille stem into the hole. Working in one direction (clockwise or counterclockwise), thread the chenille stem onto each remaining strip as shown.
7. Adjust the height of the chenille stem as desired and open the ends to secure it.

Nancy Kirchmeier, McDonald Elementary School, Moscow, ID

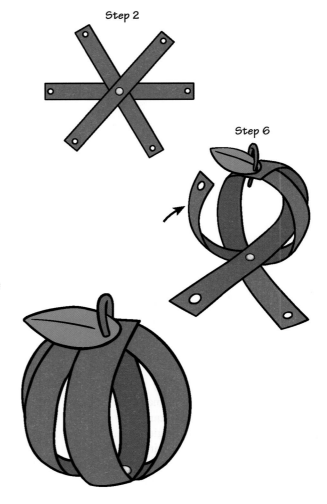

Step 2

Step 6

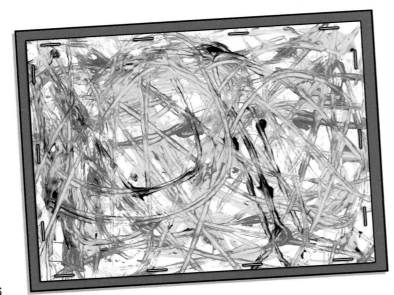

Colorful Tracks

Cruise into a color investigation with a toy car or two! To begin, place a sheet of white paper on a newspaper-covered surface. Squeeze drops of yellow paint in several different spots on the paper. Then push a toy car through the paint to make tracks. While the paint is wet, add a few drops of red and blue paint. Push the car through the different-colored paints, allowing the colors to mix and produce orange and green prints. Add more drops of yellow, red, or blue paint to achieve the desired results. After the artwork dries, staple it to a larger piece of construction paper to frame it. Impressive!

Shirley Tanaka
Francis Scott Key Elementary
San Francisco, CA

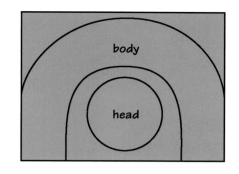

Cool Cat

Use this "purr-fect" project to complement a favorite cat story, a study of the letter *c,* or practice with the *-at* word family. To prepare tracers for students to share, cut a cat body and head from each of several 9" x 12" tagboard sheets (see the illustration).

To begin, use the tracers to make a construction paper body and head. Trim the ends of the body to resemble paws. From different-colored construction paper, cut several triangular shapes to use as stripes. Glue them onto the body so that the bases of the triangles extend slightly beyond the back of the cat. Allow the stripes to dry, and then trim the excess paper. From construction paper scraps, cut a tail and two ears. Use white paper and a marker to make two eyes. Glue the eyes and ears in place, and then glue on the head, tail, and several construction paper whiskers. Complete the colorful feline with marker details. Meow!

Johanna Litts
North Central Elementary
Hermansville, MI

Friendship Fish

Dazzle youngsters with this partner approach to painting! In advance, use eight-inch tagboard squares to make fish tracers for students to share. If desired, begin by reading aloud *The Rainbow Fish* by Marcus Pfister. Pair students and have the partners sit beside one another at a newspaper-covered surface. To make multicolored fish, the partners position a 12" x 18" sheet of white paper between them. They use watercolor paints to completely cover the paper with two or more colors. Then they allow the paint to dry. Next, they use a tracer to make two fish on the back of the paper. After they cut out the tracings, they add desired marker details to the front of their fish. Finally, they cut several small shapes from a piece of aluminum foil and glue them in place to resemble shimmery scales. How pretty!

adapted from an idea by Holly Romosier
Saint Paul School
Westerville, OH

7

Arts & Crafts

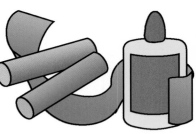

Freshly Picked!

Create a colorful window display with a crop of these apples and pumpkins. In advance, use 9" x 12" sheets of tagboard to prepare apple and pumpkin tracers for students to share. In the center of each tracer cut an opening that is smaller than a sandwich bag (see the illustration).

To begin, cut several seed shapes from construction paper or craft foam. Squeeze a small amount of glitter glue into a resealable plastic sandwich bag and then drop in the seeds. Press the bag to spread the glue; position the seeds as desired. Press out any air bubbles and then seal the bag. Next, use a tracer to prepare two apple or pumpkin shapes. Position the bag on one shape so that it covers the opening in the center. Tape the bag in place along all four sides. Glue on a construction paper stem. Then glue on the second apple (pumpkin) shape, aligning the edges. Add construction paper leaves if desired.

Sue Fleischmann, Sussex, WI

Wide-Eyed Owl

"Whooo" can resist such an adorable owl?

Materials for one owl:
brown paper lunch bag
two 2" yellow construction paper circles
two 4" x 8" brown construction paper rectangles
two 2" yellow construction paper squares
construction paper scraps (black, white, orange)
supply of brown and white tissue paper feathers
   (approximately 1½" x 2")
scissors
ruler
glue

Steps:
1. Cut about two inches from the open end of the bag.
2. Position the bag so that the flap is at the top. Glue on the yellow circles as shown. Cut smaller circles from the black and white paper. Glue them on to resemble eyes (see the illustration).
3. To make a beak, fold a piece of orange paper in half. Cut a triangle along the fold as shown. Glue the beak to the bag.
4. Beginning at the bottom of the project, glue on rows of feathers.
5. Draw a wing shape on each brown rectangle. Cut out the wings. On each side of the bag, tuck a wing between the folds and then glue it to the bottom fold.
6. Draw a foot on each yellow square. Cut it out and then glue it in place.

Step 3

Did You Know?
Some owls have wings that span 60 inches!

Kathleen Rose, Park Falls Elementary, Park Falls, WI

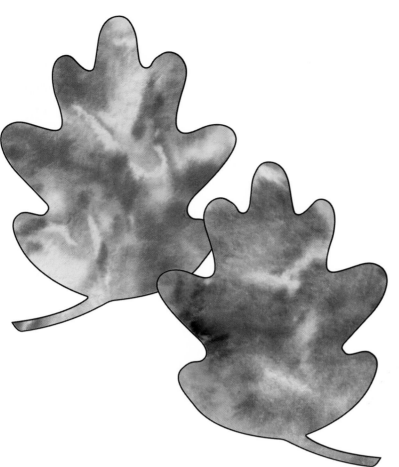

Fabulous Foliage

Whether you use these leaves to complete a fall display or to remind students of the letter *L,* they're sure to brighten your classroom! To make one leaf, place a coffee filter on a paper plate. Color the entire filter with watercolor markers in a variety of fall colors (green, orange, red, yellow). Next, use a water bottle to spray the filter just until there are no dry areas. Allow the filter to dry overnight. Then trace a tagboard leaf on the filter and cut out the tracing. It looks like fall!

Mandy Bayles
Watkins Magnet Elementary School
Hollywood, FL

Gobble! Gobble!

This totally cute turkey is the talk of the barnyard!

Materials for one turkey:
copy of the patterns on page 17
three 7" brown construction paper circles
4½" brown construction paper circle
1½ brown pipe cleaners
various colors of construction paper
   (for beak, wattle, feathers, feet)
scissors
glue
marker
access to a hole puncher

Steps:
1. Cut out the patterns. Use them to make a beak, a wattle, two feet, and four feathers from construction paper.
2. Use the marker to draw two eyes on the small circle. Fold the beak in half. Glue the beak and wattle to the circle.
3. Glue the feathers to one large circle as shown. Cut another large circle in half to make wings. Glue on the wings.
4. Cut the whole pipe cleaner in half. Wrap each of the three halves around the marker and then remove it.
5. Hole-punch the bottom of the head and the top of the third large circle. Connect them with a pipe cleaner as shown. Glue the large circle to the circle that has feathers.
6. Use a hole puncher and the pipe cleaners to connect the feet to the turkey as shown.

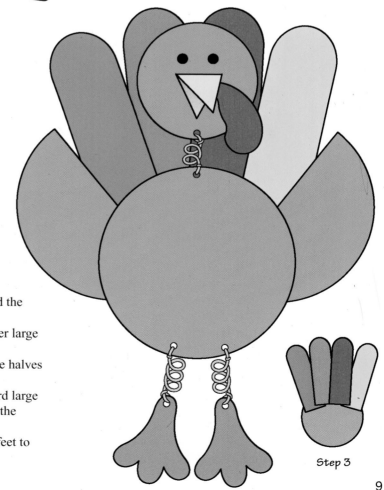

Step 3

Linda Oesterle, Eggert Road Elementary, Orchard Park, NY

9

Arts & Crafts

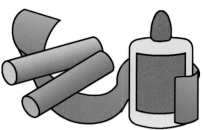

Tiny Toy Soldier

This adorable toy soldier can be made in a twinkling! For each student, make a white construction paper copy of the toy soldier pattern (page 18) and obtain a four-inch-long cardboard tube. To make a soldier, color the top stripe of a pattern black, the next stripe flesh tone, and the last two stripes red and blue as shown. Cut out the pattern. Squeeze a line of glue along each edge on the back of the pattern. Then roll the pattern around a cardboard tube so that the edges are aligned. Use the completed soldier as a tabletop decoration, or use a hole puncher and a six-inch pipe cleaner length to make it into an ornament. How cute!

Susan Brown, Southside Elementary, Tuscumbia, AL

"Hand-some" Reindeer

Clip, clop! It must be reindeer! If desired, showcase several reindeer on a rooftop display that you have posted on a hallway wall. Then use lengths of crepe paper to hook up the team.

Materials for one reindeer:
two 9" x 12" sheets of brown construction paper
9" x 12" sheet of tan construction paper
3" x 9" red construction paper rectangle
2" x 9" green construction paper rectangle
three 2" yellow circles
construction paper scraps (white, black, red, and brown)
black crayon
glue
scissors
ruler

Step 2

Steps:
1. Fold one sheet of brown paper in half to 6" x 9". Then unfold it.
2. Draw a reindeer head on one half of the paper, as shown, and then use the ruler to draw four legs on the other half. Cut out the head and legs.
3. Use construction paper scraps to make two eyes and a nose. Glue them in place.
4. Make two hand tracings on the tan paper. Cut out the tracings and then glue them to the head to resemble antlers.
5. Glue the red and green rectangles on the second sheet of brown paper, as shown, to resemble a harness.
6. Draw an X on each yellow circle. Glue the circles onto the harness.
7. Glue the legs in place. Cut our four black hooves and then glue them to the legs.
8. Fashion a tail from brown construction paper. Glue the tail and head to the body.

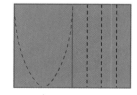

Did You Know?
Adult reindeer are about three or four feet tall and weigh up to 400 pounds!

Johanna Litts, North Central Area Schools, Hermansville, MI

Painted Pine

This "tree-rific" project is a perfect addition to a winter or holiday display. To begin, place a white paper triangle on a newspaper-covered surface. Pour a small amount of green tempera paint in a shallow dish. Dip a plastic fork into the paint and then press it on the paper repeatedly to make branchlike prints. Make additional prints to achieve a desired effect, reloading the paint as needed. Allow the paint to dry. Then glue on a brown construction paper trunk. If desired, decorate the tree with glitter and construction paper ornaments.

Sandra Patane, Fulton, NY

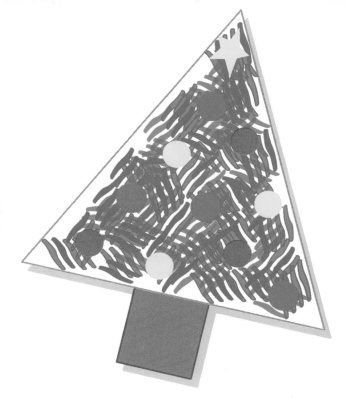

Birds of Peace

Create a reminder of Dr. Martin Luther King Jr.'s dream of peace with a flock of easy-to-make doves. To make one dove, cut out a white construction paper copy of the dove pattern on page 18. Carefully make several cuts in the tail to fringe it. Cut a beak shape from yellow construction paper and then glue it in place. Draw an eye on each side of the dove. Next, make two hand tracings on white construction paper and then cut them out. Glue the palm of a construction paper hand on each side of the dove's body, leaving the fingers free (see the illustration). Use a hole puncher and length of string to make a hanger. Then suspend the dove from the ceiling.

Susan DeRiso, Barrington, RI

Greetings!

A fluffy white snowpal peeks out from this wintry card! To make a card, fold a sheet of colorful construction paper in half. Trace a snowpal shape (with no arms) on the front of the card. Carefully cut out the tracing. Then, with the card closed, trace the inner edges of the opening. Next, open the card and use a black marker to trace the snowpal shape inside. Use a cotton swab and white paint to fill the shape with dot prints. After the paint dries, use provided arts-and-crafts materials to add facial features, a hat, a scarf, and any other desired details. Write a message to a loved one, and the snowy greeting will be ready for hand delivery!

adapted from an idea by Jelena Djordjic
Largo, FL

Arts & Crafts

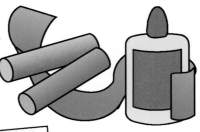

Cute Cards

Fancy fliers adorn these Valentine's Day greetings! In advance, prepare a supply of die-cut hearts. In the assortment, include double hearts (with the centers removed) or hearts of various sizes and shapes. To make one card, fold a 12" x 18" sheet of white construction paper in half to 9" x 12". Then use the side of an unwrapped blue crayon to lightly color the front of the folded paper. Next, glue on selected hearts in pairs to resemble butterflies as shown. Cut butterfly bodies, antennae, and spots from additional hearts or scrap paper. Then glue them in place. Inside the card, write a holiday message to a loved one and add desired heart decorations.

Annie Fitch
Echo Mountain Elementary School
Phoenix, AZ

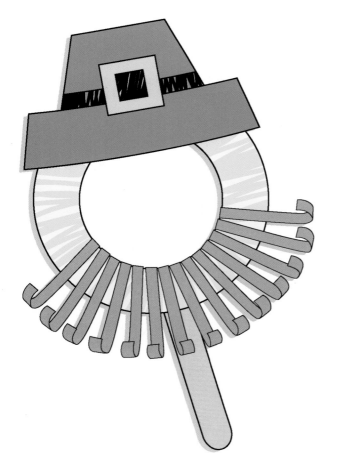

Leprechaun Look-Alikes

Leprechauns appear in a twinkling with this mask project!

Materials for one mask:
two 8" tagboard rings, each with a 4-inch opening
3" x 7" orange construction paper rectangle
5" x 8" green construction paper hat
2" square of yellow construction paper
crayons
glue
scissors
jumbo craft stick
masking tape

Steps:
1. Use a flesh-toned crayon to color one tagboard ring.
2. Glue the colored ring atop the second tagboard ring (colored side out).
3. Cut the orange construction paper into narrow, three-inch-long strips. Roll one end of each strip around a crayon and then unroll it.
4. Glue the strips onto the prepared ring to resemble a beard.
5. Color a black stripe on the hat. Color a black rectangle in the center of the yellow square to resemble a buckle.
6. Glue the buckle onto the hat. Glue the hat in place.
7. Tape the craft stick to the back of the mask to use as a handle.

Johanna Litts
North Central Elementary
Hermansville, MI

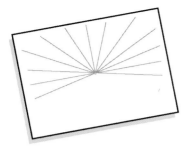

Proud Peacocks

Here's a fine feathered idea that's perfect for reinforcing the letter *p* or for inspiring alliterative writing. From 4" x 6" tagboard rectangles, cut bird templates similar to the one shown for students to share.

To begin, trace a template on construction paper and then cut out the tracing. Draw two eyes and glue on a construction paper beak. Draw a dot in the center of a 9" x 12" sheet of white paper. Use a ruler to draw several lines from the dot toward the top and sides of the paper (see the illustration). Make an ink thumbprint at the end of each line and ink fingerprints along the lines. Add more fingerprints as desired. Glue the bird in the center of the paper and then draw two legs.

Pam Baker
Lighthouse Education Center
St. Joseph, MI

Basket Buddies

These adorable bears and bunnies make nifty carriers for flash cards or holiday treats. For easy management, help students complete the project in small groups.

To make a bunny, fold up the bottom edge of a nine-inch white paper plate about 1¾ inches and then unfold it. Fold and unfold each side and the top edge in the same manner. Then staple the corners together as shown. (If desired, provide child-size staplers.) Next, cut out the center circle of a six-inch white paper plate. Draw a bunny face on it, glue on two construction paper bunny ears, and then glue the resulting head to the basket. Cut two paws from the paper plate scraps. Glue the paws and a pom-pom tail in place. Finally, make a handle by hole-punching the sides of the basket, threading a chenille stem through the holes, and then twisting the ends to secure it.

To make a bear, color the back of a nine-inch paper plate. With the colored side down, fold and staple the plate as described above. Next, draw a bear face on a 3½" construction paper circle and glue on two bear ears. Glue the resulting head to the basket. Cut two paws from the fluted portion of a six-inch white paper plate. Color the paws and then glue them on. Complete the basket with a chenille stem handle as stated above.

Shirley Tanaka
Francis Scott Key Elementary
San Francisco, CA

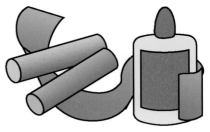

Arts & Crafts

Brilliant Butterflies

Your youngsters are sure to be all aflutter when they make these sparkly butterflies! To prepare, make a supply of butterfly templates sized to fit on large coffee filters (see the illustration). To make a butterfly, paint an entire coffee filter with watercolor paints. After the paint is dry, trace a template on the filter. Cut out the tracing. Next, cut two narrow construction paper strips to make antennae. Curl one end of each strip around a pencil and then glue the strips to one end of a jumbo craft stick as shown. Glue the craft stick in the center of the butterfly to resemble a body and then glue on colorful sequins to decorate it.

Leanne Gibbons
Boston Public Schools
Mattapan, MA

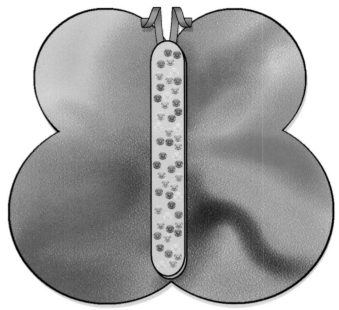

Bouquet of Blooms

This colorful card is perfect for Mother's Day or other springtime occasions! Have each child decorate the front of a card as described below. After the decorations are dry, help him complete his card with a desired message.

Materials for one card:
12" x 18" sheet of white construction paper
small amount of glue diluted with water
construction paper triangle cut from a six-inch square
12-inch length of curling ribbon, tied into a bow
several flowers cut from colorful tissue paper (approximately two inches across)
paintbrush

Steps:
1. Fold the paper in half to 9" x 12". Position the resulting card so that the fold is on the left-hand side.
2. Brush glue on the upper portion of the card's front cover.
3. Arrange the flowers on the glue, overlapping them as desired. Carefully brush on more glue, as needed, to secure the flowers.
4. Glue on the triangle as shown.
5. Glue the bow to the triangle.

adapted from an idea by Kristen Flaherty
Presumpscot Elementary School
Portland, ME

Fabulous Forsythia

If your youngsters see a bush with yellow blooms in the spring, it just might be a forsythia bush! Invite them to bring the springtime sight into the classroom with these striking pictures. To make a picture, carefully tear one long edge of a 5" x 12" strip of brown construction paper to resemble soil. Vertically position a 12" x 18" sheet of blue construction paper and then glue the brown paper along the bottom of it. Use a brown marker to draw several branches emerging from the soil. Gently twist narrow strips of yellow crepe paper (approximately ¾" x 2") to make blossoms as shown. Then glue the blossoms to the branches.

adapted from an idea by Beverly McCormick
East Brainerd Elementary
Chattanooga, TN

Nifty Nests

These delightful birds' nests are a terrific complement to a study of baby animals.

Materials for one nest:
brown paper lunch bag
piece of waxed paper to use as a workmat
small amount of brown shredded paper
2 blue cotton balls or medium-size pom-poms
orange and black construction paper scraps
glue
scissors
hole puncher

Steps:
1. Open the bag. Roll down the sides of the bag and crumple it until it resembles a bird's nest.
2. Set the nest on the waxed paper. Drizzle glue on the nest and then arrange pieces of shredded paper in the glue.
3. Glue one cotton ball atop the second cotton ball to represent a bird.
4. Fold a small piece of orange paper in half. Cut along the fold, as shown, to make a beak. Glue the beak in place.
5. Hole-punch the black paper to make two circles (eyes). Glue on the eyes.
6. Glue the bird in the nest.

Lynette Blonquist
North Summit Elementary
Coalville, UT

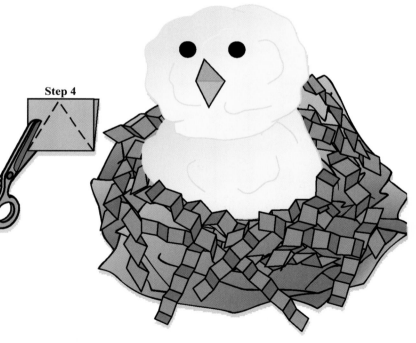

Step 4

Did You Know?
Some bird nests have been found containing unusual items such as bath towels, tin cans, paper clips, and boots!

"Hand-some" Flower

Brighten your classroom with a patch of painted posies! Set out paintbrushes and shallow dishes of tempera paint in various colors, including green. Also provide paper towels for easy cleanup.

To make one flower, vertically position a 12" x 18" sheet of white paper. Squeeze together the fingers of one of your hands. Brush a thin layer of colorful paint on your fingers and palm, keeping your thumb free of paint. Then, near the top of your paper, make a print with your fingers pointing toward the middle of the paper. Make several more prints to resemble flower petals, as shown, reapplying the paint as needed. Use a fingertip to paint a green stem and then make two handprint leaves. After the paint dries, make colorful fingerprints to create the center of the flower.

Samantha Moyer, Oskaloosa Elementary, Oskaloosa, IA

Patriotic Hearts

Gear up for the Fourth of July by suspending several of these red, white, and blue mobiles from the ceiling.

Materials for one mobile:
7½" x 10" white construction paper heart
9" x 12" sheet of blue construction paper,
   cut in half lengthwise
red crayon
several small white stars
scissors
glue
string
access to a hole puncher

Steps:
1. Use a red crayon to draw several vertical stripes on both sides of the heart.
2. Glue the heart to a piece of blue paper as shown. Trim the excess blue paper.
3. Turn the heart over and then glue it to a second piece of blue paper. Trim the excess.
4. On each side of the heart, glue several stars to the blue paper.
5. Hole-punch the top of the heart. Thread a length of string through the hole and then tie the ends to make a hanger.

Johanna Litts, North Central Elementary, Hermansville, MI

Step 2

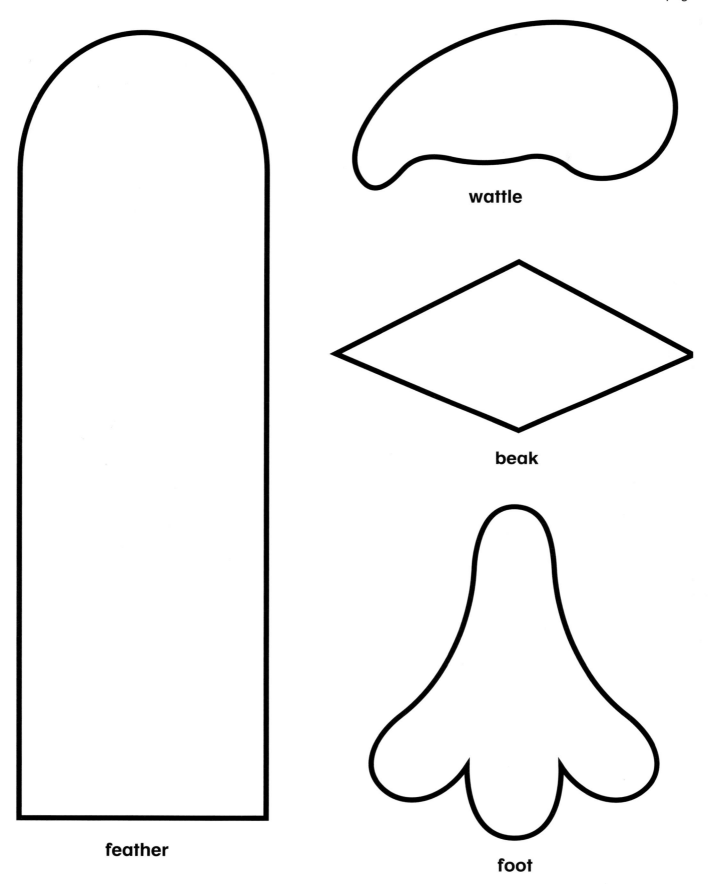

wattle

beak

feather

foot

Toy Soldier Pattern
Use with "Tiny Toy Soldier" on page 10.

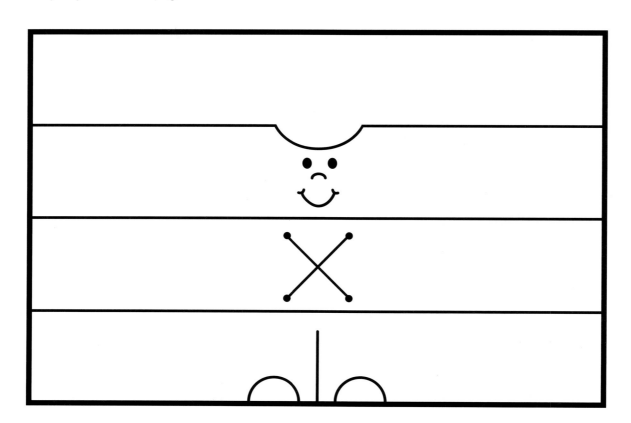

Dove Pattern
Use with "Birds of Peace" on page 11.

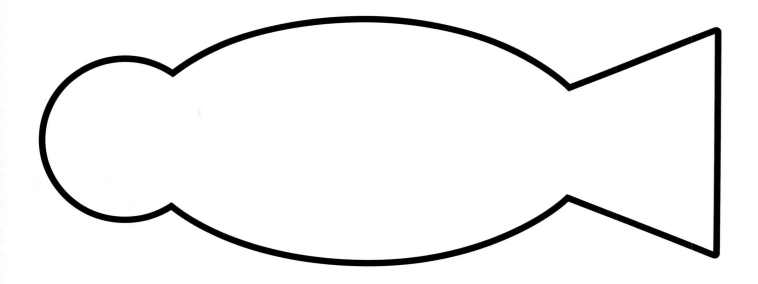

©The Education Center, Inc. • *The Mailbox*® • TEC42016 • Dec./Jan. 2004–5

Building Math Skills

Building

Round and Round
Counting

Add pizzazz to math time with a counting wand! To make a wand, cover a paper towel tube with colorful paper. Embellish the tube with numbers and then secure a decorated tagboard star to one end. To begin, stand with students in a circle and hold the wand. Explain that the number 10 is the special number for the first round. Then have students count off around the circle, beginning with the number 1, until a student says the special number. Present this youngster with the counting wand, and invite him to name a new special number to start another round. Continue in this manner as time allows.

adapted from an idea by Janet Bryce
Just Children School
Trevose, PA

Fancy Footwork
Sorting, comparing sets

Help students step ahead with sorting! Ask each child to remove one of her shoes. Then announce a sorting criterion, such as color, size, or type of shoe. Guide youngsters to sort their shoes into the corresponding categories. After each shoe is categorized, have students count the number of shoes in each group and compare the totals. Invite students to name a different criterion for more sorting fun!

adapted from an idea by Karen M. Smith
Pace, FL

Sidewalk Math
Addition, subtraction

With this outdoor activity, students will jump at the chance to explore addition. On a sidewalk or blacktopped surface, use chalk to prepare a number line with a grade-appropriate range of numbers. Ask students to stand along one side of the line. Then have each child take a turn solving an addition problem on the number line. For example, if the problem is 5 + 3, a student stands on the number 5 and jumps forward three spaces as his classmates count from 5. More advanced students may enjoy trying some simple subtraction problems too!

Betsy Lott, Davis Elementary, Greenwood, MS

Math Skills

Square by Square
Patterning

Make patterning a part of each day with colorful samples of student work. To prepare, give each child a paper strip divided into eight squares. Ask her to use two or three different-colored crayons to color the squares in a pattern of her choice. After each student signs the back of her completed pattern, collect students' strips. Each morning, post a randomly selected strip. Below the strip, display within student reach a length of adding machine tape that you have divided into blank squares—one per student. Throughout the morning, encourage each youngster to visit the display and color in the first blank square according to the pattern. Now that's a kid-pleasing way to practice copying and continuing patterns!

adapted from an idea by Jan Servideo, Stoneham, MA

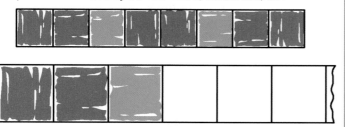

"Order-ly" Mice
Ordinal numbers

Ordinal numbers are the focus of this bright follow-up to *Seven Blind Mice* by Ed Young. Prepare a mouse cutout in each of these colors: red, green, yellow, purple, orange, blue, and white. Label each mouse with an ordinal number to show the order in which the mice check out the strange Something in the story. After reading the story aloud, scramble the mice and then guide volunteers to tape them on the board in order. Follow up with several relevant questions that include ordinal numbers, such as "Which mouse looks at the strange Something first?" or "What color is the third mouse?" Students are sure to strengthen their ordinal number skills in short order!

Laurie Mills, Stevenson Elementary, Stevenson, AL

first second third fourth fifth sixth seventh

Fishy Geometry
Shape identification

Students pair art and math with this fishy display idea. Have each youngster trace a fish template on the upper portion of a vertically positioned sheet of drawing paper. After he draws a face and colors his fish, have him glue on chosen construction paper shapes for decoration. Then instruct him to write how many of each shape he used (or ask him to dictate the information for you to write). Showcase students' completed work on a bulletin board titled "Shapely Fish."

Jane Hoogerwerf
St. Mary's Academy
Englewood, CO

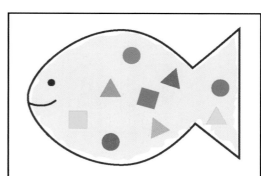

3 circles

4 triangles

2 squares

Building

Pumpkin Poll
Counting tally marks, comparing numbers

Here's a fresh way to introduce your students to the idea of an election. Display a pumpkin and tell students that they will vote on the following day to determine what type of face to give it. Present the choices and prompt discussion to build anticipation. On the election day, have each youngster complete a ballot similar to the one shown and then deposit it in a decorated box. After all of the votes are cast, ceremoniously remove the ballots one by one, and use tally marks to record the votes on the board. Ask students to determine the totals and compare the numbers to identify the winning choice. Then serve cider or another seasonal treat as you decorate the pumpkin!

Ada Goren
Winston-Salem, NC

Count On Caterpillars!
Comparing sets

They can creep and they can crawl, but that's not all. Caterpillars can also help your students compare sets! Give each student a large construction paper leaf and ten spiral pasta pieces (caterpillars). Write a number from 1 to 10 on the board; then have each child place that many caterpillars on her leaf. Lead students in counting their caterpillars to check their work. Next, guide students to determine whether they have more caterpillars on or off their leaves. Then ask each youngster to help her caterpillars "crawl" off her leaf to prepare for another number.

Jennifer Stinnett
Arlington Elementary
Arlington, TN

Cereal Lineup
Patterning

Sweeten color-patterning practice! Divide students into small groups. Give each group a bowl of Froot Loops cereal, several paper towels, and half of a pipe cleaner for each student. (Set aside some cereal for later student snacks.) On the paper towels, have the groups sort their cereal pieces by color. Next, instruct each student to curl up one end of his pipe cleaner. Ask him to thread several cereal pieces onto the opposite end to create a desired color pattern. Then have each group member, in turn, invite the rest of his group to identify his pattern. For more patterning fun, pair students and have each youngster create a pattern for his partner to copy. Math has never been so tempting!

Michele Michalski
Calvary Academy
Lakewood, NJ

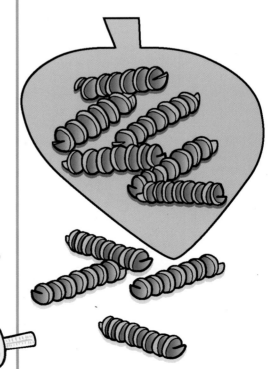

Math Skills

Mouse Math
Addition, subtraction

No doubt students will scurry to model math problems with this literature-based idea. Read aloud *Mouse Count* by Ellen Stoll Walsh for students' listening enjoyment. Then give each youngster a clear plastic cup and ten pom-poms to represent the jar and mice in the story. Pose story-related addition and subtraction problems for students to solve with their manipulatives. For example, you might say, "Ten mice are in the jar. Three mice climbed out. How many are left in the jar?" After students determine the answer to a problem, ask a volunteer to write the corresponding number sentence on the board.

Lisa A. Kelly
Orchard Lake, MI

Clueing In to Numbers
Number sense

This clue-filled version of number lotto is sure to be a hit! Prepare a set of number cards (1 to 12). Give each child a handful of game markers and a grid with four rows and three columns. Ask him to randomly label his grid spaces with the numbers 1 to 12. Shuffle the prepared cards and stack them facedown. If desired, draw a number line on the board for student reference.

To play one round, draw a card. Without revealing the number, give students a clue, such as "The number is between six and eight." Have each student place a game marker on her corresponding grid space. Then ask a volunteer to announce the described number; encourage students to check their grids. Place the card in a discard pile, draw another card, and continue in the same manner. Declare a child the winner after she marks four numbers in one column and calls out, "Number-o!"

Eva L. Graves
Derita Elementary School
Charlotte, NC

Measuring on the Move
Nonstandard measurement

Invite students to size up their math skills with a take-home kit. Place in a shoebox a supply of two different types of manipulatives, such as math links and drinking straws, and a recording sheet similar to the one shown. Add a parent note explaining that each student should measure three household items with each type of manipulative and complete the recording sheet. Establish a rotating schedule to ensure that each student has regular opportunities to use the kit. Replenish the materials as needed, and periodically substitute different manipulatives to keep student interest high.

Lindsey A. Vail
Highlands School
Braintree, MA

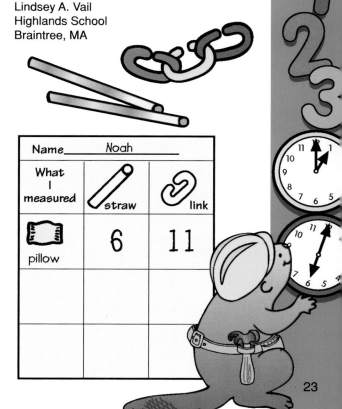

Name	Noah	
What I measured	straw	link
pillow	6	11

23

Shapely Pretzels
Geometry

This shape exploration is hard to resist! Give each student 12 pretzel sticks on a paper towel. Then announce various shape-related tasks for students to complete with their pretzels (see the suggestions below). After a desired number of tasks, invite each youngster to eat his tempting manipulatives!

- Make as many different triangles as you can.
- Make one triangle with all of your pretzels.
- Make one triangle and then compare it with a class-mate's triangle.
- Make a square and a rectangle.
- Make a rectangle with six pretzels.
- Make a rectangle with eight pretzels.

Carol Jacobs
Mountain View School
Ontario, CA

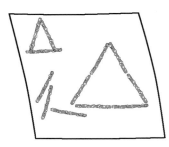

Dotty Over Addition!
Addition

Lots of dots add up to lots of math fun! Prepare a recording sheet, similar to the one shown, with four blank dominos and programming for number sentences. Copy the recording sheet to make a class supply. To complete the activity, a student presses the eraser of an unsharpened pencil on a black ink pad. He stamps up to six dots on each section of his first domino. Then he writes the corresponding number sentence. He prepares the remaining dominoes and writes the matching number sentences in a similar manner.

Wende Dickey
Trenton Elementary
Trenton, FL

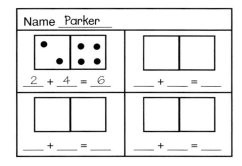

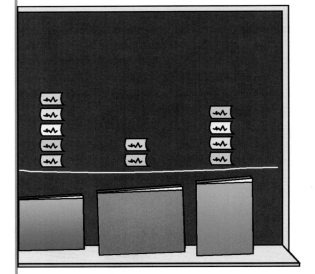

Which Book?
Data analysis

Here's a math activity that has a real-life purpose—deciding which storytime book to read next. At the beginning of a five-day school week, choose five books. Briefly tell students about each book and then set the books on your chalkboard ledge.

Next, draw a line above the books as shown. Give each student two sticky notes and have her write her name on them. Invite a few students at a time to post their sticky notes above their top two book choices so that columns are created. After all of the sticky notes are in place, guide students to interpret the displayed data. Then have them determine the order in which to read the books by identifying the book with the greatest number of votes, the book with the second greatest number of votes, and so on. (Decide with student input how to handle any ties.) Now that's a reading plan to count on!

Lisa Walcott
Schuylkill Haven Elementary
Schuylkill Haven, PA

Math Skills

Roll and Compare
Number sense

Two dice and 12 counters are the only supplies needed for this partner game. To begin, the players set the counters between them. Each player takes a die and rolls it. The player who rolls the greater number takes one counter. (If there is a tie, the players roll again.) The players continue rolling the dice and comparing numbers in this manner until all of the counters are claimed. The player who has the most counters wins. For a more challenging version, each player uses two dice and the players compare sums instead of individual numbers.

Eileen Miller
Olivet Elementary
Pittsgrove, NJ

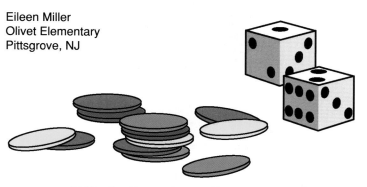

High-Scoring Teamwork
Review

Take aim at improved math skills with this easy-to-adapt activity. Prepare a class supply of flash cards to review a chosen skill such as identifying numbers or adding. Set a laundry basket in an open classroom area. Use masking tape to establish a throwing line a desired distance from the basket. Have students sit side by side alongside the throwing area.

To begin, explain that students will earn points as a team. Display a flash card and have the first student respond to it as appropriate. Then invite her to stand behind the line and toss a small foam ball into the basket. Award one point to the class for a correct response and a second point if the youngster makes the basket. After each student takes a turn, announce the total number of points. Challenge students to top their score during a later round of play!

Hilarie Hutt
Summit School
Summit, SD

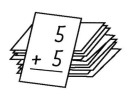

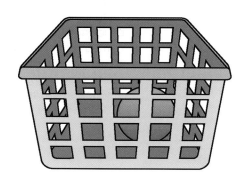

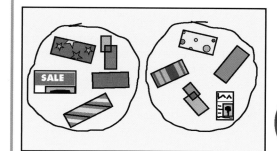

All Sorts of Paper!
Sorting by one attribute

Use this hands-on activity to focus on similarities and differences. Cut a large supply of strips (or rectangles) from various types of paper, such as construction paper, wrapping paper, wallpaper, tissue paper, and newspaper. Include strips that are the same color or size but different types of paper. Divide students into small groups. Give each group an assortment of strips, glue, and a large sheet of paper.

Next, invite students to compare and contrast the strips. Then have the students in each group sort their strips on their paper by an attribute of their choice. Instruct them to glue the strips in place and draw a ring around each set. After students complete their work, invite each group to show its paper to the class and tell how the strips are sorted. Showcase students' work on a bulletin board titled "Same and Different" to encourage additional discussion.

Lucia Kemp Henry
Fallon, NV

Building

Seasonal Search
Number sense, graphing

A number-related search launches this versatile idea! In advance, use various colors of construction paper to prepare two seasonal cutouts per student. (Or purchase seasonal craft foam cutouts.) Number the cutouts sequentially and then hide them throughout your classroom when your students are not present. Later, set your students in search of the cutouts, asking each youngster to find two of them. After the search, have students work together to complete one or more of the activities below.

- Estimate the number of cutouts. Count by twos to determine the actual number.
- Use reusable adhesive to arrange the cutouts on a wall in numerical order.
- Sort the cutouts by color and then prepare a graph to show how many cutouts there are of each color.

Shannon Adams
Waxahachie Faith Family Academy
Waxahachie, TX

Rainbow Rulers
Measurement

Try this bright approach to linear measurement. Give each child a copy of page 32. Have her color the boxes as indicated and then cut along the bold lines to make a rainbow ruler. Next, demonstrate how to use the ruler. To do this, position the red end of a ruler at the first dot on a chosen figure. Then announce the color of the section that is at the opposite dot and explain that the figure should be colored this color to indicate the length. Allow time for students to practice using their rulers. Then have each youngster measure her figures and color them as described.

Robbin Kemp
Happy World
East Windsor, NJ

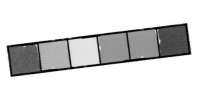

Lakeesha	Aaron
63	42
31	22
54	55

On a Roll!
Number sense

Sizing up numbers is twice as fun with a partner! Give each twosome two dice and one sheet of paper. In each pair, the students divide their paper into two columns and label their columns with their names as shown. Next, each partner, in turn, rolls both dice, arranges them to represent a two-digit number, and then writes the number below his name. The partners identify the greater two-digit number and circle it. They continue forming and comparing numbers in this manner as time allows. **For an easier version,** have each twosome use one die and compare one-digit numbers.

Heather Volkman
Messiah Lutheran School
St. Louis, MO

Math Skills

Sweet Combinations
Addition

Here's an addition activity that's simply irresistible! Give each child 15 M&M's candies, making sure that he has at least one candy of each color. Also give him a paper towel and a blank booklet that has three or more pages. Have each child sort his candies by color on his paper towel. Next, call out two colors and ask each youngster to determine how many candies he has of each color. Instruct him to illustrate the candies and write a corresponding addition sentence on a blank booklet page. Continue in this manner with different pairs of colors until each student's booklet is complete. Then invite youngsters to eat their manipulatives. Yum!

Teresa O'Brien-Tidy and Wendy Beaty
St. Helen School
Mississauga, Ontario, Canada

$4 + 2 = 6$

Quilt Blocks
Geometry

A colorful quilt takes shape with this pattern block project. Prepare a supply of construction paper pattern blocks. Give each child an eight-inch white square, glue, and access to the prepared pattern blocks. Have her glue selected pattern blocks on her square to form a desired design. After each student completes her work, invite her to show her square to the class and identify the types of shapes she used. Arrange students' completed squares on a bulletin board to resemble a quilt.

For more advanced students, label the displayed squares with letters for easy identification. Describe secretly chosen squares with math-related clues and challenge students to identify them.

Lara Renfroe
Heber Springs Elementary
Heber Springs, AR

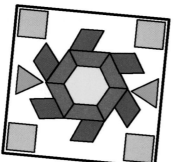

An Orderly Day
Time

Put students in the spotlight from time to time! Take photos of students engaged in various activities throughout one day, such as journal writing, calendar time, snack, lunch, recess, and centers. Display the developed photos in random order. After students identify each activity, help them arrange the photos on a bulletin board in chronological order. As students work, prompt them to use time-related vocabulary such as *morning, afternoon, before,* and *after.* If desired, label blank cards with the corresponding times; have students read each card and post it by the appropriate photo. My, how time flies!

Lindsey Vail
Birthplace of John Quincy Adams School
Quincy, MA

Building

Stick Lineup
Number sense

Tailor this small-group activity to reinforce any range of numbers. Obtain a supply of jumbo craft sticks. Number the sticks with a chosen sequence of numbers, labeling both sides of each stick. Label a canister with the number range and then stand the sticks in the canister.

To begin, one student spills the sticks from the canister. Then each student, in turn, picks up one stick and sets it on a work surface to help arrange the numbers in a row from least to greatest. The youngsters continue taking turns until the sequence is complete. To modify the activity for skip-counting practice, number the sticks by twos, fives, or tens.

Heather Graley
Grace Christian School
Blacklick, OH

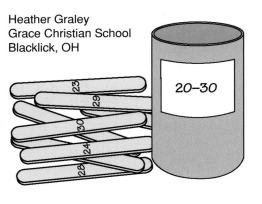

Flitter, Flutter!
Subtraction

Spring into subtraction with fancy flyers! Prepare a form similar to the one shown and then copy it to make a class supply. In the first two blanks on each child's copy, write numbers appropriate for the youngster's skill level. After familiarizing students with the poem, have each student glue his poem near the top of a large sheet of drawing paper. Ask him to draw himself and the number of butterflies first mentioned in the poem. Instruct him to cross out the appropriate number of butterflies to show how many fly away. Then have him complete his form with the corresponding subtraction sentence.

Brenda Sharpe
Fairview Early Childhood
  Center
Rocky Mount, NC

> ___ butterflies fluttering by me.
>
> ___ fly away as you can see.
>
> How many butterflies are left by me?
>
> ___ — ___ = ___

Veggie Sums
Addition

Here's a "soup-er" approach to addition! Place in a cooking pan a ladle and several orange and white Unifix cubes (diced carrots and potatoes). Give each student an individual chalkboard or whiteboard and writing supplies.

Next, invite volunteers to remove two or three scoops of cubes. Have them sort the cubes by color and then announce the number of cubes in each set. After each youngster adds the two numbers on his board, call out, "Soup's on!" At this signal, each student displays her work for your approval. Confirm the correct answer and then return the cubes to the pot for more addition fun. **For more advanced students,** add green Unifix cubes (green beans), and have the youngsters cook up problems with three addends.

Deborah Patrick
Park Forest Elementary
State College, PA

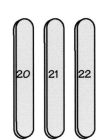

Math Skills

Presenting the Facts!
Fact families

With this class activity, every student will be eager to be part of the family—the fact family, that is! Write each number in a chosen fact family on a separate blank card. Also prepare a plus sign, a minus sign, and an equal sign card. Give each card to a different student and have the cardholders stand at the front of the classroom. Guide the youngsters to form a number sentence with the cards. Have the remaining students read the number sentence aloud; ask a volunteer to write it on the board. Encourage the youngsters to continue forming number sentences until the entire fact family is written. Assign new roles to explore different fact families!

Jill Hetsler
West Carlisle School
LaGrange, OH

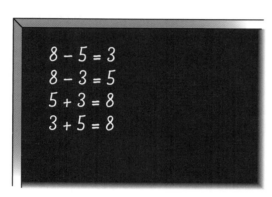

$$8 - 5 = 3$$
$$8 - 3 = 5$$
$$5 + 3 = 8$$
$$3 + 5 = 8$$

What's in the Bug Jar?
Data analysis

Creepy-crawly critters are the topic of this graphing activity! Obtain a supply of three different types of small toy insects. Place them in a plastic bug jar or another unbreakable container. Give each student in a small group a copy of an appropriately labeled graph (see the illustration). Have the youngsters remove the bugs from the jar, sort them, and then record on their graphs the number of each type of bug. Prompt discussion to help students interpret their completed graphs. **For more advanced students,** ask each youngster to write two sentences about his graph.

Shelly Lanier
Reeds Elementary School
Lexington, NC

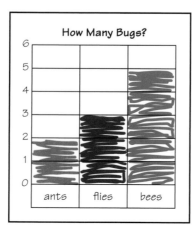

How Many Bugs?

(bar graph with categories: ants, flies, bees; y-axis 0–6)

Pizza Wheel
Fractions

Serve up a slice of fractions with this hands-on idea. For each student, draw two lines to visually divide a white paper plate into quarters. To begin, ask each child to color a white paper plate so that it resembles a pizza. Then have her place her divided plate atop her colored plate. Help her cut the stack along one line from the outer edge to the center. Separate the plates and then fit the two slits together as shown. Demonstrate how to turn one of the plates so that varying amounts of the pizza are visible. Then lead students in using their pizzas to explore fractions. For example, prompt each youngster to show one-fourth or one-half of her pizza. For added fun, have each student imagine that she ate her whole pizza, and have her manipulate her plates to make it disappear!

Angela Van Beveren
Alvin, TX

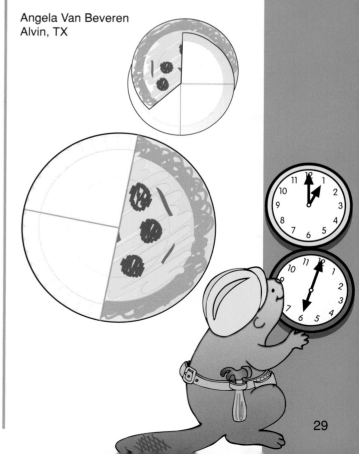

29

Jump, Students, Jump!
Measuring distance

Invite students to size up their jumps! To begin, read aloud *Jump, Frog, Jump!* by Robert Kalan. Then set out a supply of math links that students have linked together for easy handling. Invite each child, in turn, to stand at a designated starting point and then jump as far as he can. Mark where the youngster lands. Next, help the student use the links to measure how far he jumped. Ask him to complete a recording sheet similar to the one shown with his name, the measurement, and an illustration of himself jumping. **For more advanced students,** provide rulers or yardsticks instead of links.

Brenda Sharpe
Fairview Early Childhood Center
Rocky Mount, NC

Jump, _Max_ , jump!

My jump was _20_ links long.

Sold!
Addition and subtraction

Use this bargain of an idea to sharpen both addition and subtraction skills. Gather several plastic foods or other items appropriate for use as store items. Give each student an individual chalkboard or whiteboard and writing supplies. To reinforce addition, designate two students to be buyers and one student to be a seller. Have each buyer, in turn, pretend to purchase some items. Then ask each remaining student to write an addition sentence on his board to show how many items were purchased in all. After you confirm the correct answer, continue with different students in the roles of buyers and seller.

To reinforce subtraction, designate one buyer and one seller. Ask each youngster to subtract the number of items purchased from the total number of store items.

Amy Adams
Lindbergh Elementary
Madison, WI

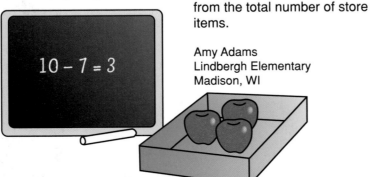

$10 - 7 = 3$

Bowling for Sums
Addition

Take aim at writing number sentences! Set up plastic bowling pins or several empty two-liter soda bottles. On a sheet of chart paper, prepare a score sheet similar to the one shown. To begin, have a pair of students bowl to complete the first number sentence. To do this, each partner, in turn, rolls a small ball, counts how many pins he knocks down, and then writes the number in a circle. The partners write the total in the square. (If the first partner knocks down all of the pins, he completes the number sentence and the second partner bowls without recording the result.) To continue, set up the pins again and invite a different pair of students to bowl.

Nancy Tangorra
Dolgeville Elementary
Dolgeville, NY

$3 + 4 = 7$
$5 + 1 = 6$
$2 + 8 = 10$

Math Skills

Speedy Lineup
Number order

Students try to beat the clock with this number card mix-up! Sequentially number a class supply of large blank cards, beginning with 0. Randomly distribute the cards. Once each child has a card, announce, "Go!" and begin timing the students. The child who has the card labeled "0" goes to the front of the classroom; the child who has the card labeled "1" immediately follows and stands beside the first student. The remaining students quickly join the line in number order. When all of the students are in place, announce how long it took for the students to line up. Repeat the activity later, challenging students to beat their time. **For more advanced students,** use cards numbered by twos or fives.

Louise Hoogstra, Calvin Christian School, Wyoming, MI

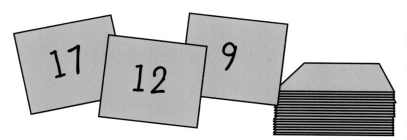

Shoes by Twos
Skip-counting

Step ahead with number patterns! Give each child two construction paper shoe cutouts. Invite him to add crayon details and to glue on yarn shoelaces. Arrange students' completed shoes in pairs on a wall or a length of bulletin board paper. Then, to number the shoes by twos, have students help you add number cards to the display or write directly on the paper. Invite students to practice skip-counting whenever they walk by!

Patrick Festa, McNichols Plaza Elementary, Scranton, PA

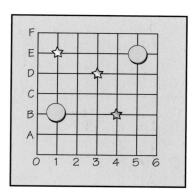

Mark the Spot!
Grid coordinates

This small-group version of bingo puts a playful twist on reading grids. To prepare, make student copies of a lettered and numbered grid similar to the one shown. On each grid, place a small sticker on each of five different coordinates, making each grid unique.

To play, give each child in the group a grid and five game markers. Call out a coordinate and jot it down on a sheet of paper for your reference. Have each child who has a sticker on the coordinate place a game marker on it. Then call out a different coordinate. Continue in this manner until one student marks all of her stickers and calls out, "Grid-o!" After confirming the placement of her markers, declare her the winner. Then have each youngster clear her grid to prepare for another round of play!

Karen Langdon
St. Margaret Mary Grade School
Neenah, WI

Colorful Lengths

Listen and do.

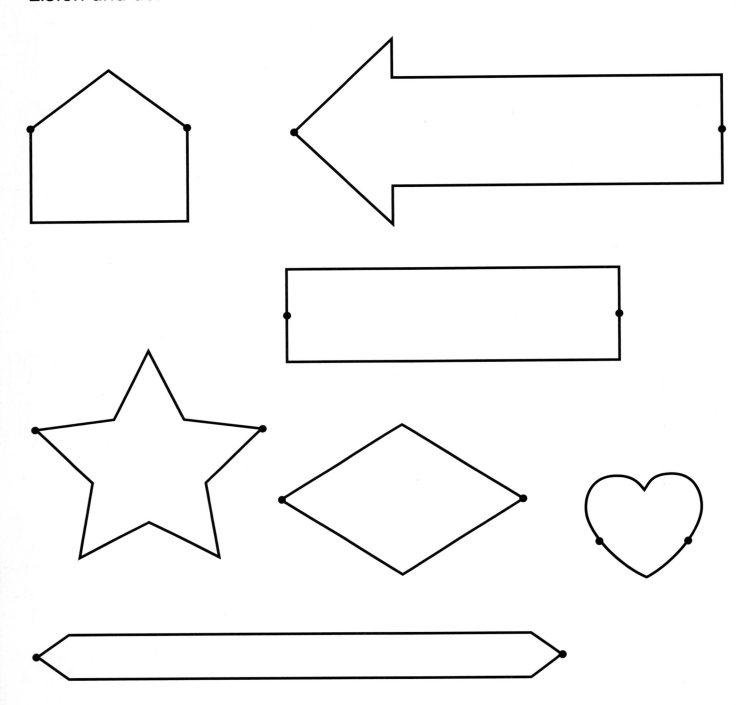

red	orange	yellow	green	blue	purple

Classroom Café

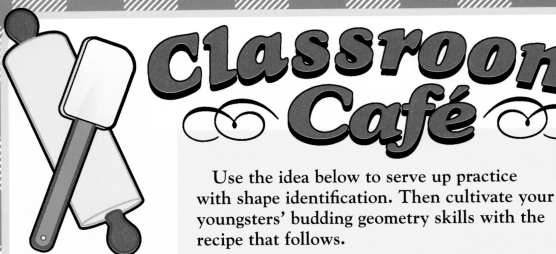

Classroom Café

Use the idea below to serve up practice with shape identification. Then cultivate your youngsters' budding geometry skills with the recipe that follows.

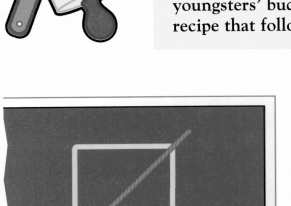

Before the Recipe

Round up your students for an intriguing shape exploration! On a flannelboard, use lengths of yarn to form each of the following shapes one at a time: circle, square, and triangle. After forming each shape, ask students to name it and tell how many sides it has. Then invite each of several volunteers to take a turn forming a chosen shape; have his classmates identify it. Next, clear the flannelboard and form a square once again. Claim that the square has two triangles inside it. After students express their disbelief, use a length of yarn to divide the square in half diagonally. Then trace the resulting triangles with your finger. Interesting!

Sunflower Snack

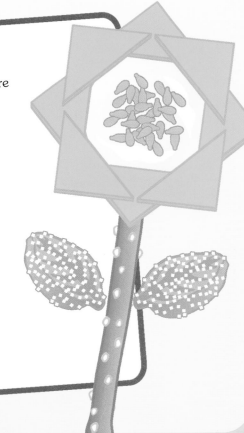

Ingredients for one:
rice cake
softened cream cheese
slice of American cheese
spoonful of sunflower seeds
pretzel rod
2 spearmint leaves

Utensils and supplies:
paper towel for each student (to prepare the snack on)
small paper plate for each student (for the American cheese)
plastic knives
plastic spoons

Teacher preparation:
- Arrange the supplies and ingredients for easy student access.
- Post a copy of the recipe (page 40) as desired. Or give each student a copy; then ask him to cut apart the cards and staple them to make a booklet.
- Have students identify the shapes of the rice cake and cheese slice. Remind them that a square can be divided into triangles.

adapted from an idea by Jeri Daugherity
Mother Seton School
Emmitsburg, MD

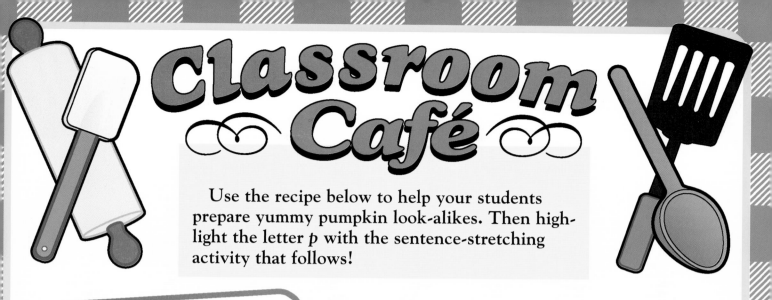

Classroom Café

Use the recipe below to help your students prepare yummy pumpkin look-alikes. Then highlight the letter *p* with the sentence-stretching activity that follows!

Pair of Pumpkins

Ingredients for one:
2 tsp. whipped topping
1 tsp. pumpkin pie filling
2 vanilla wafers
2 green gumdrop pieces (stems)

Utensils and supplies:
disposable cup for each student
2 measuring teaspoons
small paper plate for each student
plastic spoons
plastic knives

Teacher preparation:
- Cut green gumdrops vertically to make two gumdrop stems for each child.
- Arrange the supplies and ingredients for easy student access.
- Post a copy of the recipe (page 41) as desired. Or give each student a copy; then ask her to cut apart the cards and staple them to make a booklet.

adapted from an idea by Judi Lesnansky
New Hope Academy
Youngstown, OH

Please pass a piece of pumpkin pie to Peter.

The pretty pig ate pickles at the picnic.

After the Recipe
P is for *pumpkin, patch,* and plenty of other pleasing words! As students enjoy the snacks that they prepared, point out that the words *pair* and *pumpkins* have the same beginning letter. Post a jumbo letter *P* that you have cut from white paper. Have students name words that begin with *p;* write them on the displayed letter. Next, say a sentence with two of the words. Guide students to revise the sentence to include more *p* words; write the revision on a sheet of chart paper. Then have volunteers underline the *p* words with an orange marker. After you prepare a few more alliterative sentences in this manner, invite students to practice reading them with a pumpkin-decorated pointer!

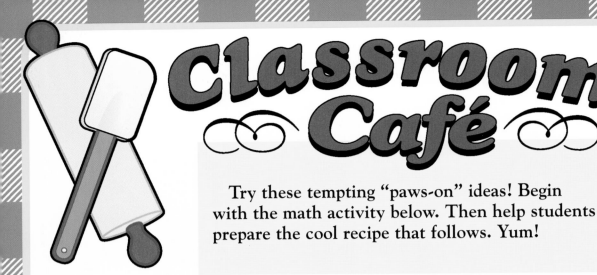

Classroom Café

Try these tempting "paws-on" ideas! Begin with the math activity below. Then help students prepare the cool recipe that follows. Yum!

Before the Recipe

Use this mouthwatering idea to give students practice with counting by fives. Explain that each youngster will prepare a snack that resembles a bear's pawprint. Reveal that each student will need five chocolate chips; wonder aloud how many chocolate chips two students will need. To determine the answer, have two volunteers stand in front of the class. Ask each volunteer to hold up five fingers as you lead students in counting by fives. Write the answer on the board. In a similar manner, help students determine how many chocolate chips are needed for three students, four students, and so on. After several numbers are listed, point out the number pattern. Then assure students that you have plenty of chocolate chips for each youngster to make his own chocolaty pawprint!

5, 10, 15, 20!

Bear Pawprint

Ingredients for one:
graham cracker square
1 tbsp. whipped topping
chocolate cookie
5 chocolate chips

Utensils and supplies:
small paper plate for each student
measuring tablespoon
plastic knives

Teacher preparation:
- Arrange the supplies and ingredients for easy student access.
- Post a copy of the recipe (page 42) as desired. Or give each student a copy; then ask her to cut apart the cards and staple them to make a booklet.

adapted from an idea by Michelle Miles
Early Childhood Development Center
Charlottesville, VA

Classroom Café

These sweet ideas are perfect for February! Whether you make the activities part of a Valentine's Day celebration or try them after telling students the legend of George Washington and the cherry tree, they're sure to hit the spot!

Cherry Delight

Ingredients for one:
graham cracker square
⅓ c. prepared vanilla pudding
2 spoonfuls cherry pie filling
1 spoonful whipped topping

Utensils and supplies:
resealable plastic sandwich bag for each student
rolling pin
9 oz. clear plastic cup for each student
⅓-cup measuring cup
2 serving spoons
plastic spoon for each student

Teacher preparation:
• Arrange the supplies and ingredients for easy student access.
• Display a copy of the recipe (page 43) as desired. Or give each student a copy; then ask her to cut apart the cards and staple them to make a booklet.

Nancy Karpyk, Weirton Heights School, Weirton, WV

Red
Red is a pretty valentine,
A juicy apple,
A tiny ladybug,
And sweet cherries!

After the Recipe

Think red—cherry red! Tell students that they will write a poem about the color red. Title a sheet of chart paper with the color word and begin the first line of the poem with the phrase "Red is." Continue the poem with student input and in the format shown. Conclude the poem after a desired number of lines.

Later, prepare a computer-generated copy of the poem, leaving space for student illustrations. Give each youngster a copy. Then read the poem with students and reinforce chosen phonics or word recognition skills. After each student illustrates his poem, help him staple it to a sheet of red construction paper.

Classroom Café

Reinforce reading and sequencing skills with these cute caterpillar ideas!

Caterpillar Roll-Up

Ingredients for one:
slice of bread, crust removed
whipped cream cheese, tinted green
decorating gel

Utensils and supplies:
piece of waxed paper for each student
rolling pin
plastic knives
small disposable plate for each student

Teacher preparation:
- Tint the cream cheese with green food coloring.
- Cut the crust from each slice of bread.
- Arrange the supplies and ingredients for easy student access.
- Display a copy of the recipe (page 44) as desired. Or give each student a copy; then ask her to cut apart the cards and staple them to make a booklet.

adapted from an idea by Virginia Zeletzki
Banyan Creek Elementary
Delray Beach, FL

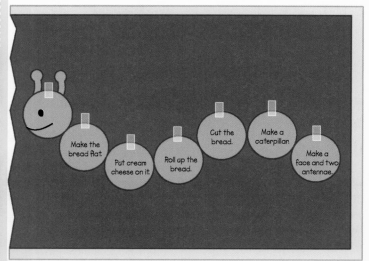

Make the bread flat.

Put cream cheese on it

Roll up the bread.

Cut the bread.

Make a caterpillan

Make a face and two antennae.

After the Recipe

As this caterpillar grows, students' sequencing skills grow too! Prepare seven large paper circles. Embellish one circle to resemble a caterpillar head. Loosely tape the head and one blank circle to the board to begin forming a caterpillar. Next, have students recall the first step for preparing a caterpillar roll-up. Write the step on the displayed blank circle. Then tape up another circle and program it with the second step that students recall. Continue in this manner until all of the steps are posted. When the caterpillar is complete, read the steps with students.

For additional reinforcement, place the programmed circles at a center. Have students sequence them to help the caterpillar grow—step by step!

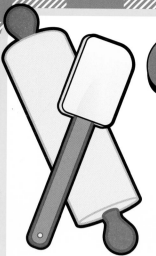

Classroom Café

Make a splash with the snack idea below. Then dive into a fishy vowel review with the activity that follows!

Funny Fishbowl

Ingredients for one:
rice cake
softened cream cheese, tinted blue
rainbow sprinkles
five Goldfish crackers

Utensils and supplies:
small disposable plate for each student
plastic knives

Teacher preparation:
- Tint the cream cheese with blue food coloring.
- Arrange the ingredients and supplies for easy student access.
- Display a copy of the recipe (page 45) as desired. Or give each student a copy; then ask him to cut apart the cards and staple them to make a booklet.

Cori Collins
Howe School
Green Bay, WI

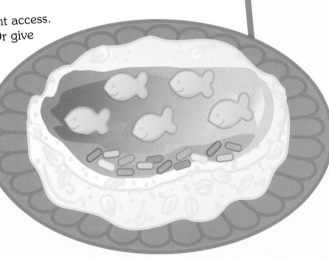

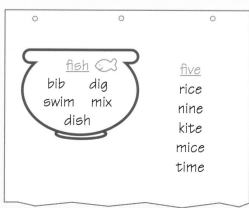

After the Recipe

This fun follow-up is sure to get students into the swim of identifying vowel sounds! Draw a large fishbowl on a sheet of chart paper. Label it "fish" and add a fish illustration. Write "five" beside the fishbowl. Underline both words. Then read them aloud and confirm that students can identify the vowel sounds. Next, announce a word that has either a short or long *i* sound. If the word has a short *i* sound, each student makes a swimming motion with his hand to imitate a fish. If the word has a long *i* sound, he holds up five fingers. Confirm the correct response and then write the word below the correct heading. Continue with additional words as time allows. **For an easier version,** adapt the activity to focus on initial consonants by having students signal whether chosen words begin with *f*.

Recipe Cards

Use with "Sunflower Snack" on page 34.

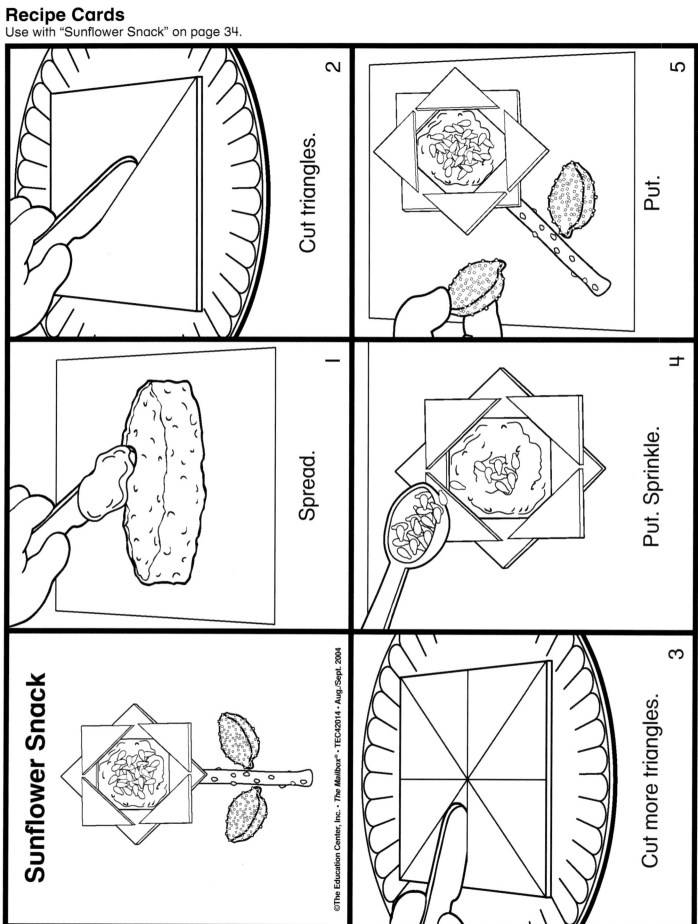

2 Cut triangles.

5 Put.

1 Spread.

4 Put. Sprinkle.

Sunflower Snack

3 Cut more triangles.

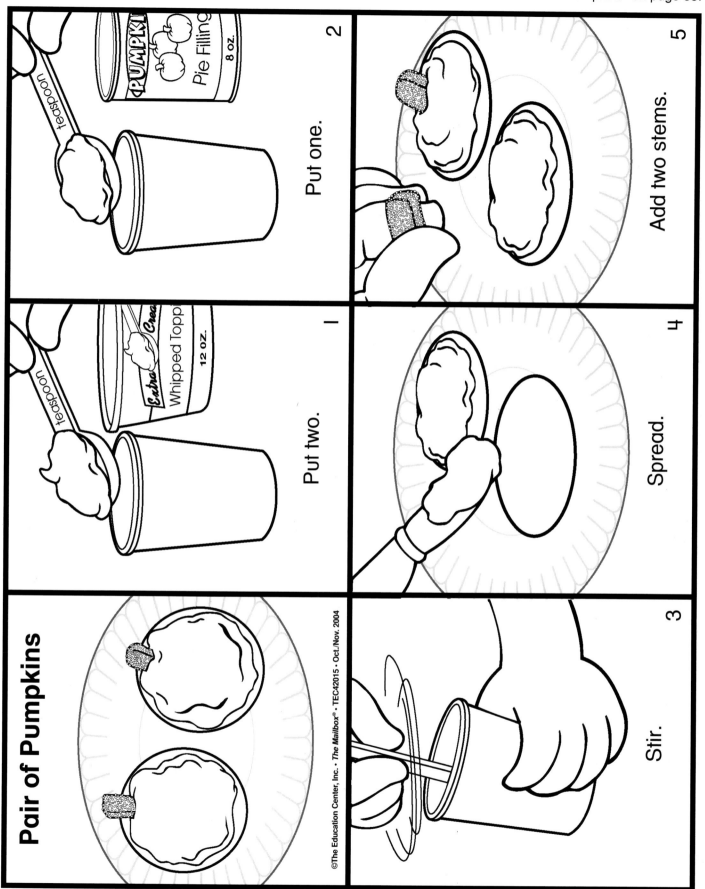

2

Put one.

1

Put two.

Pair of Pumpkins

5

Add two stems.

4

Spread.

3

Stir.

Recipe Cards
Use with "Bear Pawprint" on page 36.

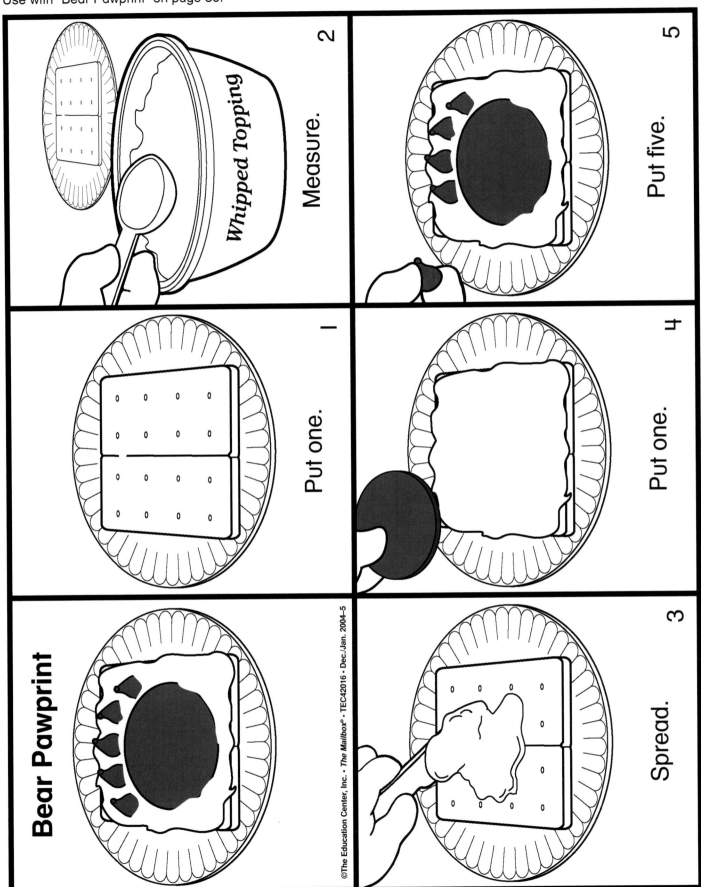

2 Whipped Topping. Measure.

1 Put one.

Bear Pawprint

5 Put five.

4 Put one.

3 Spread.

2

Pour it into the cup.

5

Whipped Topping

Add one spoonful whipped topping.

1

Crush the cracker.

4

Cherry Pie Filling

Add two spoonfuls pie filling.

Cherry Delight

3

1/3 cup

Measure the pudding. Add it to the cup.

©The Mailbox® · TEC42017 · Feb./Mar. 2005

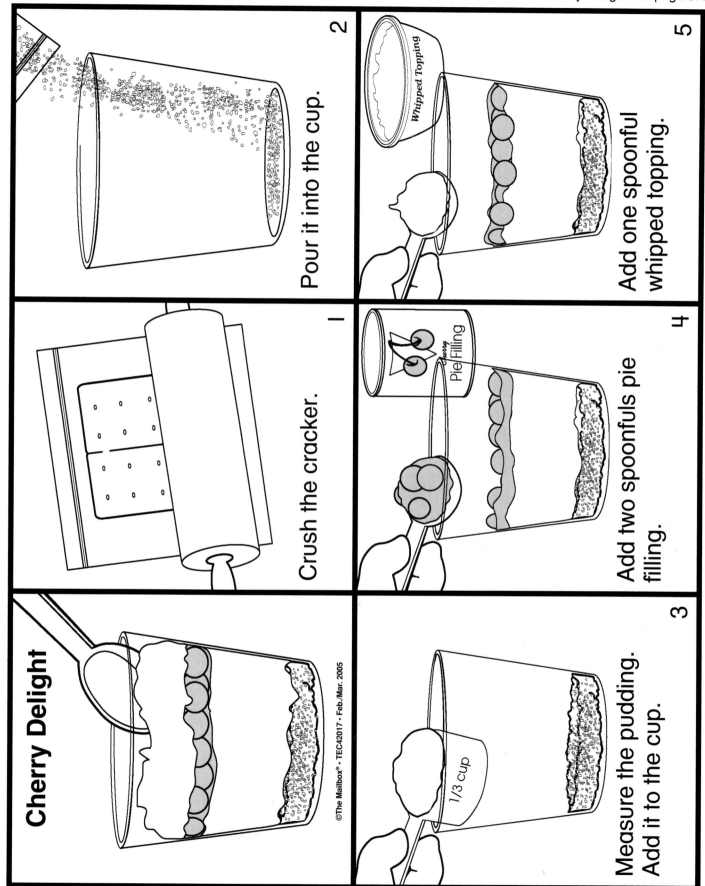

Recipe Cards

Use with "Caterpillar Roll-Up" on page 38.

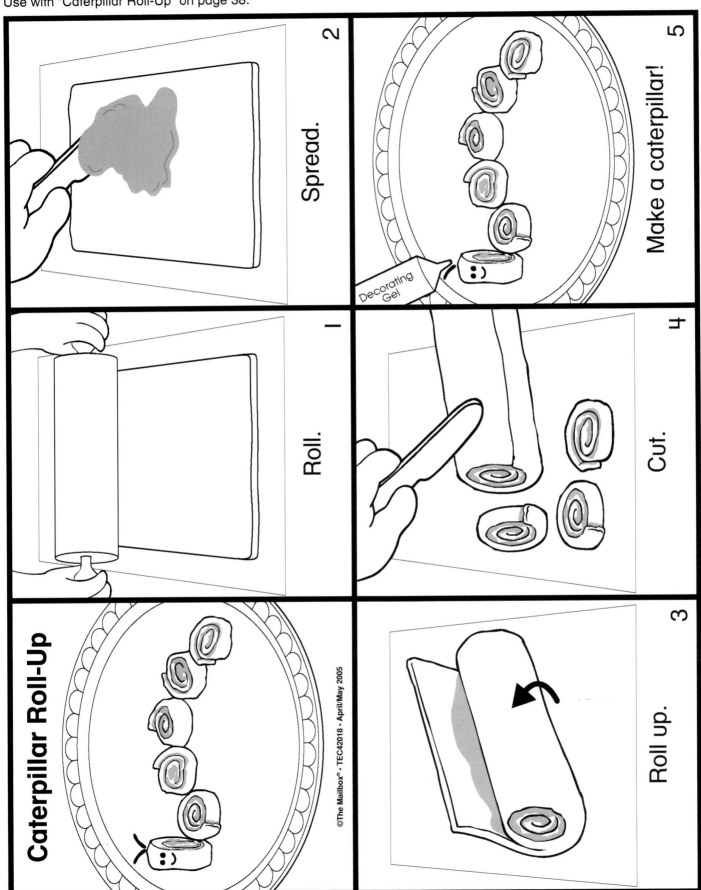

2
Spread.

5
Make a caterpillar!

Decorating Gel

1
Roll.

4
Cut.

Caterpillar Roll-Up

3
Roll up.

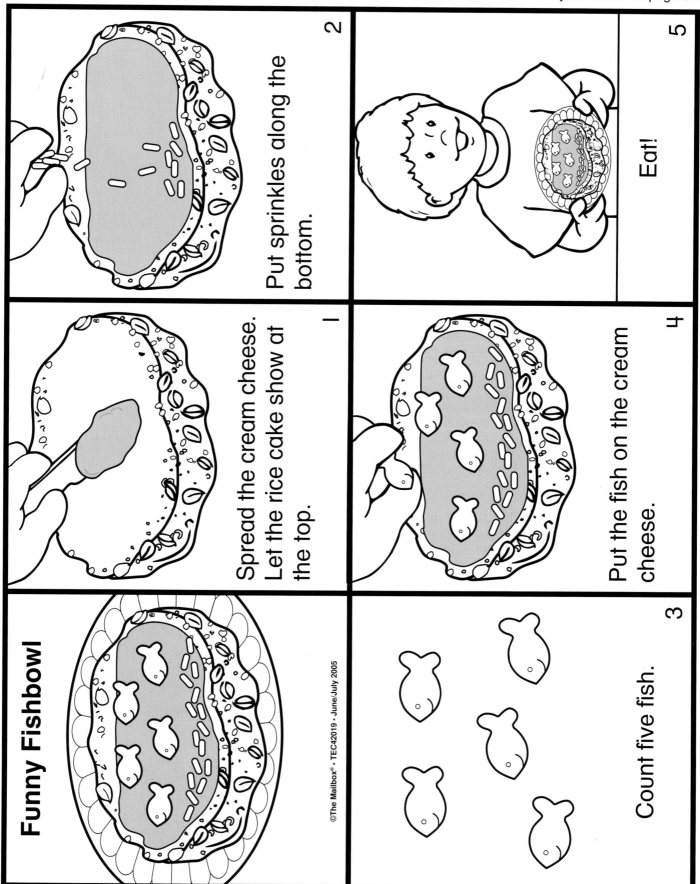

2 Put sprinkles along the bottom.

5 Eat!

1 Spread the cream cheese. Let the rice cake show at the top.

4 Put the fish on the cream cheese.

Funny Fishbowl

3 Count five fish.

Dear Parent,

This week we are making _____. We would
be grateful if you could help by providing the following ingredient(s):

_____

_____

_____

We need the ingredient(s) listed above by _____
                                                              date

Please let me know if you are able to send the ingredient(s).

                        Thank you,

                        _____
                                    teacher

☐ Yes, I am able to send the ingredient(s).
☐ No, I am unable to send the ingredient(s) at this time.

                        _____
                                parent signature

©The Mailbox®

Dear Parent,

This week we are making _____. We would
be grateful if you could help by providing the following ingredient(s):

_____

_____

_____

We need the ingredient(s) listed above by _____
                                                              date

Please let me know if you are able to send the ingredient(s).

                        Thank you,

                        _____
                                    teacher

☐ Yes, I am able to send the ingredient(s).
☐ No, I am unable to send the ingredient(s) at this time.

                        _____
                                parent signature

©The Mailbox®

CLASSROOM DISPLAYS

Celebrate summer vacation with this bright look back! Embellish a paper-covered bulletin board with blue waves and tissue paper sand. Then title it as shown. Have each youngster write about a fond summer memory on a sand pail cutout, or ask her to decorate the cutout with a summertime illustration. Add a chenille stem handle and a personalized shovel to each pail. Showcase students' pails as desired.

Jana Sanderson, Stockton, CA

This "tree-mendous" display helps a spirit of camaraderie grow in your classroom. Prepare a tree trunk and leafy top; label the trunk as shown. Assemble the tree on a bulletin board, tucking a small amount of tissue paper behind it to create a three-dimensional effect. Have each student sign his name on an apple cutout and use provided arts-and-crafts materials to add leaves and a stem. Then tack each apple to the tree.

Rhonda Pearce
Anne Watson Elementary
Bigelow, AR

Tammy Riche
Kaplan Elementary
Kaplan, LA

Students meet at this coconut tree to share favorite books! Display a coconut tree and the title shown. Help each student label a sheet of drawing paper with the title of a book she recently enjoyed. Have her add a story-related illustration and then mount her work on colorful paper. Post her work with a personalized construction paper coconut. And, of course, make *Chicka Chicka Boom Boom* by Bill Martin Jr. and John Archambault one of your first read-alouds of the year!

adapted from an idea by Gayle Lormand, Martin Pettijean Elementary, Rayne, LA

No doubt students will be tickled pink to contribute to this display! Staple twisted lengths of colorful tissue paper along the edges of a bulletin board as shown. Instruct each youngster to sponge-paint an entire sheet of paper in a chosen color. After her painting dries, have her cut from the paper a large figure that resembles something of that color. Invite her to add marker details. Display each student's artwork along with a caption formatted as shown.

Maryann Schroeder, Northwoods Elementary School, Cary, NC

Do the Monster Mash!

Symmetry gets into the act with these colorful monsters! Cover the top portion of a bulletin board with black paper and the lower portion with brown paper to establish a stage area. Add paper curtains and the title. Then have each youngster cut a folded piece of construction paper as desired to create a symmetrical monster body. Ask her to glue on construction paper facial features, arms, and legs. Showcase students' completed monsters on the stage. It's show time!

Pam Ingram, Davenport A+ School, Lenoir, NC

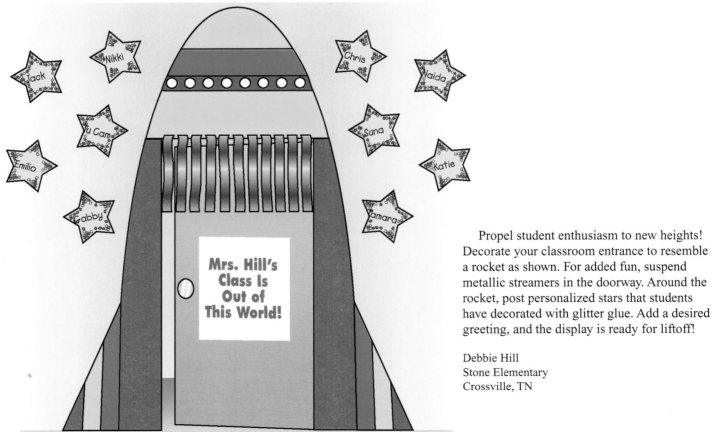

Propel student enthusiasm to new heights! Decorate your classroom entrance to resemble a rocket as shown. For added fun, suspend metallic streamers in the doorway. Around the rocket, post personalized stars that students have decorated with glitter glue. Add a desired greeting, and the display is ready for liftoff!

Debbie Hill
Stone Elementary
Crossville, TN

This quiltlike display is a warm Thanksgiving reminder. Post paper rectangles in a patchwork pattern and then frame them with paper strips to resemble a quilt. Help each youngster write a response to a holiday-related prompt on provided paper. Next, have him sponge-paint a small paper plate and add construction paper details to make a turkey similar to the one shown. Post each youngster's writing and turkey in adjacent sections of the display. Happy Thanksgiving!

adapted from an idea by Taryn Lynn Way, Los Molinos Elementary School, Los Molinos, CA

Here's an easy-to-maintain display that's perfect for spotlighting your youngsters' artwork! Post the title on a wall and embellish it with jumbo crayon or paintbrush cutouts. Personalize a small crayon cutout for each student and mount it near the bottom of a large sheet of paper. Then laminate the paper. Use removable adhesive to mount samples of students' artwork on the appropriate papers and post them below the title. Periodically replace the samples to keep the exhibit current.

Shelly Fales, Whittemore-Prescott Early Childhood Center, Whittemore, MI

Think winter! Post the title shown on a bulletin board covered with blue paper. Have each student create a wintertime illustration on a six-inch construction paper circle. Instruct him to mount his illustration on a ten-inch white paper doily. Then help him prepare a caption with a word-processing program or sentence strip. Showcase each youngster's artwork with his caption as desired.

Janet Pincus and Suzanne Davidson, Washington Hebrew Early Childhood and Primary School, Potomac, MD

Imagine how handy it would be if mittens grew on trees! If desired, share Steven Kellogg's *The Missing Mitten Mystery* to spark students' imaginations. Have each youngster use provided arts-and-crafts materials to decorate a construction paper mitten as desired. Showcase the completed mittens on a leafless tree and post the title shown.

Cathy Fontana—RNSZ Homeschool
Clifton, NJ

Students warm up their estimation skills as they prepare this cool display! Present a jumbo snowpal shape and one paper circle (snowball). Ask students to estimate how many snowballs it would take to cover the shape. Then have them prepare construction paper snowballs and glue them in place. After comparing the estimates and the actual total, point out how the size and shape of the snowballs influence the total. Embellish the snowpal as desired. Then post it on a hallway wall along with a labeled folder that has the snowball total inside.

Judith Wrenick
Fraser Valley Elementary
Fraser, CO

Guess How Many Snowballs!
* * * * * *

This motivating display keeps students moving on the road to success! Mount a traffic light on a titled board. Have each student personalize a car cutout. Then post each car along with a sample of the corresponding student's best work. Vroom!

Lydia Hess, Chambersburg, PA

This alliterative display comes straight from the heart! Help each student write an alliterative sentence with the format shown. Then have him decorate a paper doll cutout (pattern on page 59) to resemble himself. Ask him to glue the likeness on a red-backed heart similar to the ones shown and invite him to add crayon details. Arrange each student's completed work as desired on a prepared board. Happy Valentine's Day!

Felice Kestenbaum, Goosehill Primary School, Cold Spring Harbor, NY

Mirror, mirror, on the wall, here are the most popular fairy tales of all! Glue a length of aluminum foil on a jumbo mirror. Post the mirror and the title shown. On the outside of a construction paper folder, have each student write the title of her favorite fairy tale and draw a story-related illustration. Ask her to write inside the folder about the tale. Post students' completed work on the board, and embellish the display with glitter-decorated stars.

Debbie Hill, Stone Elementary, Crossville, TN

Spark students' imaginations with this follow-up to *It Looked Like Spilt Milk* by Charles G. Shaw. Combine equal parts of white tempera paint and white glue; then thin the mixture slightly with water. Have each youngster "spill" a small amount of the mixture on a blue paper plate and then tilt the plate back and forth to achieve a desired effect. After the paint dries, help him label his plate. Display students' eye-catching artwork as shown.

Julia Mashburn, Black's Mill Elementary, Dawsonville, GA

Here's a pride-boosting idea for spotlighting the results of your students' hard work! Title a board with a sign similar to the one shown and add desired construction site items for decoration. Have each student write her name on a construction paper hard hat (pattern on page 59) and cut it out. Then post each hat with a sample of the corresponding student's best work. Now that's a display constructed with care!

adapted from an idea by Susan J. H. Johnson, Zion Lutheran School, Belleville, IL

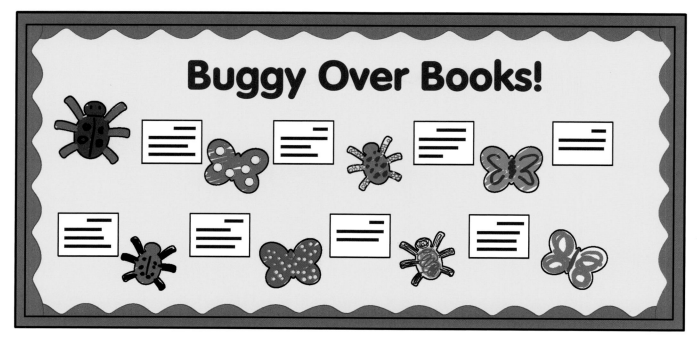

Watch interest in books soar at this springtime display! After a chosen storytime, have each student write about her favorite part of the book. Then invite her to decorate a bug cutout with provided arts-and-crafts materials. Post students' completed writings and bugs on a board titled as shown. Periodically encourage students to update the display with comments about different books.

Brooke Shaw, Columbia, SC

April, National Poetry Month, is a perfect time to bring the outdoors indoors with a student-illustrated sidewalk! Have each student use colored chalk to sign his name on a sheet of gray construction paper and create a desired illustration. As youngsters work, read aloud poetry by Shel Silverstein. When the students' artwork is finished, use hairspray to set the chalk. Then, beginning at your classroom door, display the papers in a row on a hallway wall. Add the title shown.

Cindy Barber, Fredonia, WI

Guess Who Is Ready for Summer!

Your students are the stars of this intriguing summer display. Have each student draw a summertime self-portrait and then mount it on a slightly larger piece of colorful paper. Write each youngster's name in small letters at the bottom of her artwork. Then staple a rectangle labeled with a question mark over each name so that the rectangle can be lifted as shown. Display the mystery portraits on a hallway wall below a desired title.

Angelena Pritchard, Waterloo Elementary, Waterloo, SC

Transform a classroom window or bulletin board into a watery wonder! Tack up blue and brown paper to create the background of an underwater scene. Add student-decorated fish and shells, and draw desired details such as seaweed. Then secure lengths of blue crepe paper to the top of the display. Gently twist the crepe paper and then tack it to the bottom of the scene. Look what's under the sea!

Jo Fryer, Kildeer Countryside School, Long Grove, IL

A Winning Team

Eliana — Lights
Joe — Plants
Ariel — Line Leader
Han — Librarian
Leigh — Messenger
Nate — Papers

Promote teamwork with this easy-to-maintain job display. On a titled board, post one baseball mitt (pattern on page 60) per classroom job. Display the names of the jobs as shown. Have each student sign a white construction paper baseball (pattern on page 60). Use Velcro fastener dots to secure a baseball to each mitt, and store the extra baseballs nearby. When it's time to have a different lineup of classroom helpers, simply switch the baseballs!

Jennifer L. Kohnke
Nature Ridge Elementary
Bartlett, IL

Watch Our Garden Grow!

hop, stop, mop, pop
-op

sing, king, ring
-ing

van, man, tan, ran
-an

Cultivate reading skills with a word family review! Post a length of paper on a classroom wall and add the title shown. Post several flowerpots that you have labeled with familiar rimes. Ask students to program blossoms with words that have the rimes and add them to the display. Then have volunteers draw stems and leaves. How pretty!

Sarah Bajema, White Pine Academy, Leslie, MI

Paper Doll Pattern
Use with "Things We Love" on page 54.

Construction Hat Pattern
Use with "We Have Been Hard at Work!" on page 55.

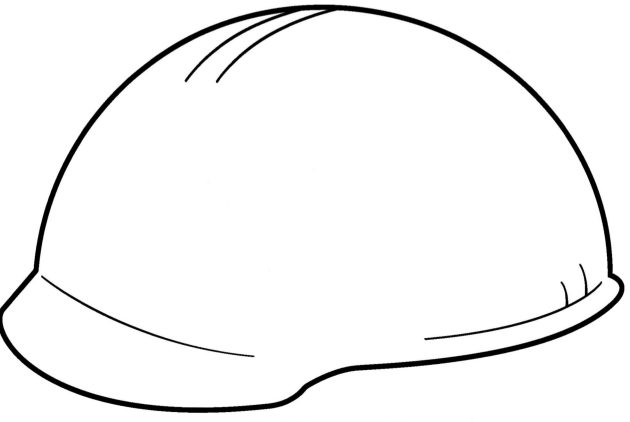

Baseball and Mitt Patterns

Use with "A Winning Team" on page 58.

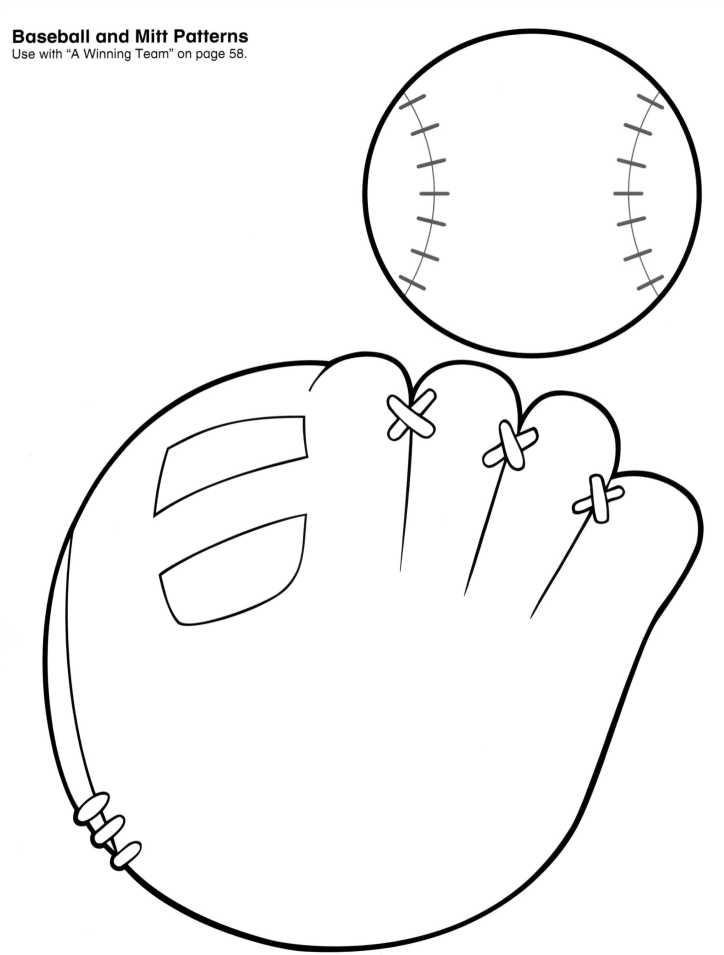

GROUP TIME!

Group Time!

Tune in to Names!
• • • • • Word Identification • • • • •

Help students get acquainted with this name-recognition activity. Use a marker to print each child's name in large letters on a separate paper plate. Spread out the plates on the floor in your group area. After each child finds his paper plate, ask him to hold it as he sits with you in a circle.

Next, play some lively music and have students quickly pass the plates around the circle. Stop the music after a few moments. At this signal, have students stop passing the plates. Invite each of several children to read aloud the plate he holds and show the name to his classmates. (If reading assistance is needed, encourage him to hold up the plate so that the corresponding student can identify his own name.) Start the music again to resume play. What a nifty way to develop reading vocabularies!

Shirley Tanaka
Francis Scott Key School
San Francisco, CA

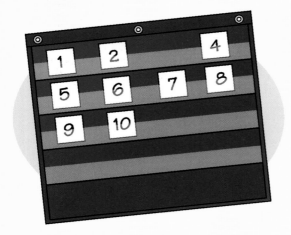

Numbers in Place
• • • • • Number Order • • • • •

Improved number sense is in the cards! Prepare a sequence of number cards that is suitable for your youngsters' abilities. Arrange the cards in order in a pocket chart. To begin, ask students to cover their eyes as you remove one number from the chart and conceal it. Then have students study the chart and encourage them to guess which number is missing. When a child correctly identifies the number, return the card. Invite the youngster to secretly remove a card of her choice to present a new missing number challenge.

Bonnie Elizabeth Vontz
Cheshire Country Day School
Milldale, CT

Aim for Shapes!
• • • • • Geometry • • • • •

Toss some fun into shape identification! Program several large blank cards with various shapes, one shape per card. Stand with students in a circle and spread out the cards faceup in the center of it. Have one child toss a provided beanbag onto a card and name the shape on which it lands. Then instruct her to retrieve the beanbag and hand it to the next child for his turn. Continue in this manner until each child has had a turn identifying a shape. To modify the activity for other skill areas, use cards labeled with colors, letters, numbers, or sight words.

Brandy Bowen
Iowa Elementary
Nampa, ID

Group Time!

Alphabet Soup
• • • • • Letter Knowledge • • • • •

Here's a "soup-er" way to serve up letter-sound associations! Cover the cut edges of a clean and empty coffee can with heavy tape. Decorate the can to resemble a soup can and then place a supply of letter manipulatives inside. To begin, sit with students in a circle and pass the can to a child beside you. The child removes a letter, identifies it, and names a word that begins with it. He holds the letter and gives the can to the next student. This youngster names a different word that begins with the letter and passes the can. Students continue around the circle in this manner until one youngster cannot name a word. Then this child takes a different letter to start a new round.

Cheryl Mesch
Northwood Elementary
West Seneca, NY

Teacher:	[Katie, Katie], what will you do? If we go to [the farm], what will you do?
Response:	If we go to [the farm], here's what I'll do; I'll [milk the big cow]. How about you?
Final Response:	If we go to [the farm], here's what I'll do; I'll [pick some corn] and have fun with you!

Going Places!
• • • • • Oral Vocabulary • • • • •

Use this language-boosting idea to take a field trip without leaving the classroom! Sit with students in a circle and establish a steady clapping rhythm. Next, say the chant shown, inserting a student's name and a chosen location. Have the child respond as indicated and then point to a classmate. Repeat the chant with the classmate's name. Continue until every youngster has responded, having the last child point to you. Then give the final response and gesture toward the entire class. What fun!

Katie Carter
Punkin' Place Child Development Center
Jacksonville, FL

Hoop-de-doo Sums
• • • • • Addition, Number Sense • • • • •

Get students on a roll with number comparisons! Place two large plastic hoop toys on the floor. Have half of your students sit side by side facing one hoop and the other half sit facing the other hoop. Assign the two groups names. Then give the first two students in each group a pair of large dice. Ask each twosome to toss its dice into its hoop and announce the sum rolled. Have students tell which group has the greater sum or whether the sums are equal; record the information to keep score. Then invite the next two students in each group to roll the dice. After each child takes a turn or two, help students determine which group had more greater sums.

Lindsey Vail, Highlands School, Braintree, MA

Group Time!

Good Morning!
• • • • • Letter Knowledge, Speaking in a Group • • • • •

Here's a letter-perfect approach to morning greetings. Prepare a set of letter cards and a set of picture cards that correspond with the letter sounds. Give each child either a letter or picture card so that each card has a match. Plan to participate if you have an odd number of students.

To begin, invite a child to stand in front of the class and announce his letter or picture. The child with the corresponding card comes forward and names her letter or picture. Then the two students greet one another with a previously modeled exchange. They deposit their cards in a designated container and return to their places. To continue, invite a different student to come forward. Welcome, everyone!

Deborah Patrick
Park Forest Elementary
State College, PA

Dear Ms. Hagerty's Class,
I hear you are good at solving problems. Can you help me? I lost 9 sheep. Then I found 4 of them. How many sheep are still missing?

Sincerely,
Little Bo-Peep

$$\begin{array}{r} 9 \\ -4 \\ \hline 5 \end{array}$$

Mailbox Math
• • • • • Problem Solving • • • • •

Deliver first-class math problems! Decorate a mailbox with number stickers and display it in a prominent classroom location. Every few days, secretly write a letter to your class from the point of view of a storybook or nursery rhyme character. Present in the letter a math problem for students to solve. Place the letter in the mailbox and raise the flag. During group time, announce the delivery and ask a volunteer to remove the letter from the mailbox. After you read the letter aloud, have students solve the problem using provided paper or manipulatives. Then discuss the solution and write a reply as a class. "Send-sational"!

Cara Hagerty
Hickey Elementary
Plano, TX

block

Reading With Music
• • • • • Word Families • • • • •

This version of musical chairs keeps reading skills on the move. Arrange two rows of chairs back-to-back so that there is one chair per child and ample walking room. Place on each chair a word card that shows a familiar word family. To begin, play some lively music and have students walk in an established path around the chairs. After several moments, pause the music. At this signal, each student takes the card that is on the nearest chair and sits down. Then she reads her card to a neighboring classmate. For another round of reading fun, simply restart the music!

Tammy Minnick, Rockwood Elementary, Rockwood, PA

Group Time!

Packed With Clues!
• • • • • **Critical Thinking** • • • • •

Stretch students' thinking skills with this twist on traditional show-and-tell. For take-home use, decorate a lidded box and place a supply of paper inside it. Tape a parent note to the box asking that a child place a chosen item in the box, write three clues about it with adult assistance, and then return the box. Establish a rotating schedule for students to take the box home. When a child returns it, help him give the clues to the class, one at a time, and encourage his classmates to guess what the item is. Then invite the youngster to reveal the item and tell the class about it. Mystery solved!

Barbara Hollis
Las Flores Elementary
Rancho Santa Margarita, CA

1. It is silver.
2. You squeeze it.
3. It makes holes.

Pass the Letters!

(sung to the tune of "The Muffin Man")

Oh, look who has the letter bag,
The letter bag, the letter bag.
Oh, look who has the letter bag.
Now please take a letter!

The Letter Bag
• • • • • **Letter Knowledge** • • • • •

Tune up students' letter-sound associations! Gather several objects (or pictures of objects) whose names begin with different consonant sounds, and place the corresponding magnetic letters in an opaque bag. Sit with students in a circle and then set the objects in the center. Next, lead students in the song shown as they pass the bag. Have the youngster who is holding the bag at the song's conclusion randomly remove a letter and then pair it with the corresponding object. Begin another round of the song to resume the activity.

Treena Ferguson
Edgewood Elementary
Pottstown, PA

Fishing for Punctuation
• • • • • **Language Arts** • • • • •

Reel in improved punctuation skills! Place in a pocket chart several telling, asking, and exclamatory sentences without end marks. Program cards similar to the one shown with the missing punctuation marks, one mark per card. Then slide a large paper clip onto each card. Attach a length of string to a dowel and tie a magnet to the end of it. To begin, spread the cards facedown on the floor. Have students take turns fishing for the end mark needed for the first sentence. When a student makes the catch, ask him to set the card in the pocket chart. Invite your young fishers to punctuate the remaining sentences in a similar manner.

adapted from an idea by Andrea Selking
Lantern Farms School
Fishers, IN

Group Time!

Six minus three.

Domino Differences
••••• Subtraction •••••

A bag of dominoes holds lots of dots and loads of subtraction possibilities! Place a class supply of dominoes in an opaque bag. Give the bag to a student and have her randomly remove a domino. Ask her to tell how many dots are on each section of the domino. Then guide her to announce a subtraction problem that uses the corresponding numbers. Write the problem on a sheet of chart paper. After a volunteer gives the correct answer, record it on the paper. Have the domino holder set the domino aside and then pass the bag to a different student. When each student has had a turn, lead the group in reading the subtraction sentences you've written.

Angie Kutzer
Garrett Elementary
Mebane, NC

Letter by Letter
••••• Reading •••••

Here's a kid-pleasing approach to decoding words. Prepare several large letter cards that can be used to form decodable CVC words. Ask three children to stand in front of the group. Then give the first letter of a chosen word to the first child. Have him show the letter to his seated classmates. After they tell what sound it represents, give the second letter to the second student. Prompt his classmates to announce the corresponding sound. Introduce the last letter in the same manner.

Next, instruct the three cardholders to link arms. Lead students in blending the letter sounds to name the word. Then invite a different trio of students to present another word. "Sound-sational"!

Lindsey Vail, Highlands Elementary, Braintree, MA

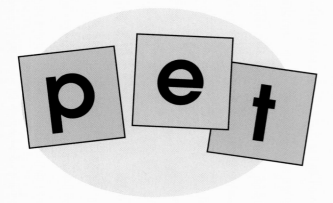

Buggy Math Toss
••••• Computation, Number Sense •••••

Use a jumbo ladybug to help your students practice addition, subtraction, or number comparisons. Here's how! Prepare a large paper ladybug (or decorate a red Christmas tree skirt so that it resembles a ladybug). Label each spot with a different number. To begin, place the ladybug on the floor. Have a student stand a designated distance from it and ask her to toss two beanbags onto different numbers. Instruct her to add the numbers, announce their difference, or tell which number is greater. Then give each remaining student a turn, modifying the task as appropriate for each youngster's abilities.

Cynthia D. Davis, Kathleen, GA

LEARNING CENTERS

Learning Centers

Cookies to Share
Dramatic-Play Area

After students are familiar with *The Doorbell Rang* by Pat Hutchins, no doubt they'll be eager to make pretend batches of yummy cookies! Stock your dramatic-play area with baking supplies such as cookie sheets, spatulas, plastic mixing bowls, wooden spoons, and pot holders. Provide markers, scissors, and craft foam for students to fashion into cookies. Add to the area some blank recipe cards, pencils, and crayons to encourage young bakers to write recipes. Then watch as the baking and sharing begin!

Christy Owens
Centerville Kindergarten Village
Centerville, OH

Beyond Compare!
Math Center

More apples or pumpkins? That's what students decide at this easy-to-prepare center. Program a blank sheet of paper with the provided sentence as shown, keeping the two boxes blank. Place copies of the sheet at a center. Also set out red and orange ink pads, fine-tip markers, and wet wipes for easy cleanup. A child completes the sentence on her paper by making an orange fingerprint pumpkin in one box and a red fingerprint apple in the other box. Then, above the sentence, she makes a desired number of fingerprint pumpkins and apples to make the statement true. After the prints dry, she uses the markers to add desired details.

Katie Zuehlke
Bendix Elementary
Annandale, MN

Spin a Word!
Reading Center

Put a spin on high-frequency words! To prepare a spinner, divide a tagboard circle into six sections. Program each section with a different word. Use a metal brad and a paper clip to assemble the spinner as shown. Next, draw a six-column grid with a desired number of rows. Label the columns with the words (see the illustration). Place the spinner and copies of the grid at a center stocked with crayons.

Arrange for students to visit the center in pairs. To take a turn, a student spins the spinner. He reads the word aloud with his partner's assistance, if needed. Then he colors the appropriate space on the grid. The partners alternate turns until one column is full. Wow! Look what word won!

Tina Beeler
Lincoln Center Elementary
South St. Paul, MN

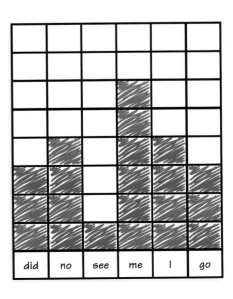

did	no	see	me	I	go

Roll Out the Letters!
Literacy Center

This letter-formation idea doubles as a way to strengthen youngsters' fine-motor skills. On each of several large tagboard rectangles, write the uppercase and lowercase forms of a chosen letter with a broad-tip marker. Laminate the resulting letter cards for repeated use. Place the cards and a supply of play dough at a center. A child sets a card on a tabletop. She rolls the play dough into snake shapes and then places them atop the marker lines to form the letters. She traces her play dough letters with her finger several times before moving on to a different letter card!

Jara Tharp
Northside Elementary
Nebraska City, NE

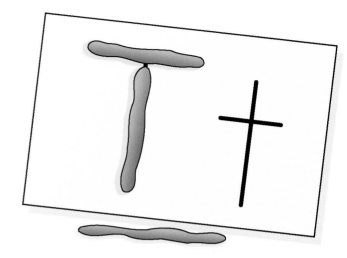

Now Serving Addition
Math Center

Use plastic plates for addition practice? You bet! Obtain a few disposable plates that are divided into three compartments. Program several blank cards with addition problems and then put them in a resealable plastic bag. Place the bag, plates, and a supply of manipulatives at a center stocked with paper and pencils.

A child takes an addition problem and a plate. He sets the appropriate number of manipulatives in the two smaller compartments of his plate to represent the problem. For example, if the problem is five plus two, he puts five manipulatives in one compartment and two in another compartment. Next, he writes the addition problem on his paper. Then he places both sets of manipulatives in the large compartment, counts them to determine the sum, and writes the sum. Finally, he clears his plate and helps himself to another problem!

Jo Montgomery
John C. French Elementary
Cuero, TX

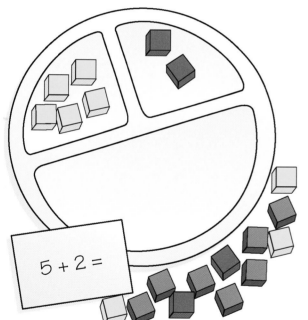

Animal Cracker Captions
Writing Center

Students will be wild about writing at this unique center! Set out one animal cracker for each student. Also provide drawing paper, glue, crayons, and pencils. A youngster draws a line across her paper a few inches from the bottom. She illustrates a setting for her animal cracker above the line. When she is satisfied with her artwork, she glues her animal cracker in place. She writes a caption below the line to complete her work.

Jody Steed
La Vega Primary Center
Waco, TX

The tiger is roaring.

Learning Centers

Memorable Words
Reading Center

This high-frequency-word game is a winner any time of year. Prepare a 20-space poster board grid and 20 identical seasonal cutouts sized to fit the grid. Program the cutouts with ten familiar high-frequency words so that there are two cutouts for each word. Place the cutouts in a seasonal gift bag; then set the bag and grid at a center. Arrange for two or three students to use the center at a time.

The players randomly arrange the cutouts facedown on the grid. To take a turn, a player turns over two cutouts and reads the words aloud. If the words are the same, he keeps the cutouts. If they are not, he turns them facedown in their grid spaces. Players alternate turns until all of the cutouts have been paired. The player with the most pairs wins. **For an easier version,** reduce the number of grid spaces and words. How simple!

Christine Jojola
Rock Ridge Elementary
Castle Rock, CO

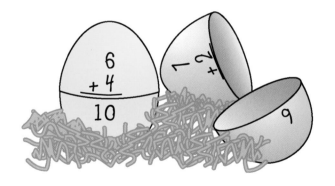

Scrambled Addition
Math Center

Invite students to cook up "sum-thing" fun! Obtain a supply of plastic eggs. Use a permanent marker to label the top half of each egg with a vertical addition problem and the bottom half with the sum. Separate the egg halves and then place them in a basket lined with cellophane grass. Set the basket at a center. A student reads each problem, finds a matching answer, and then puts the two halves together. After she assembles all of the eggs, she cracks them open and scrambles them for the next mathematician!

Kelly Finch
Vaughan Elementary
Powder Springs, GA

Appetizing Artwork
Art Center

Creativity is in the forecast! After sharing Judi Barrett's *Cloudy With a Chance of Meatballs,* invite students to create illustrations of the legendary town Chewandswallow. Stock a center with large sheets of drawing paper, grocery store flyers, glue, scissors, and crayons. To begin, a student illustrates a town scene that includes details such as buildings, roads, trees, and people. Then he cuts images of food from the flyers. He arranges the food on his paper so that it appears to be falling from the sky. When he is pleased with the arrangement, he glues the food in place. Why, it's raining cookies and cake!

Leanne Gibbons
Sacred Heart School
Quincy, MA

Pets for Sale!
Dramatic-Play Area

Transform your dramatic-play area into a "purr-fect" little pet shop! Invite students to bring in stuffed animals and empty pet food boxes. Prepare several construction paper pawprints. Then label them with a student-generated shop name to make nametags for shop clerks. Provide books about pets to help the clerks advise shoppers about pet care and blocks that the workers can use to make animal pens. Also set out materials for making animal and shop signs. Add a toy cash register and some play money, and the shop will be ready for business!

Jenny Baker
South Penn Elementary
Cumberland, MD

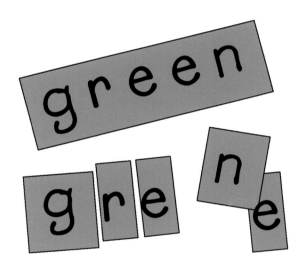

Letter-Perfect Colors
Spelling Center

"R-e-d" spells *red;* "b-l-u-e" spells *blue;* here's an activity that's fun to do! To make a color-word puzzle and spelling guide, cut two strips from a chosen color of construction paper. Write the corresponding color word on each strip. Keep one strip intact and cut apart the letters on the other strip. Place the intact strip and the letters in an envelope. Prepare a puzzle and spelling guide for each of several colors. Set all of the prepared envelopes at a center. Have students refer to the spelling guides as they form the words with the letters. Or ask students to form the words before they check the guides.

Cindy Holzschuher
Laura Farrell Elementary
Franklin, OH

March Math
Math Center

Give students some wild and woolly estimation practice. Place copies of page 76, pencils, a supply of small tan or brown pom-poms, and a supply of small white pom-poms at a center. A child writes her name on her paper. Next, she estimates how many tan or brown pom-poms fit in one layer on the lion. After she writes her estimate, she fills the lion figure with pom-poms, counts them, and then records the actual number. In a similar manner, she estimates how many white pom-poms fit on her lamb and checks her estimate. Now that's an idea worth roaring about!

Nancy M. B. Betler
Montclaire Elementary
Charlotte, NC

Learning Centers

Fishy Combinations
Math Center

Make number combinations the catch of the day! Label a plastic pail with a numeral from 5 to 12. Place the corresponding number of fish cutouts in the pail. Then set the pail at a center stocked with paper. A student writes the featured number at the top of her paper and then circles it. Next, she arranges the fish on a work surface to represent a combination that equals the number. After she writes the combination on her paper, she rearranges the fish to show a different combination. She continues in this manner until she has written several combinations.

Sandra O'Connell
M. M. Pierce Elementary
Remington, VA

Picturing Words
Spelling Center

CVC words are the focus of this hands-on spelling activity. Use clip art to prepare several picture cards that represent chosen words. Label the back of each card with the word. Place the cards and a supply of letter manipulatives at a center. A student selects a card, says the name of the picture, and then spells the word with the manipulatives. After she flips the card to check her work, she chooses a different word to spell. **To make the activity easier,** place each card and the corresponding letters in a separate resealable plastic bag.

Lynne Nelson
Sherrills Ford Elementary
Sherrills Ford, NC

Books at the Beach
Reading Area

Spark students' interest in books with this "sun-sational" idea. In a corner of the classroom or another cozy area, place a couple of beach towels, an old portable radio, and a few pairs of sunglasses (with the lenses removed, if necessary, to allow for easy reading). Also set out a picnic basket that you have stocked with beach-themed books and other appropriate reading selections. As students relax with the books they chose from the basket, encourage them to quietly talk with one another about their selections. Ah, nothing's better than a day at the beach with good books!

Scarlett Murphy
Moorhead Elementary
Indianapolis, IN

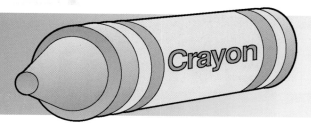

Classy Picture Prompts
Writing Center

Inspire young writers with picture-perfect word banks! Select several photos of your students involved in various school activities. Mount each photo near the top of a separate sheet of paper. Below each photo, write a few related words for students' spelling reference. Slide each paper into a plastic sheet protector to keep the photos free of fingerprints. When it's time for a youngster to write, the ideas are sure to start flowing!

Erin Green
Rosewood Elementary
Rock Hill, SC

swing
friend
recess

Price List	
Draw a face.	1¢
Draw 2 antennae.	2¢
Draw 6 legs.	4¢
Color the head.	5¢
Color the body.	6¢

Buggy Buying
Game Center

Players race to complete bug illustrations with this money game. For each student, make a copy of a simple bug illustration similar to the one shown (without antennae, a face, or legs). Color a copy of the gameboard on page 77 and cut it out. Glue the gameboard and a price list in a file folder (see the illustration). Set out a die, two different-colored counters, and a supply of imitation pennies. Arrange for two children to play the game at a time.

Each player places his counter on a Buy space. To take a turn, a player rolls the die and then moves his counter in a clockwise direction. If he lands on a money space, he takes the corresponding money amount. If he lands on a Buy space, he may pay for a chosen type of bug part and then illustrate or color it. The players alternate turns until one player wins by completing his bug illustration. The players add any desired crayon details to their papers before taking them home.

adapted from an idea by Suzanne Frey
Frankford Elementary
Biglerville, PA

Peekaboo Words
Reading Center

With these lift-the-flap cards, young readers get feedback right away! Program the upper portion of each of several blank cards with chosen clip art. At the bottom of each card, write the corresponding word. Laminate the cards for durability. Then cover the clip art with sticky notes, leaving the words visible. A student chooses a card and reads the word. She lifts the flap to see whether she is correct and then chooses another card to read. What a simple way to build students' reading vocabularies!

Susan Page
Thompsontown-Delaware Elementary
Mifflintown, PA

house

Learning Centers

Shop and Sort!
Literacy Center

A trip to this grocery-themed center boosts phonological awareness. Make a white construction paper copy of the picture cards on page 78 and then color them. If desired, laminate the cards for durability. Cut out the cards and place them in a resealable plastic bag. Number three paper lunch bags from 1 to 3. Place the lunch bags and cards at a center. A student opens the bags and stands them. As she names the picture on a chosen card, she claps the word parts (syllables). Then she drops the card into the bag with the corresponding number. She bags the remaining groceries in a similar manner.

Lydia Hess, Chambersburg, PA

WKID News
Dramatic-Play Area

News flash: students will be eager to tune in to this center! To transform your dramatic-play area into a television news station, turn a bookshelf backward to be used as an anchor desk. Set out stools or chairs. Provide clipboards, pencils, and paper for writing news scripts. Display a laminated wall map on a nearby wall to provide a backdrop for the weather segment. Supply a pointer, illustrated weather word cards, and wipe-off markers for drawing weather symbols on the map. Mount a toy video camera (or a camera fashioned from a cardboard box and a disposable cup) on a tripod, and everything will be in place for young camerapersons to capture all of the latest news!

Pam Safrit
Hurley Elementary
Salisbury, NC

Easy as 1, 2, 3!
Math Center

Shake up practice with number order! Place at a partner center copies of a recording sheet similar to the one shown. Also provide a disposable cup containing four number cubes, a piece of felt, and a number line. The two partners sign one paper. Then Partner 1 shakes the cup and spills the number cubes onto the felt. If any cubes have duplicate numbers, he rolls them again. Partner 1 arranges the cubes in order from least to greatest. Partner 2 uses the number line to check his partner's work before writing the number sequence. The partners trade roles to continue.

Jodi Specht
Jefferson Elementary
Clinton, IA

Names Jack Sean

Recording Sheet

2, 3, 4, 6

___, ___, ___, ___

___, ___, ___, ___

___, ___, ___, ___

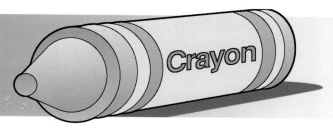

Word Mix-Up
Spelling Center

Forming words is a snap at this center! Use clip art to prepare several picture cards that represent grade-appropriate spelling words. Write the words on the backs of the cards to make the activity self-checking. Program Unifix cubes with the letters needed to spell each word. Place each card and the corresponding cubes in a separate resealable plastic bag. Set all of the bags at a center stocked with paper.

A child chooses a bag, names the picture, and then connects the cubes to spell the word. After he checks his work, he writes the word on his paper. Then he selects another bag.

Joyce Randall, Keshequa Elementary, Dalton, NY

Insect Inspiration
Writing Center

What's the buzz? This buggy project sparks young writers' imaginations! Set out chosen arts-and-crafts materials, such as craft foam cutouts, chenille stems, and pom-poms. Also provide story paper, crayons, and pencils. A child creates a bug with selected materials. She illustrates her creation on a sheet of paper (or tapes a photo of it to her paper). Then she writes about her bug, including details such as its name, what the bug looks like, and what it can do.

If desired, compile students' completed papers into a class book and add it to your classroom library. Or post each child's writing with her buggy creation.

Fern Satin, Mamaroneck Avenue School, White Plains, NY

My bug is a
dragonfly. It is
long. It is skinny. It
can fly really fast!

Scrambled Facts
Math Center

Provide a hands-on review of fact families! Write a chosen addition sentence on a sentence strip, leaving extra space between each number and sign. Also write a subtraction sign. (You may wish to write the numbers and symbols in different colors.) Cut between the numbers and symbols and then place the resulting cards in an envelope. Prepare a desired number of additional fact family envelopes. Set the envelopes at a center stocked with paper and pencils.

A student removes the cards from an envelope. He forms a number sentence with the cards and writes it on his paper. Then he rearranges the cards to form a different number sentence. He continues in this manner until he completes the fact family.

Antoinette Griffin, John G. Shedd Elementary, Chicago, IL

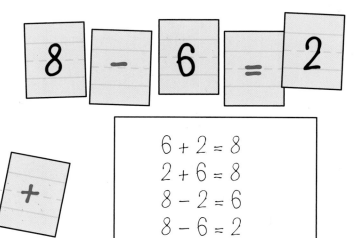

$$8 - 6 = 2$$

$$6 + 2 = 8$$
$$2 + 6 = 8$$
$$8 - 2 = 6$$
$$8 - 6 = 2$$

March Math

How many pom-poms fit on the lion?

Estimate _____

Check _____

How many pom-poms fit on the lamb?

Estimate _____

Check _____

Note to the teacher: Use with "March Math" on page 71.

Buggy Buying

©The Mailbox® • TEC42018 • April/May 2005

Picture Cards

Use with "Shop and Sort!" on page 74.

Management Tips
& Timesavers

Arrival Buddies

Get the first days of school off to a smooth start with the help of some older students. Arrange for a couple of fifth- or sixth-grade students to help your youngsters on each of several mornings. Ask the buddies to assist children with tasks such as putting away backpacks and taking care of any milk or lunch money. Also encourage them to provide a listening ear for any children who need help making the transition. Your youngsters will quickly settle in to the morning routine!
Lynne Nelson, Sherrills Ford Elementary Sherrills Ford, NC

Lunch Money

Delightful Dismissal

Pack learning into every minute, even the last few minutes of the day! As students prepare to go home, lead them in singing familiar songs related to your curriculum. Off-task behavior will be minimized, and the day will end on a happy note.
Shelly Fales
Whittemore-Prescott Early Childhood Center
Whittemore, MI

Friday Folders

Friday folders not only help ensure that students' papers make it home, but they also help guarantee safe delivery of parent communication! To prepare one folder, glue a copy of the poem shown to the front of a file folder and then laminate the folder for durability. Each Friday, have each youngster take his papers home in a prepared folder. Check students' folders for any parent notes on Monday, and collect the folders for safekeeping until the week's end.
Katie Zuehlke, Bendix Elementary, Annandale, MN

Friday Folder

Through every season of the school year,
This folder goes home when Friday is here.
Read, enjoy, even write a note back;
Then simply return in your child's backpack!

Center System

Keep track of the centers students visit with this simple strategy. At each center, place a list of student names and a highlighter. When a student completes a center, have her highlight her name. Or, for more capable students, have each student place her signature beside her name on a prepared list. You'll know at a glance who worked at each center, plus students are sure to enjoy their responsibility! *Denise Clay*
St. Columbkille Parish School Parma, OH

Sarah
Ben
Tamika
Josh
Tomas
Aleah
Rosine
Alex

Circle Round!

Make it easy for students to form a group-time circle. Here's how! Join hands with students to make a ring. Then guide them to move in toward the center. Ask students to pretend that they are a giant balloon being inflated, and have them blow out air as they slowly step further and further back. When their arms are stretched wide, send everyone to the floor by exclaiming, "Pop!" After blowing up and popping a few balloons in this manner, help students blow up a balloon without popping it. Then ask youngsters to drop their hands and sit for group time. What a great-looking circle! *Cynthia Helinski, Nocatee Elementary, Nocatee, FL*

Management Tips & Timesavers

Picture-Perfect Centers

Do your youngsters often forget where they're headed at center time? Photos can help! Take a photo of each center and laminate it for durability. Use Sticky-Tac or magnetic tape to post the photos on the board; then label the photos. Each day, write students' names beside the photos of their assigned centers. Even nonreaders will be able to tell where they should be at center time! *Abigail Jimenez, Henderson School, Midland, TX*

Jenna
Daniel
Aviana

Listening
Center

Transitions on Cue

Students will be all ears when you use this transition tip! Announce literacy-related directions to have your students move to the next activity a few youngsters at a time. For example, you might say, "If your name begins with *J*, line up," or "If you have a long *a* sound in your name, come to calendar time." Not only will you avoid the confusion of having all of your students move at once, but you'll also pack learning into spare moments! *Suzanne Navo, Greenville Elementary, Baton Rouge, LA*

Take Note!

Keep on top of anecdotal notes in just ten minutes a day! At the end of each school day, spend five minutes thinking about each of two students and jotting down relevant observations in a notebook designated for this purpose. Check off the youngsters' names on a class list to ensure that you eventually take notes on each student. When it's time to prepare report cards or hold conferences, you'll have valuable information at your fingertips! *Susan Bragg, Falling Creek Elementary School, Richmond, VA*

Time for Inspection!

A neat classroom is guaranteed with the help of classroom inspectors! After a chosen cleanup time, ask two children to be inspectors. Present them with magnifying glasses and novelty eyeglasses to wear. Have them look over the room and tidy up anything that needs it while you move on with the next activity. No paper scraps on the floor? Good work, inspectors! *Pat Barney-Hicks, Putman Elementary, Blanchester, OH*

Simply Organized

Here's an easy way to organize materials you'll need for upcoming activities. Collect six shallow cardboard containers, such as lids from paper boxes or flats used for flowers. Cover the sides of the containers with colorful Con-Tact paper. Then label a separate container for each day of the school week and one container "Next Week." In each container, store the appropriate reproducibles, project supplies, or other needed materials. Stack the containers out of the way when they're not in use. How handy! *Terry Schreiber, Holy Family School, Norwood, NJ*

Management Tips & Timesavers

Snapshots for Subs

Make it a snap for substitute teachers to find their way around your classroom! Take photos of commonly used classroom areas, such as your calendar area, computer center, and journal storage area. Mount the photos on paper as desired and add notes of explanation. Then tuck the resulting visual reference in your substitute folder. A picture really is worth a thousand words! *Susan Braverman, Council Rock School, Rochester, NY*

Technology Tip

If you keep folders on themes or topics of study, this technology tip is for you. Whenever you come across a relevant Web site, write the Web address inside the corresponding folder. Secure a clasp envelope to the inside of the folder and use it for storing a floppy disk on which you have saved lesson plans, skill sheets, or other teaching materials. At planning time, you'll have helpful resources and materials at your fingertips! *Pam Clark, Parker Mathis Elementary, Valdosta, GA*

High and Low Storage

A magnetic chalkboard or whiteboard has attractive storage possibilities! Obtain two magnetic storage containers such as those for use on refrigerators or filing cabinets. Secure one container to the board within students' reach and stock it with chosen materials for student use. Secure the second container high on the board and store selected teacher supplies in it. High or low, the containers are sure to come in handy! *Kim Mullis, Pearson Elementary, Pearson, GA*

Ready Game Markers

Try this winning idea for managing game markers. In advance, gather a class supply of empty film canisters. Place in each canister a desired number of game markers. Simply have each youngster take a canister at game time; then, when game time is over, ask him to return his markers to his canister. Now that's a timesaving game plan! *Emily Koch, Columbus Grove Local Schools, Columbus Grove, OH*

Changing Choices

Respond to the question "What do I do now?" with a free-time choice list. Display an illustrated poster that lists all of your free-time activities. Each day, use large sticky notes to cover any choices that are not available to students. When a student finishes her work with time to spare, she'll know just what to do! *Sabrina Zaman, Campus School, Memphis, TN*

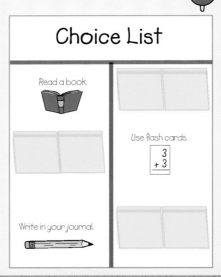

Choice List

Read a book.

Use flash cards.

$$\frac{3}{+\ 3}$$

Write in your journal.

Management Tips & Timesavers

Library Markers

Encourage students to keep your classroom library in order with this simple plan. Personalize a jumbo craft stick for each child and decorate it with a sticker. When a child removes a book from the library, have her put her craft stick in its place. She'll know exactly where to return her selection!
Andrea LaBonte, PS 58, Maspeth, NY

Print and Save

This idea makes it a snap to organize the online extenders from www.the mailboxcompanion.com. For each issue of the magazine, label a tabbed divider page with the corresponding months and year. Secure the divider pages and a supply of top-loading page protectors in a three-ring binder. After you print an extender, slip it into a page protector in the appropriate section. How handy!
Cynthia Nehrbass, Resurrection Parish School, Jacksonville, FL

Eye for Good Behavior

This pride-boosting twist on the traditional I Spy game ends each day on a positive note. Near the end of each day, gather your students and then share a positive observation about their behavior. For example, you might say, "Today I spied all of you walking quietly to the library." Then invite students to report on good behaviors that they spied during the day. You're sure to see lots of smiles and an increase in praiseworthy behavior! *Jo Fryer, Kildeer Countryside School, Long Grove, IL*

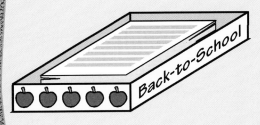

Fall in the Spring?

Get a jump start on the next school year! During the last few weeks of school, duplicate parent notes and other papers that you'll need for the opening weeks of school. You'll have one less thing to do in the fall! *Jo Fryer*

Flannelboard Folders

Here's a convenient way to store your flannelboard materials. For each story or poem, obtain a two-pocket folder. On the front of the folder, add an illustration to aid nonreaders and write the title and the relevant skills. Open the folder and then glue a piece of felt on the left-hand side, covering the pocket. Tuck the flannelboard pieces and a copy of the book or poem in the right-hand pocket. The folders will be easy for students to use at their seats, at home, or at centers! *Catherine Dinse, Errick Road Elementary, N. Tonawanda, NY*

Management Tips & Timesavers

Preparing Centers

Reduce the time you spend preparing centers by teaming up with colleagues. Each week, plan for each teacher at your grade level, including yourself, to prepare the materials and any needed instruction sheets for one or more different center activities. Place all of the center supplies on a rolling cart. The cart can be rolled to each classroom as needed, and the instruction sheets will be helpful to any colleagues or volunteers who are unfamiliar with the activities. *Chris Holmstrom, Bristol Elementary, Bristol, WI*

Magazines at a Glance

Speed up lesson planning with a few notes! When you receive a new issue of *The Mailbox*® magazine, staple a sheet of paper to the inside front cover. As you use ideas in the issue, jot down the titles, page numbers, and any other helpful information. List the ideas you want to try in the future too. The notes will make quick work of your planning! *Jacqueline Feldman, Timothy School, Berwyn, PA*

Teams and Turns

Here's a quick strategy for designating teams or choosing groups of students. Place in a box a class supply of Unifix cubes in two or more colors (one color for each team or group). Have each child remove a cube at random. Then use the colors to sort students. For example, you might have red and blue teams for a class game, or you might announce that the students with the blue cubes will go to the computer lab first. *Susan Johnson, Zion Lutheran School, Belleville, IL*

Namely, Filing

If you have student portfolios, try this letter-perfect tip for keeping up with the filing. Arrange the portfolios alphabetically by students' first names and have your youngsters file their own work. It's one less task for you, and students will get valuable practice with alphabetical order! *Barbara Cohen, Horace Mann Elementary, Cherry Hill, NJ*

How Neat!

Inspire your students to keep their work areas tidy. Here's how! Obtain a small stuffed animal for use as a class mascot and name it with students' input. Explain that the mascot likes to spend time in tidy areas. After students leave for the day, place the mascot on the neatest desk (or table). The next day, congratulate the corresponding student(s) and, if desired, award a privilege such as getting to be first in line for recess. No doubt youngsters will work hard to earn visits from the mascot! *Monica Schroeder, Central Elementary, Toledo, OH*

OUR READERS WRITE

Our Readers Write

Keepsake Kiss

This literature follow-up results in sweet reminders of the new school year! Read aloud *The Kissing Hand* by Audrey Penn during the first week of school. Then help each child use a large, colorful stamp pad to make a handprint on a white construction paper square. Have her glue a red paper heart in the center of the handprint. After she mounts the artwork onto a larger piece of construction paper, ask her to add the poem shown and sign her name. Showcase students' heartwarming projects during your open house.

Sherri Gustine, Limestone Elementary School, Kankakee, IL

Liv

This kissing hand helped me start
The new school year with love in my heart!

Welcome Arch

Here's an eye-catching way to welcome students. Obtain an inexpensive metal arch (available at craft stores). Position the arch in front of your classroom door. Add silk greenery, ribbon, and small back-to-school items such as pencils and novelty erasers. Plan to keep the arch in place all year, redecorating it with students' artwork or seasonal decorations.

Ronda Watts, Southport Elementary School, Southport, NC

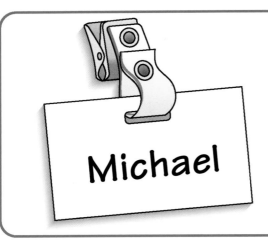

Michael

Nifty Nametags

These nametags are not only handy, but they're also durable! For each child, prepare a business card–size tagboard rectangle. Label one side with the child's name and one side with your school information. Laminate the nametag. Then cut a slit near the top and attach an alligator clip (available at office supply stores). Have students wear their nametags to help office staff and specialists learn each child's name. Use the nametags for field trips too; simply have students wear them with the school information facing out.

Laura Hamons, Pawnee Elementary, Overland Park, KS

Colossal Cupcake

It's a piece of cake to celebrate students' birthdays with this idea! A day or two before a child's birthday, prepare a giant white tagboard cupcake. Arrange for each classmate to color part of it. Then invite students to glue on crumpled bits of colored tissue paper to resemble sprinkles. On the birthday child's special day, present her with the cupcake and numbered paper candles that correspond with her age. Have her glue on the candles in order. Then honor her with a rousing birthday song!

Kathy Brand, St. Paul's Preschool, K–1 Center
Monroe, NY

Where Is the Worm?

This display is just "ripe" for reviewing positional words! Staple a large paper apple to a bulletin board, tucking a bit of paper stuffing behind it. Title the display and use pushpins to add a green paper worm. On each of several days, tack the worm in a different spot in relation to the apple—such as *on, above,* or *beside* it—and then prompt students to use positional words to describe the worm's location. On the last day, cut a small slit in the apple and tuck the worm *inside* so that it is peeking out!

Jana Sanderson, Rainbow School, Stockton, CA

Bonus Books

Looking for good ways to use the books you earn with club bonus points? Check out these suggestions! Save bonus books in a decorated box and invite each child to choose a book on his birthday. Or surprise each student with a bonus book at the end of the year. If you know a student teacher, consider giving her bonus books for a starter library. Books make such wonderful gifts!

Barbara Cohen, Horace Mann Elementary School, Cherry Hill, NJ

My name is <u>Meredith.</u>

My favorite color is <u>green.</u>

The thing I like most about school is <u>science.</u>

At home, I like to <u>ride my bike.</u>

Classy Introductions

Help students get to know one another with this easy-to-make book project. Prepare a student information form similar to the one shown. Have each child fill out the form at home with an adult and then attach a photo of herself. After a child returns the form, invite her to make a self-portrait on provided paper. Then place the form and self-portrait back-to-back and slide them into a plastic page protector. Secure students' resulting pages in a binder. After each youngster contributes to the book, read it with students and then add it to your classroom library.

Lauren Voshell, Mulberry Child Care and Preschool, Glen Mills, PA

Straight Titles

Make crooked bulletin board titles a thing of the past! Here's how! Tack a length of yarn to one side of a bulletin board. Stretch the yarn across the board and secure it to the opposite side. Adjust the yarn end as needed to straighten it. Post desired die-cut letters directly above the yarn and then remove it. What a handy tip!

Tiffany Gosseen, Polo Elementary, Polo, MO

Boxes of Words

Transform a word wall into a word grid! First, use paper strips to divide the wall space into 24 boxes. Then label each box alphabetically, using the last box for three letters: *X, Y,* and *Z.* The boxes make it easy to display words. Plus, they help students quickly find the words they need!

Jo Fryer, Kildeer Countryside School, Long Grove, IL

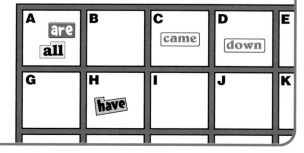

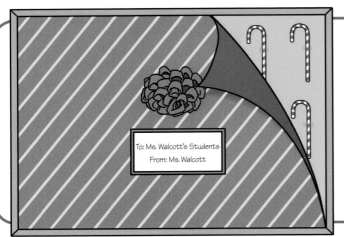

A Sweet Gift

This festive display doubles as a holiday gift for your students. Attach a class supply of small candy canes or other holiday treats to a blank bulletin board. Then cover the bulletin board with colorful gift wrap. Add a bow and gift tag so that the display resembles a present. On the last day of school before your holiday break, invite students to tear away the gift wrap and reveal the surprise!

Lisa Walcott
Schuylkill Haven Elementary Center, Schuylkill Haven, PA

What a Treat!

Instead of serving cookies and cake during classroom holiday parties, try this creative alternative. Serve each child a flat-bottomed ice-cream cone containing a snack such as pudding, mini marshmallows, or trail mix. Students can eat the entire treat, container and all!

Jan Robbins, Fairview Elementary, Richmond, IN

Mobiles in a Jiffy

Here's a neat twist on assembling mobiles that not only saves time but also helps youngsters be more independent! Rather than attaching parts of a mobile with yarn or string, use twist-ties. To connect two hole-punched sections of a mobile, a child bends a twist-tie into a U shape. He pokes one end of the twist-tie through each section, loosely crosses the ends, and then gently twists the ends to secure them.

Jean Horton
Threadgill Primary School
Sheffield, AL

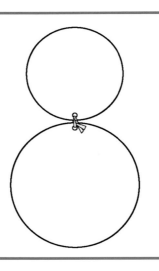

Cheery Chains

Deck the halls—or at least your classroom—and reinforce patterning in the process! Choose two or more holiday colors. Then group students so that the number of students in each group is equal to the number of colors. Give each group member a supply of different-colored 1" x 12" paper strips and access to a glue stick. Then have each group create a paper chain with a designated color pattern. Link all of the completed chains and see how far your class's teamwork can stretch!

Betty Silkunas, Lower Gwynedd Elementary, Ambler, PA

Frosty Gift Tags

These adorable gift tags are perfect for student-made presents. To make one, a child arranges three white hole reinforcers on a construction paper rectangle to resemble a snowpal. She uses fine-tip markers to add details such as a hat, a nose, and some buttons. Then she labels the tag, with adult assistance as needed. How simple!

Betty Silkunas
Lower Gwynedd Elementary, Ambler, PA

Recycle for Writing

Don't throw away the holiday cards you receive; have your youngsters use them next year! If desired, ask colleagues to save their cards for you too. Cut off the signed portion of each card and recycle it. Invite students to cut selected illustrations and messages from the remaining portions and then use them to embellish construction paper cards for their loved ones.

Christy Inman, Brooklet Elementary, Brooklet, GA

Bright Resolutions

Usher in the new year with this eye-catching writing project! Prompt a class discussion about New Year's resolutions. Then ask each child to write a resolution on a half sheet of writing paper (or dictate one for you to write). Help the youngster staple his resolution onto a sheet of construction paper as shown. Instruct him to glue on die-cut numbers to label his work with the new year and then decorate the numbers with glitter glue and bits of foil paper. Impressive!

Phoebe Sharp
Gillette School
Gillette, NJ

Words on the Move

Keep important words in students' view with a portable word wall. List desired words on a folding science project board. Move the prepared board to various classroom areas as needed. For example, you might display the words in your circle-time area and then move the board to a table during small-group instruction. Now that's a ready reference!

Erin Brettel, Springfield Elementary, Springfield, LA

Months of Numbers

Count on outdated and free calendars for practice with number formation! If desired, laminate several calendar pages and provide wipe-off markers for repeated use. Have a child write the appropriate number in each calendar box. For example, ask her to write the number 1 in the box for the first day of the month. Students' writing skills are sure to improve day by day!

Joelle Quimby, Kids & Kreations School, New Berlin, WI

DECEMBER

Sunday	Monday	Tuesday	Wednesday	Thursday	Friday	Saturday
			1	2	3	4
5	6	7	8	9	10	11
12	13	14	15	16	17	18
19	20	21	22	23	24	25
26	27	28	29	30	31	

"Heart-y" Greetings

What's in the cards? Heartfelt gifts! From unwanted decks of playing cards, collect a class supply of cards with hearts. Have each child glue a card onto a sheet of white paper, leaving space at the top and bottom of her paper. Encourage her to imagine that the card is the body of a person, and instruct her to use crayons or markers to draw a head, two arms, and two legs. After she completes her artwork with desired details, help her add a holiday message for a loved one. How adorable!

Sue Lewis Lein, St. Pius X Grade School, Wauwatosa, WI

A Community of Readers

Take note of the Read Across America event with the help of guest readers. Ask various community members—such as the police chief, a postal worker, and a local TV celebrity—to visit your classroom. During each visit, have the guest read aloud a favorite childhood selection or a book that relates to his or her occupation. Snap a photo of each read-aloud session. Compile all of the photos in an album and add student-generated captions. The completed album is sure to be a popular addition to your classroom library!

Kathy Lajoie, Pepin School, Easthampton, MA and Susanna Walz, Center School, Easthampton, MA

The ABCs of Valentines

Distributing valentines is a great opportunity to reinforce alphabetical order! Make sure that each child's valentine holder is clearly labeled with his name. Then arrange the holders alphabetically by first names. As children deliver their cards to the holders, encourage them to use ABC order to help them quickly find each name.

Peg Swanton, Archbishop Howard School, Portland, OR

Treasured Volunteers

Don't wait until the end of the year to tell your classroom volunteers how much you appreciate them. Tell them in March! Near St. Patrick's Day, prepare for each volunteer a small plastic bag of gold foil-wrapped chocolate coins. Use green curling ribbon to attach a note similar to the one shown. Then plan to present each treat to the intended recipient.

Laura Oneto, Kindercare 1124, Eldresburg, MD

Sizable Blocks

Build students' measurement skills in your block center! After lessons on linear measurement, give your block builders standard rulers, a yardstick, a measuring tape, and a carpenter's ruler. After lessons on weight, set out balance scales and a bathroom scale. Provide paper, pencils, and crayons for recording measurements. No doubt students will be eager to see how their construction site measures up!

Jill Palmer, William J. Thorton Elementary, San Antonio, TX

Ready Flash Cards

Use this tip for keeping flash cards within easy reach, and increase skills practice in the process. Hole-punch one corner of each flash card and then thread all of the cards in one set onto a metal ring. Display each set of flash cards on a hook in a convenient location such as the side of a bookcase. When you need a filler activity or a student has free time, the flash cards will be close at hand!

Leslea Walker, Ridgeway Alliance School, White Plains, NY

Celebrate With Headbands

Add a festive touch to a classroom celebration or culminating activity with these easy-to-make headbands. Obtain bulletin board trim with a design that complements a chosen season, holiday, or topic. For each student, size a length of trim to fit her head and then staple the ends together. It's time to celebrate!

Emily Cutrer, Crabapple Crossing Elementary, Alpharetta, GA

Week's End Note

Here's a simple way to keep parents up-to-date. Each Friday, send home a parent note with information such as student birthdays, upcoming events, and requests for classroom items. Briefly describe current and upcoming topics of study. To promote at-home skill reinforcement, list student-appropriate Web sites that you have previewed. Parents are certain to appreciate the information!

Sheila Criqui-Kelley, Lebo Elementary, Lebo, KS

Guess Who!

Reinforce literacy skills as you create anticipation for a coveted class job. Here's how! Secretly choose a student to be the class helper. Draw boxes on the board to represent the letters in his name (see the illustration) and then underline the boxes that represent vowels. Prompt youngsters to guess the letters, encouraging them to refer to any classroom displays that include student names. List each incorrect guess nearby and write each correct guess in the appropriate box. When the entire name is spelled, congratulate the helper!

Mary Spratt, McKinley School, Muscatine, IA

Poetry Picnic

Rain or shine, celebrate National Poetry Month this April with an indoor poetry picnic. On the day of the event, arrange for students and invited guests to sit on the floor with blankets. Serve refreshments as each youngster shares selected poetry with his guests. He might share poems that he can recite, poems that he wrote, or poems that he recently learned to read. If desired, take photos during the event, and plan to send a snapshot to each guest along with a student-prepared thank-you note.

Samantha Engoglia, Westwood Elementary, Novelty, OH

You're Invited to a
Poetry Picnic!

Mark Your Calendar!

Keep calendar skills up-to-date with an idea that can be used again and again! Give each child in a small group an outdated monthly calendar and several counters. Then announce chosen dates or give clues for certain dates; have youngsters mark the corresponding calendar spaces with counters. For example, you might have students mark the 15th or the first Thursday of the month. Timely math reinforcement is guaranteed!

Cheryl Martin, Woodlake Elementary, San Antonio, TX

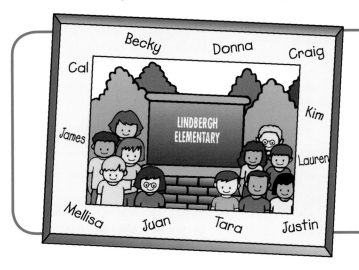

Becky   Donna   Craig
Cal
Kim
James   LINDBERGH ELEMENTARY
Lauren
Mellisa   Juan   Tara   Justin

Goodbye Gift

When it's time to say goodbye to a student teacher, present her with a "class-y" keepsake. To prepare the gift, purchase a picture frame and mat suitable for a class photo. Have each student write his name on the mat. Then place the mat and photo in the frame. What memorable names and faces!

Cindy Casillas, Lindbergh Elementary, Little Falls, MN

Umbrella Day

April showers not only bring flowers, they also bring learning fun! Encourage each child to bring an umbrella to school on a designated day. (Have several umbrellas available for youngsters who do not bring any.) On the special day, have students complete various umbrella-themed activities such as the ones shown. It looks like rain!

Rhonda Urfey, Allan A. Greenleaf School Waterdown, Ontario, Canada

- Sort the umbrellas by color, size, or type of handle.
- Measure the length of each umbrella.
- Sit by open umbrellas and write *u* words.
- Create umbrella-shaped booklets.

Five-Minute Fillers

No preparation is required for this time filler! Simply announce a topic such as one of the ones shown. Have students brainstorm a corresponding list as a class, or encourage them to work independently. There's sure to be plenty of creative thinking!

Suzanne B. Madero
S. M. Anderson Kindergarten Center
Big Spring, TX

List Topics
• things that fly
• places you may see numbers
• things that have wheels
• things that are wet
• reasons to be happy
• things that come in boxes

Special Reader

Give each of your young readers a turn in the spotlight! Each Friday, invite a child to read a chosen book to the class the following week. When the youngster is ready to read to the class, have her sit in a chair designated for the occasion. After the reading session, help students create a response booklet. To do this, have the reader prepare a titled cover and ask each classmate to prepare a page about his favorite part of the story. Present the assembled booklet to the reader along with a photo of her reading.

Sheila Criqui-Kelley, Lebo Elementary, Lebo, KS

That's Important!

Culminate a science or social studies unit with this project modeled on Margaret Wise Brown's *The Important Book*. Help each youngster use the format shown to write several facts on the topic. After each student illustrates his paper, bind youngsters' work into a class book. The project will not only be fun for students, but it will also help you check what students have learned!

Susan Winter, Shekou International School, Shekou, China

The important thing about a ladybug is that it is helpful in a garden.
It has black spots.
It is tiny.
And it can fly.
But the important thing about a ladybug is that it is helpful in a garden.

People, Places, and Things

Nouns are the focus of this ongoing idea. Title a sheet of chart paper for each of the following: people, places, and things. Add a small, representative illustration beside each title and then display the posters within student reach. Have students find nouns in their reading books and list them on the appropriate posters. *Noun* will quickly become a familiar word!

Kim DeNeefe, Oakmont Elementary, Fort Worth, TX

Delightful Book Display

Here's an inexpensive way to show off student-made books. Stand a wooden clothes-drying rack in an easily accessible classroom location. Bind the books with metal rings. Then use a clothespin to clip each book to the drying rack as shown.

Kim Mattoli, Big Tree Elementary, Hamburg, NY

Magnificent Memories

Showcase wonderful school memories with this year-end project. Read aloud Judith Viorst's *Alexander and the Terrible, Horrible, No Good, Very Bad Day.* Point out to students that just as people have memorable bad days, they have memorable great days too. Then have each child write about a great school day from the past year. After each youngster illustrates her work, compile students' papers into a class book and add a title similar to the one shown. What a fantastic look back!

Susan Corino, Bear Tavern School, Titusville, NJ

Ms. Corino's Class and the Wonderful, Marvelous, Fantastic, Very Good Year

Photos for Field Trips

Here's a great tip for making sure that field trips run smoothly. Before a trip, take a photo of each child and label it with his name. Give each chaperone the photos of the children in her group. The photos will help her learn the students' names. Plus, if a child is temporarily separated from the group, his photo will be a help in finding him quickly.

Mindy Apel, Resurrection Catholic Academy, Chicago, IL

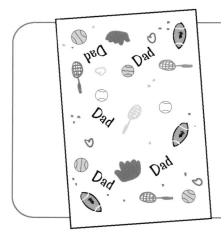

Unique Gift Wrap

Whether you use this gift wrap idea for Father's Day or for another special occasion, it's sure to be a hit! Use a word-processing program to type "Dad" or another relevant word or phrase several times. Print the words. Cut them out and then tape them in a desired arrangement on an 11" x 17" sheet of paper. Make a copy of the prepared paper for each student. Then have her illustrate her resulting gift wrap as desired. How sweet!

Tina Bellotti, George A. Jackson Elementary, Jericho, NY

Summertime Folders

Help students maintain their skills this summer with take-home folders. For each child, glue a poem similar to the one shown to the front of a manila file folder. Stock the folder with grade-appropriate supplies, such as writing paper, drawing paper, a book list, word wall words, and math practice sheets. Parents will appreciate the folders on rainy days or long trips!

Jane Williams, Stratford Academy, Macon, GA

When it's raining or there's nothing to do,
Take out this folder of fun things for you!
We've learned so much we want to remember,
So keep in practice until September!

A Timely Center

Time-telling practice isn't just for math—it can be part of dramatic play too! Set up a desk and chair. Provide toy phones, a manipulative clock, pencils, and a notebook for scheduling appointments. Supply additional props so that the area resembles a chosen type of office. Encourage children to make and record appointments. To keep the appointments running like clockwork, invite a youngster to use the clock to display each time in turn.

Gail Marsh, St. Mark's Lutheran School, Eureka, MO

Action!

Bring action words onto the scene! Tape a large piece of white bulletin board paper to a tabletop. Sketch on the paper a setting—such as a park, zoo, or neighborhood—without any people or animals. Arrange for students to add illustrations of animals or people engaged in various activities. Then help the youngsters label their artwork with the appropriate verbs. An action-packed mural will be the result!

Pam Susman, The Shlenker School, Houston, TX

New Use for Old Books

Make the most of tattered books with this recycling suggestion. Cut out chosen illustrations from each book. Mount the illustrations onto separate pieces of construction paper and then label each illustration with an appropriate word or phrase. Place the resulting picture-word cards at your writing center to give your young authors writing inspiration and spelling help!

Melanie Strohecker, Merry Oaks School, Charlotte, NC

Who's the Helper?

Instead of simply announcing the day's helper, give clues to the youngster's identity. It's a great way to boost students' listening skills! Each morning, secretly write the name of the helper on a blank card. Ask all of the students to stand. Then announce several clues about the helper, one at a time. For example, you might say that the helper is a girl or the helper is wearing tie shoes. After each clue, have each youngster who does not match the description sit down. When only one child remains standing, reveal the name on the card. Hooray! You're the helper of the day!

Angie Kutzer, Garrett Elementary, Mebane, NC

Waiting With Words

A word-making station near your desk is a perfect tool for maximizing learning time. Set out a rimmed tray and a supply of letter manipulatives. Encourage students to form words or messages as they wait for your attention.

Jo Fryer, Kildeer Countryside School, Long Grove, IL

Picture-Perfect Game Markers

This winning idea for board games helps each youngster remember which game marker is his. Obtain a small school photo of each student. Secure the hook side of a Velcro dot to the back of each photo, and attach the loop side of a Velcro dot to each game marker. Before students start a game, each player attaches his picture to a game marker. No more moving another player's game marker by accident!

Elizabeth DeChellis, Victor Mravlag School No. 21, Elizabeth, NJ

Take Five!

When your students are waiting in line, why not use the time to sharpen their skip-counting skills? To practice counting by fives, for example, point to yourself and say, "Five." Then point to your students and have them respond, "Ten." Continue by saying, "15," and then prompting your students to say, "20." Keep counting in this manner until the wait is over!

Gail Marsh, St. Mark's Lutheran School, Eureka, MO

Fun Framers

Use shapely pointers to help students zero in on letters and words. Prepare a seasonal or thematic tagboard cutout. Cut a small rectangle from the center of the cutout. Then tape the cutout to a wooden dowel. Invite students to use the resulting pointer to frame letters or words in big books or the day's morning message.

Erin Owens, West Hardeeville School, Hardeeville, SC

Lots of Lids

Looking for a supersimple way to prepare a memory game? Use juice-can lids! Program several lids as desired to prepare pairs of identical lids. For example, you might program the lids with seasonal stickers or adhesive labels on which you have written high-frequency words. You'll have a set of durable game pieces in a jiffy!

Karen Lotito, Kid's Care, Wrightstown, WI

Spell, Repeat, Erase!

Make spelling practice irresistible with the help of dry-erase markers! To prepare for a pair of students, set out a small whiteboard and a dry-erase marker that has an eraser. To begin, Partner 1 reads aloud a word from a provided spelling list and Partner 2 writes it on the board. Then Partner 1 checks the spelling. Next, the youngsters spell the word together as Partner 2 underlines it. Finally, Partner 2 spells the word again as she erases it, letter by letter. After she wipes the board clean, the partners trade roles. Spell, repeat, erase!

Jana Jilek-Wolfe, Ruahmah J. Hutchings Elementary, Howell, MI

Rhythm & Rhyme Time

Rhythm & Rhyme Time

So Many Colors!

This poem is sure to brighten a study of colors or color words. Display the poem and familiarize youngsters with it as desired. Then, for each verse, encourage students to find classroom items that are the featured colors, or mask the color words and have students guess the beginning letters.

Red is the color of apples in trees.
Yellow is the color of bumblebees.

Orange is the color of carrots in a line.
Purple is the color of grapes on a vine.

Blue is the color of a great big lake.
Green is the color of a garden snake.

Pink is the color of a little flower.
Brown is the color of a sand castle tower.

Black is the color of the sky at night.
White is the color of the moon so bright.

Take a moment to look around.
There are so many colors to be found!

Shannon Adams
Waxahachie Faith Family Academy
Waxahachie, TX

Six Little Apples

Harvest a bushel of counting practice! Display six felt apples on a flannelboard. Then lead students in the song six times, each time removing an apple when indicated and having students determine the number of apples that remain. What mouthwatering fun!

(sung to the tune of "Six Little Ducks")
[Six] little apples in a tree
Looked so very good to me.
So I picked one apple for my lunch.
I ate that apple with a crunch, crunch, crunch.
Crunch, crunch, crunch, crunch, crunch, crunch;
I ate that apple with a crunch, crunch, crunch!

Jill Davis
Kendall-Whittier Elementary
Tulsa, OK

Time to Go!

Recite this chant as a class to prepare your line of youngsters for a walk in the hall. Everybody ready?

My hands are by my side.
I'm standing straight and tall.
My eyes are looking toward the front.
I'm ready for the hall!

Lauren Eisnor
Walker Charter Academy
Walker, MI

Rhythm & Rhyme Time

Time to Go!

Whether you're observing Fire Prevention Week or saluting community helpers, this song is sure to receive a warm reception from your youngsters! Lead students in singing the verse below. Then continue by singing it four more times, each time replacing the first, second, and fourth lines with the next line in the sequence shown.

(sung to the tune of "The Farmer in the Dell")

[The firefighters hear the bell.]
[The firefighters hear the bell.]
Hey, ho, it's time to go!
[The firefighters hear the bell.]

They put on their boots.
They put on their coats.
They put on their helmets.
They get in the truck.

Johnna Lewis
St. Agnes Central School
Mingo Junction, OH

Giving Thanks

Serve up this Thanksgiving tune to get students in the holiday spirit!

(sung to the tune of "She'll Be Comin' Round the Mountain")

We will cook Thanksgiving dinner for our guests. (Mmm, mmm!)
We will cook Thanksgiving dinner for our guests. (Mmm, mmm!)
Oh, the turkey has been basting.
We are tempted to start tasting.
We will cook Thanksgiving dinner for our guests. (Mmm, mmm!)

We will gather round the table when they come. (Oh yes!)
We will gather round the table when they come. (Oh yes!)
We are thankful for each other,
Every cousin, sister, and brother!
We will gather round the table when they come. (Oh yes!)

Lisa Friesen, Pam Fostano,
  Debbie Casey
YMCA Wraparound Kindergarten
Hilton, NY

Batty Banter

What do five little bats banter about on a Halloween night? That's what students find out with this playful poem! After children are familiar with the poem, encourage them to add movements to create a "spook-tacular" performance!

Five little bats hanging upside down.   *Hold up five fingers.*
The first one said, "Let's go look around!"   *Place hand above eyes and look around.*
The second one said, "What do you think we'll see?"   *Throw hands outward.*
The third one said, "Maybe owls in a tree!"   *Pantomime looking through binoculars.*
The fourth one said, "Or some pumpkins round and fat!"   *Make a circle with arms.*
The fifth one said, "Or a big black cat!"   *Pretend to scratch with claws.*
Then with a flap, flap, flap, they flew off in the night.   *Flap arms.*
Five little bats—such a spooky sight!   *Shiver.*

adapted from an idea by Marlene Browne
Azalea Park Elementary
Orlando, FL

Rhythm & Rhyme Time

December's Here!

Are your students beaming with festive cheer? Then it must be December! Highlight the merry month with a snappy sing-along.

(sung to the tune of the refrain in "Jingle Bells")
December's here, December's here—
The last month of the year.
Bells are ringing, people are singing,
Filled with holiday cheer!

Families meet; we all greet
People we hold dear!
We're so glad that December
Is finally right here!

Constance Bancroft
East Fairhaven School
Fairhaven, MA

A Seasonal Song

No matter what time of year it is, this song is always in season! Lead youngsters in singing the verse shown. Then use the suggestions that follow to compose a verse for each remaining season.

(sung to the tune of "When the Saints Go Marching In")
Oh, when we build a big snowpal,
Oh, when we build a big snowpal,
The season is called winter
When we build a big snowpal.

Suggestions for additional verses:
Spring: *Oh, when we plant some tiny seeds...*
Summer: *Oh, when we all go to the beach...*
Autumn: *Oh, when we rake up all the leaves...*

adapted from an idea by Bonnie Elizabeth Vontz
Cheshire Country Day School, Milldale, CT

Cupcake Chorus

This tempting math chant really takes the cake! Lead children in performing the verse below. Then perform it four more times, each time decreasing the numbers by one and replacing the underlined words with the next line in the sequence. If desired, add flannelboard props so children can see the subtraction in action. How sweet!

Five cupcake(s) in a bakery pan,
Waiting to be frosted by the baker man.
[A fox crept in through an open door.]
It ate one up, and that left four.

A crow flew in from a nearby tree.
A tiger walked in—it had escaped from the zoo.
A lion charged in—it was on the run.
A chimp climbed in—it was having fun.

Elizabeth Schneller
Kehoe France School
Metairie, LA

Rhythm & Rhyme Time

A Coyote Chorus

Five howling coyotes are the stars of this playful song! Select five youngsters (coyotes) to sit together. Lead the class in singing the first verse, directing one coyote to leave the group during the third line to join his other classmates. Repeat the verse four times, decreasing the numbers and prompting one coyote to leave during each repetition. Then sing the final verse with students. No more coyotes!

(sung to the tune of "Five Green and Speckled Frogs")

[Five] little coyotes sitting by mesquite trees,
Howling up at the big full moon—ah-woo!
One chased a jackrabbit, a very bad habit.
Now there are [four] coyotes left—ah-woo!

Final verse:
No little coyotes sitting by mesquite trees,
Howling up at the big full moon—ah-woo!
Now those jackrabbits can play until the break of day.
All the coyotes went away—ah-woo!

Sue Creason
Highland Plaza United Methodist
Preschool and Kindergarten
Hixson, TN

Buying Bubble Gum

Here's a "cent-sational" approach to counting by tens. Lead students in the chant shown, prompting them to loudly clap their hands once when they say, "Pop!" Then, if desired, invite students to suggest different bubble gum flavors during later repetitions. How tempting!

I'm going to the store with my pocket full of
    dimes.
I want to buy some bubble gum; there are so many
    kinds.
I'll choose strawberry—it's so tasty and sweet.
Then I'll count out my dimes to pay for my treat!
10, 20, 30, 40, 50, 60, 70, 80, 90, 100—pop!

adapted from an idea by Ginger Viets
South Heights Elementary
Henderson, KY

Lucky Leprechaun

Enrich a St. Patrick's Day celebration with this wee action poem!

I found a little leprechaun; a tiny man was he.
He sat under a rainbow near an old oak tree.
I walked right up to him, and he looked me over.
Then he winked and handed me a four-leaf clover!

Hold up thumb and forefinger to show height.
Hold arms over head to make an arch.
Walk in place.
Wink; then pretend to hold out a four-leaf clover.

Ann Fisher, Toledo, OH

101

Rhythm & Rhyme Time

Little Lighthouse

Pay tribute to the beacons of the night with this cheerful song!

(sung to the tune of the chorus of "Down by the Station")

Down by the lighthouse
Standing near the ocean,
See the yellow light shine brightly
For ships to see.

It guides them safely home
On the darkest evenings.
Blink, blink, blink, blink,
Safely home!

Margaret Southard
Cleveland, NY

Bugs Galore

Here's a poetic look at bugs that's sure to help students identify insects! Prepare a picture card of a spider and each featured insect for flannelboard use. As you teach the poem to your students, place each card on your flannelboard when appropriate.

Ants are insects that may live underground.
Grasshoppers are insects that hop all around.
Butterflies are insects with beautiful wings.
Crickets are insects that sing, sing, sing!
Ladybugs are insects that are easy to spot.
Are spiders insects? No, they're not!

Robbin Stook Williams
Montclair Elementary School
Orange Park, FL

American Pride

This patriotic song is a perfect addition to a Fourth of July celebration.

(sung to the tune of "I'm a Little Teapot")

It's great to live in the USA
Where many people work, rest, and play.
The USA is free—yes, it's true.
So give a cheer for the red, white, and blue!

SIMPLE SCIENCE

Remarkable Rocks!

Dig into this nitty-gritty investigation of rocks to sharpen students' observation skills!

by Kimberly A. Brugger, Staff Editor

Rock-Solid Introduction

Making predictions, describing observations

Promote interest in rock exploration with this gem of an introduction! In advance, collect a class supply of rocks that vary in appearance and then place them in a lidded box. Display the box and ask students to listen for clues to its contents as you recite the poem shown. Then invite youngsters to guess what is in the box. After several students share their ideas, open the box and reveal its contents with great fanfare.

Next, hand a rock to each child. Allow time for students to examine their rocks with their classmates. Prompt children to use descriptive words, such as the ones in the poem, as they discuss the properties of the rocks. Then collect the rocks and place them at a center along with nonbreakable magnifying glasses for further exploration. Rock on!

What's Inside?

The things we'll study may have speckles or stripes.
Some are bumpy, some are smooth, and there are many types.
Some are made inside the earth where it's very hot.
Some are as big as can be; some are as small as a dot.
You may find them on a mountaintop or under the sea.
What is in this box? What could these things be?

● **FUN FACT** ●
Rock covers Earth like a crust. So wherever you walk, you're walking over rock!

Under Investigation

Recording observations

What better way to practice a mountain of observation skills than with rock reports? Give each child a copy of the rock report form (page 109) and a rock from the collection used in the previous idea. After youngsters examine their rocks, read aloud the questions on the form and have each child circle his answers. Then ask each student to draw and color a picture of his rock in the provided space. If desired, have students trade rocks and complete additional rock reports. Encourage your young rock hounds to take their papers home and share their observations with their families.

SIMPLE SCIENCE

A Spectrum of Possibilities

Have students try these colorful activities and "hue" won't believe the oohs and aahs that result!

ideas contributed by Beth Allison—PreK–5 Art Specialist
Decatur City Schools, Decatur, AL

Cool Shades
Making and testing predictions

With this idea, discoveries about shades of color don't come out of the blue—they come from your pint-size Picassos' observations! Divide students into small groups. Provide each group with partially filled disposable cups of blue, black, and white tempera paint. Place a plastic spoon in each cup. Give each group member a paper plate, paintbrush, and paper towel.

Next, have each student draw a line down the center of his plate and then place a spoonful of blue paint on one half. Invite students to predict what would happen if they mixed black paint in with their blue paint. Have each child test the predictions. After students share their results, instruct them to wipe the excess paint from their paintbrushes. Then ask students to predict the results of mixing blue and white paint. Have them use the empty portions of their plates to test their ideas. Afterward, invite youngsters to paint with shades of blue on provided paper. As they work, encourage them to consider whether white and black paint can make all colors lighter and darker. Provide later painting opportunities for them to test their theories!

FUN FACT
Blue, red, and yellow paint can be mixed together to make hundreds of colors.

Mix It Up!
Recording predictions and results

Combining primary colors is sure to make a vivid impression on your students! Divide youngsters into small groups. Give each group one spoon, three clear plastic cups partially filled with water, and a copy of page 110 for each child.

To begin, have each youngster color the first two bottles on her sheet the designated colors. Then ask her to predict what color results from mixing the two colors. Have her use words and pictures to record her prediction. Next, for each group, squeeze drops of yellow and blue food coloring into one cup of water. After a group member stirs the water, instruct each youngster to record the results. Explore the remaining color combinations in a similar manner. So that's how purple is made!

Read aloud *The Color Kittens* by Margaret Wise Brown.

SIMPLE SCIENCE

Chilly Explorations

Brrr! Use these ideas to warm up students' observation skills and to investigate how wintry weather affects people's lives.

ideas by Laurie Gibbons, Huntsville, AL

So Slippery!
Observing changes in ice

Slide into a discussion about winter weather with this intriguing experiment. In advance, prepare a large pan of ice and a supply of ice cubes. Post a two-column chart with one column titled "Before" and one column titled "After." Display the pan of ice and invite youngsters to tell how the ice looks and feels. List the describing words in the first column. Then push a small toy car on the ice and comment on how it moves on the slippery surface. Tell students that some communities put salt on their roads during the winter. Have students share their ideas about why.

Next, divide students into small groups. Give each group a container of salt and two disposable bowls that each contain an ice cube. Sprinkle salt on the large pan of ice and instruct each group to sprinkle salt on one of its ice cubes. After a few minutes, invite students to share their observations. Push the toy car on the pan of salted ice and point out that it moves more slowly. List student-generated descriptions of the salted ice in the second column; then compare the two lists. Now that's a cool science lesson!

Here's why: *Salt lowers the freezing point of water, making it harder for ice to stay frozen. Salted ice melts faster than unsalted ice.*

● FUN FACT ●
Shivering makes a person's muscles work harder, which helps keep him warm.

Tracking Temperatures
Using a thermometer, collecting data

Whether it's warm or downright cold, the weather affects everyone! Help your students become weatherwise with this ongoing idea. Use a desired method to label a thermometer with the following temperature ranges: cold, cool, warm, and hot (see the illustration). Post a chart similar to the one shown and obtain a supply of adhesive dots—one color for each row. After familiarizing students with the thermometer's labels, place the thermometer outside in an easily accessible location.

At the same time on each of several days, have students predict how cold it is outside. Help one or more of your young weather watchers read the thermometer; then have a volunteer use a colored dot to record the information on the chart. Follow up with a class discussion about outdoor clothing and activities that are appropriate for the weather.

SIMPLE SCIENCE

Spotlight on Shadows

Whether or not Punxsutawney Phil sees his shadow this February, your students can make some shadow observations of their own! Familiarize youngsters with the tradition of Groundhog Day and then try the following investigations.

Shadow Watch

by Kimberly Brugger-Murphy, Staff Editor

Experimenting, discussing results

This exploration-based center is an intriguing way to introduce the topic of shadows. Make an enlarged construction paper copy of the groundhog pattern on page 111. Cut it out and then tape it to a portion of a cardboard tube to make it self-standing. Place the groundhog and a flashlight at a center. Post the questions shown, and explain that students will later share their answers with the class. If desired, provide paper for recording observations. Then arrange for students to visit the center in pairs.

To use the center, the partners stand the groundhog in an open area. They try to determine the answer to each question by shining the light on the groundhog from different distances, directions, and angles. After each youngster has visited the center, discuss students' answers and observations. Hey—look how long the shadow is now!

1. How can you make the groundhog's shadow bigger?
2. How can you make the groundhog's shadow smaller?
3. What happens when you shine the light from different directions?

> ● FUN FACT ●
> When the sun shines on one side of the earth, it casts a shadow on the other side.

Block the Light!

Recording predictions and results

Invite your young shadow investigators to put their prediction skills to the test! Place a wooden block, a transparency sheet, and a translucent lid near an overhead projector. Give each child a copy of the recording sheet on page 111. Hold up the block and ask each youngster to silently predict whether it will have a shadow when the projector light shines on it. After each student writes his prediction in the appropriate column on his paper, place the block on the overhead projector and turn the projector on. Then have each youngster record what happened. Repeat the predicting and recording process with the transparency sheet and lid. Discuss the results, leading youngsters to realize that objects that block light have shadows, while objects that let all of the light pass through do not. How enlightening!

Read aloud *Bear Shadow* by Frank Asch.

"Sense-ational" Watermelon

There's more to watermelon than meets the eye! Invite your students to use all of their senses to investigate the popular summertime treat.

ideas contributed by Lucia Kemp Henry, Fallon, NV

Inside-Out Investigation
Describing observations

No doubt your students will know watermelon inside and out after this vocabulary-boosting activity! Display a watermelon within reach of students and encourage them to examine it. Then give each youngster a copy of the recording sheet on page 112. Have him illustrate the watermelon in the first box. Ask him to write a word in the first blank to describe how the melon looks. After each youngster completes his writing, invite students to thump the melon and tell how it sounds. Then ask each student to write a describing word in the appropriate space on his paper. Have students determine how the melon smells and feels; help them write corresponding describing words.

Next, cut the watermelon and give each student a piece. Have each youngster illustrate his watermelon slice in the second box on his paper. Encourage him to use all of his senses to examine the inside of the melon. Then help him write describing words to correspond with his observations.

● FUN FACT ●
A good sense of smell helps a person taste food easily!

Touch
What feels as __smooth__ as a watermelon?

tabl
book
appl
ball
pumkin

Just Like Melon!
Using senses to classify

How are a tabletop and the outside of a watermelon alike? They're both smooth! After students examine a watermelon, they'll be ready to make similar comparisons with this poster project. Title each of five sheets of chart paper with a different sense. Then program each paper with a corresponding question similar to the one shown (without a word in the blank). With student input, complete the questions by filling in the blanks. Next, divide students into five groups and give each group a poster. Ask the students in each group to illustrate several items that fit their poster description and then label their illustrations. After students complete their work, invite each group to display its poster on a classroom wall and read it aloud.

Name_____

Rock Report

Look. Circle the correct words.

1. Is the rock big or small?

2. Is the rock speckled, striped, or plain?

3. Is the rock bumpy, smooth, or sharp?

Draw a picture of the rock.

Color.

Note to the teacher: Use with "Under Investigation" on page 104.

Name_____

Drop by Drop!

Listen for directions.

Colors	Guesses	What Happened
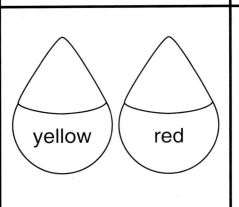 blue yellow		
yellow red		
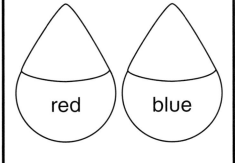 red blue		

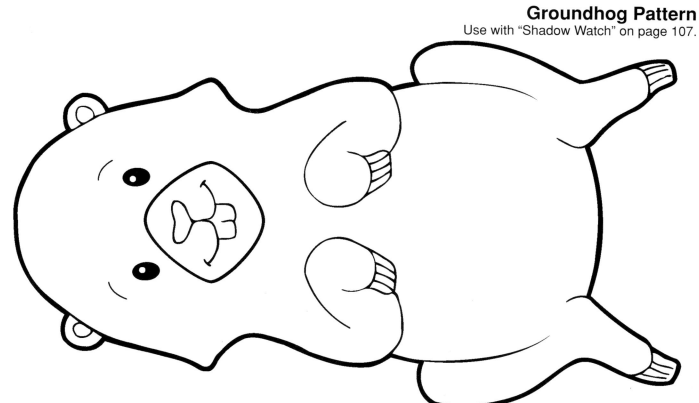

Name _____

Shadow Test

Objects	Guesses	What Happened
block		
plastic sheet		
lid		

Note to the teacher: Use with "Block the Light!" on page 107.

111

Name_____

Use Your Senses!

Listen for directions.

Outside

Inside

Note to the teacher: Use with "Inside-Out Investigation" on page 108.

SKILLS FOR BEGINNING READERS

Skills for Beginning Readers

N Nigel

NUTTY CEREAL

Letters and Logos
Environmental Print

This intriguing logo search zeroes in on beginning letters! Send a parent note home requesting that each student bring in at least one logo from a product whose name or brand name begins with the same letter as the youngster's name. For example, Michael could bring in an empty marshmallow bag, and Carter could bring in the front section of a Cap'n Crunch cereal box. After each youngster brings in at least one logo, have students sit with you in a circle and place their finds on the floor in front of them. Ask each student, in turn, to hold up a logo he found and then announce his letter and the corresponding word.

To follow up, have each student label a sheet of white paper with his letter and name and then glue on his logo(s). Display the resulting posters in alphabetical order to showcase words that students know to the letter!

Linda Newman
Washington Hebrew Early Learning Center
Potomac, MD

Who Has the Letter?
Letter Identification

Give a popular chant a letter-themed twist! Prepare a class supply of letter cards. Sit with students in a circle and distribute the letter cards, asking each youngster to place her card facedown in front of herself. Next, lead students in the first part of the chant shown, inserting a chosen letter and student name. Have the named student turn her card over at the appropriate time and show it to the class. If she has the letter, have her reply, "I sure do!" Then lead the class in a round of applause and begin the chant again with a different letter. If she does not have the letter, instruct her to place the card facedown and then resume the chant. At the chant's conclusion, return to the first part to continue. **To adapt the activity for more advanced students,** program blank cards with chosen words and modify the chant accordingly.

Kathy Halley
Rochester, NY

Missing Letter
(chanted to the rhythm of "Who Stole the Cookies?")

Part 1
Teacher and students: Who has the card with the letter [A]?
Teacher: [Student's name] has the card with the letter [A].
Named student: Who me?
Teacher and students: Yes, you!

Student turns her card over.

Part 2
Named student: Couldn't be!
Teacher and students: Then who?

Put It Together!
Phonological Awareness

Students develop an ear for words with this rhythmic activity! Sit with students in your group area. Begin by saying the chant below, establishing a beat by lightly patting your lap in a steady rhythm. Next, use the following format to present a two-syllable word, syllable by syllable: "If I say [to-day], you say…" Then have students respond with the blended form of the word. Use the same format to present different two-syllable words. After students can easily blend syllables, make the activity more challenging by presenting words divided into onsets and rimes.

> Boys and girls,
> Have you heard?
> I know a game
> Where you guess the word!

Michele Galvan
Roosevelt School, McAllen, TX

Today!

Alex wore his blue shirt.

Dressed to Read!
Predictable Text

Use this class book idea to outfit your youngsters for reading success! Share your favorite version of *Mary Wore Her Red Dress and Henry Wore His Green Sneakers.* Then, on provided paper, have each youngster draw and color a picture of himself wearing a chosen outfit. (If desired, provide a person-shaped template for each student to trace.) As students complete their illustrations, work with each youngster, in turn, to add a caption modeled after the story.

Later, bind students' completed papers between construction paper covers and title the resulting book "Colorful Clothing." Read the book with students, inviting each youngster to point to the words on his page as his classmates read it. The colorful story is bound to be a popular addition to your classroom library!

Maureen Glennon
Faller Elementary, Ridgecrest, CA

In the Neighborhood
Word Families

Students' reading vocabularies are sure to grow right along with these word-family neighborhoods. Draw on a sheet of duplicating paper a house shape similar to the one shown. After introducing a word family to students, make one copy of the house. Label the roof with the corresponding rime and the house with three words that include the rime. Give each student a white construction paper copy of the prepared house.

Next, have her read the words and trace them with a crayon. Ask her to color her roof, cut out her house, and add desired crayon details to the blank side of it. Then help her hole-punch the house and thread it onto a metal ring. As she learns different word families, have her prepare more houses for her ring. Encourage her to read her ring often and she'll soon be right at home with word families!

Shannon Roberts
Silver Strand Elementary, Coronado, CA

-at
cat
mat
hat

Skills for Beginning Readers

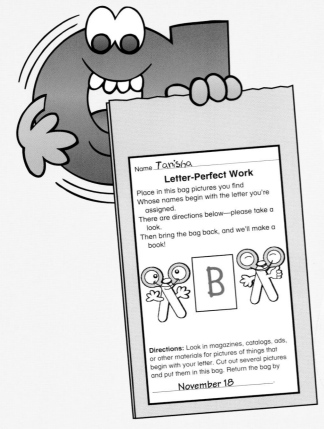

Picture This!
Letter-Sound Relationships

Learning fun is in the bag with this one-of-a-kind alphabet project! Make one copy of the bag label on page 125. Write a due date in the blank at the bottom of the label. Then copy the label to make a class supply. Program the boxes on the labels with the letters of the alphabet, omitting less commonly used letters and repeating letters as needed. Give each child a label and have her sign her name. Read the rhyme and directions aloud. Ask each youngster to glue her label onto the back of a paper lunch bag and then take the bag home.

After each student returns her bag with the pictures she found, give her a large sheet of paper. Have her write her letter in the center of her paper and then glue her pictures around it. Stack students' completed papers in alphabetical order. Bind them between two construction paper covers and add a desired title. The resulting book is letter-perfect for small-group sharing as well as independent exploration!

Sue DeRiso
John W. Horton Elementary School
Cranston, RI

Count the Claps
Phonological Awareness

Here's a handy way to help students tune in to the syllables in their names. Lead students in saying each classmate's name, in turn, as they clap the parts (syllables). For each name, have students identify the number of claps. Next, give each youngster a 12" x 18" sheet of white paper and access to copies of the clapping cards on page 125. Instruct him to fold his paper in half and then unfold it. On one half of the paper, have him write his name and place the appropriate number of clapping cards. After you check his work, ask him to glue the cards in place and draw a self-portrait on the other half of his paper. Invite youngsters to take their papers home to share with their families, or bind their work into a class book,

Fern Satin
Mamaroneck Avenue School
White Plains, NY

Sticky Matchup
High-Frequency Words

Pair sticky notes and big books to help youngsters increase their reading vocabularies. Here's how! During a small-group reading time, select a familiar big book that contains several instances of a chosen word. Display the word on a large blank card and ask students to keep an eye out for it throughout the story. As you read the story, track the print with a finger; prompt each youngster to give a thumbs-up sign whenever he sees the word. After students correctly signal a word, place a small sticky note below it. For additional reinforcement, label each sticky note with the word and move it to the corner of the page. Then place the book at a center and have students place the sticky notes atop the matching words.

Melanie Climenhage
Oakley Park Public School
Barrie, Ontario, Canada

Pack of Words
-ack Word Family

What's a perfect prop to introduce the *-ack* word family? A backpack, of course! In advance, place in a backpack a word card for each word shown. Display the backpack and ask students how the words *back* and *pack* are similar. Lead them to conclude that both words end with *-ack*. Next, ask a student to remove a card from the backpack. Have students identify the word and use it in a sentence. Then invite a different student to remove another card. Continue in this manner until the backpack is empty. Then tack the backpack to a bulletin board titled "A Pack of *-ack* Words!" and staple the cards around it to create an eye-catching student reference.

Word List
back
black
pack
sack
snack
stack
tack
track

Faith Fishkind
New Town Elementary School
Owings Mills, MD

Questions by the Book
Comprehension

Four simple questions make this take-home activity a surefire way to boost comprehension! Have a child take home a storybook and a copy of a sheet similar to the one shown with sections for who, what, where, and how story-related questions. Also send home a note asking a parent to read the book with the youngster and then help her use pictures or words to respond to the questions. After the student returns the completed paper and book, discuss the story with her individually, or read the book to the class and invite her to share her work!

Susan Lindberg, Westerly School, Long Beach, CA

Skills for Beginning Readers

Wearable Words
Sight Words

This ongoing idea is such a perfect fit for sight-word practice that it's well worth the advance preparation! Invite each family to donate one large white T-shirt. Gather additional T-shirts so that you have one for each student and a few extra for any late enrollees. Obtain fabric markers and brush-on fabric paint in assorted colors. On each T-shirt, have a classroom volunteer use fabric markers to outline large block letters that spell a different designated sight word. Arrange for each child to use a paintbrush and fabric paint to fill in the letters on a prepared shirt (provide adult assistance as needed). Set the shirts aside to dry.

Every week or so, designate a day for sight-word silliness. On the chosen day, have each youngster wear a prepared T-shirt over his clothes. Review the words with students as desired. Then explain that throughout the day each student will be called by his sight word instead of his name. What a fun strategy for keeping sight words in sight!

Barbara Embree
Coolidge Elementary
Oklahoma City, OK

Jumping Jacks
Predictable Text, Concepts of Print

Students will jump at the chance to practice reading with this class book project! Write the nursery rhyme "Jack Be Nimble" on a piece of copy paper, replacing each occurrence of Jack's name with a blank. Make one copy for each child. To begin, recite the rhyme with your youngsters. Next, give each child a prepared rhyme and have her write her name in each blank. Ask her to glue the rhyme near the bottom of a vertically positioned 12" x 18" sheet of white construction paper and then add an illustration. After each student practices reading her resulting page, bind all of the pages between two covers. Reinforce chosen concepts of print as you read the book with students. Then place the book in your classroom library for independent reading practice.

Chari Purchatzke and Kristy Reid
Denmark Elementary
Denmark, IA

Jan Leighton
Searsport Elementary School
Searsport, ME

Hannah be nimble.
Hannah be quick.
Hannah jump over the candlestick.

It's on the Box!
Environmental Print

What do boxes of crackers, cake mixes, and cereal have in common? They're all convenient sources of environmental print! Collect a variety of empty, clean food boxes. Cut away the back and sides of each box and plan to recycle them. Laminate each box front. Sit with a small group of students and give each child a box front and wipe-off marker. Then engage the students in a variety of reading-related searches. For example, have youngsters find designated letters or blends and then circle them. Or have each youngster circle one or two words that he knows how to read. Invite students to share their finds before wiping off their markings and beginning a new search.

Chris Foedisch
Paul Fly Elementary
Norristown, PA

Eye for Phonics
Phonics Review

Keep a variety of phonics skills sharp with this skill-boosting version of the I Spy game. To play, give students phonics-related clues to different classroom items. For example, you might say, "I spy with my little eye something whose name begins with *ch*." Tailor the clues to match the needs in your group, and reinforce different phonics elements such as initial or final consonants, vowel sounds, or blends. The possibilities are endless!

Kim Summers, Ontario, CA

"Egg-cellent" Vowel Sound
Short e

Try this "eggs-tra" special vowel activity as a follow-up to Keith Baker's *Big Fat Hen* or your favorite version of *The Little Red Hen*. Use a permanent marker to label each of ten plastic eggs with a short *e* word. Program a few other eggs with three-letter words that have different vowel sounds. Arrange all of the eggs in a raffia-lined basket to resemble a nest. If desired, add a hen puppet or stuffed animal. Place at a center the nest and several copies of a recording sheet with ten numbered blanks.

Two students visit the center at one time. They write their names on one recording sheet. Then Partner 1 chooses an egg and reads the word aloud. The partners determine whether it is a short *e* word. If it is, Partner 2 writes it on the paper. If it isn't, she sets the egg aside. Then the partners trade roles. They continue in this manner to complete their "eggs-traordinary" list!

Betty Lynn Scholtz, Providence Day School, Charlotte, NC

Skills for Beginning Readers

Musical March
Sight Words

Here's an upbeat approach to practicing sight words! Prepare two identical class sets of sight word cards. Place a card from one set facedown on each child's desk (or table space). Keep the second set for your use. To begin, have each student push in her chair and stand behind it. Play some lively music and ask the students to march in an established path around their desks. After a few moments, stop the music. At this signal, each child stands behind the closest unclaimed chair. Read aloud one of your cards and have each youngster check to see whether she has the same word. Ask the child who has the word to hold up her card and spell the word aloud. To continue, have students set their cards facedown; then resume the music.

For an easier version, use letter cards. When a student holds up a designated letter, have her name a word that begins with it. March on!

Yolanda Ramos, Pearl Rucker Elementary
Houston, TX

Word Slide
Onsets and Rimes

Slide into word family fun! For each child, make two parallel slits about an inch apart in a small paper plate. Then label the plate with a chosen rime as shown. Divide a 1½" x 12" strip of white construction paper into sections at one-inch intervals. Program several sections with onsets that can be used to form a word; leave one or more sections at each end of the strip blank for easy handling. (See the illustration.)

Next, help each youngster thread his strip through the slits in his plate so that words may be formed. Have him slide the strip up and down and read aloud the resulting words. Then invite him to embellish his plate with provided arts-and-crafts materials. If desired, help him decorate his plate to represent a relevant word. For example, he may fashion his plate into a cat for *-at* or a nighttime sky for *-ight*. How clever!

Julie Douglas, St. Louis, MO

Sing and Read!
Word Wall Words

Try this toe-tapping strategy for keeping word wall words fresh in students' minds. Lead students in singing the song shown, inserting chosen words from your display as you point to them. Requests for encores are guaranteed!

(sung to the tune of "He's Got the Whole World in His Hands")

We can read the word wall; yes, we can.
We can read [all] and [Alex]; yes, we can.
We can read [ant] and [Ashley]; yes, we can.
We can read a lot; yes, we can!

Barbara J. Anderson, Elyria Kindergarten Village, Elyria, OH

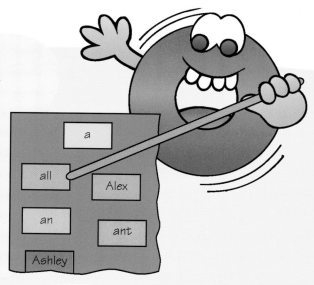

Star Surprise
Letter-Sound Relationships

No one knows who will be the star of this suspense-filled letter activity! Program jumbo craft sticks with different alphabet letters as shown. On the blank side of several of the sticks, adhere a star sticker at the lettered end. Stand all the sticks, programmed end down, in a canister. In a small group, have each student, in turn, remove a stick, name the letter, and then name a word that begins with the letter. When a child removes a starred stick, lead the rest of the group in exclaiming, "You're a star!" At this signal, the child sets the starred stick aside and all of the group members return any nonstarred sticks that they have. Continue in this manner as time allows. **For more advanced students,** program the sticks with high-frequency words.

Wendy Whittlinger, Shoal Creek Elementary, Conyers, GA

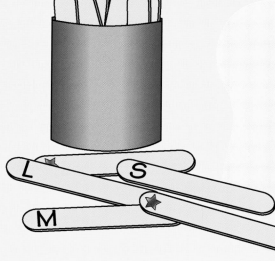

Which Hoop?
Initial Consonants or Short Vowels

Use this sorting idea to round up practice with consonants or short vowels! Place in a basket several objects or pictures of objects whose names have a chosen initial consonant or short-vowel sound. Add a few items whose names do not have this phonics element. Position two large plastic hoops in the center of your group. Then label one hoop to designate the chosen phonics element. Ask a volunteer to remove one item from the basket. Encourage her classmates to signal with a thumbs-up or thumbs-down whether its name has the featured phonics element. Then have the volunteer set the item in the appropriate hoop. Sort the remaining items in a similar manner.

For a print-related extension, give each youngster a sheet of paper. Have her illustrate a few items that are in the labeled hoop and then write the corresponding words.

Michelle Brown and Susan Fiet
Watervliet Elementary School, Watervliet, NY

Skills for Beginning Readers

Instant Words
Sight Words

Count on this small-group reading activity to be an instant hit! Label an empty instant oatmeal canister "Instant Words." Write a different sight word on each of several cards and then place the cards in the canister. To begin, tell students that instant words are words that they can read on sight. Suggest that the more instant words they know, the better readers they'll be. Next, remove each card, in turn, and prompt students to call out the word as soon as they recognize it. Then return the cards to the canister for later review. For additional reinforcement, post a chosen card before a shared-reading session and have youngsters give a predetermined signal each time they see the word in the book.

Susan Johnson, Zion Lutheran School, Belleville, IL

Chocolate, Vanilla, Chocolate
Consonant-Vowel-Consonant Words

Here's a sweet way for students to practice consonant-vowel-consonant words. Prepare five four-inch white construction paper circles and several four-inch black construction paper circles. Label each white circle with a different vowel, and program the black circles with the consonants in chosen CVC words (see the illustration). Display the circles in a pocket chart and post a jumbo construction paper cookie jar nearby. Then form a word with the circles. Have students read the word aloud; ask a volunteer to write it on the cookie jar. Form and record several words in this manner; then ask volunteers to use the circles to form designated words. Guide students to notice that the assembled words resemble Oreo cookies. Instead of vanilla frosting, a vowel is sandwiched in each one!

Dawn Fleming, West Boulevard Elementary
Boardman, OH

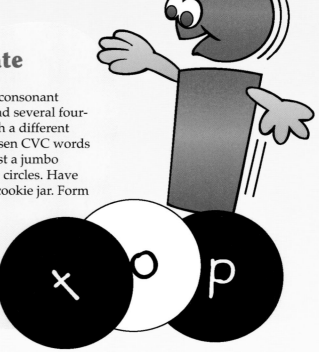

Popcorn Words
High-Frequency Words

Make reading practice irresistible with this class game! List 12 high-frequency words on the board. Tell students that since these words pop up frequently, you call them popcorn words. Then give each child a copy of the gameboard on page 126 and nine counters. Have him write a different popcorn word in each space on his gameboard. (He will not use all of the words.)

To play one round, announce a listed word and ask each child to place a counter on his corresponding space. When a child has a counter in each space, he calls out, "Popcorn Words!" Continue the game until each child has marked all of his words. Everyone's a winner!

Gina Craig, North Duplin Elementary, Calypso, NC

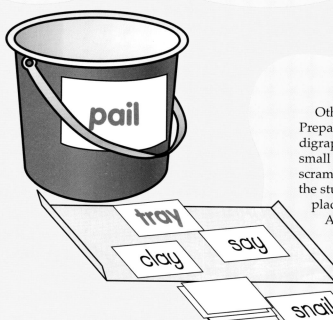

Pail or Tray?
Digraphs: ai, ay

Other word sort activities "pail" in comparison to this one! Prepare several word cards—some with words that have the *ai* digraph and some with words that have the *ay* digraph. Label a small pail and tray as shown. To begin this small-group activity, scramble the cards and then stack them facedown. Next, have the students take turns drawing a card, reading it, and then placing it in the pail or on the tray according to its digraph. After all of the cards are sorted in this manner, lead the students in reading each set of cards aloud. Wow, *ai* and *ay* stand for the same sound!

Tracey Gerkens, West Side Montessori Center, Toledo, OH

Alphabet Assessment
Letter-Sound Relationships

This two-part project is a handy tool for assessing youngsters' letter knowledge. Prepare two grids with randomly sequenced alphabet letters similar to the ones shown. Give a child a copy of each grid and have her name each letter. Then, for each letter, ask her to name a word; write it in the corresponding box. Or invite her to represent each word with an illustration. Later, have her cut apart the boxes and glue them in ABC order on a strip of paper. The result will be a letter-perfect work sample to share with her parents!

Bernette Alegre
Olive Branch Elementary
Portsmouth, VA

Skills for Beginning Readers

Welcome!
(sung to the tune of "The Farmer in the Dell")

[Michael] is here today.
[Michael] is here today.
[Mi-mo, the merry-o],
[Michael] is here today!

Who's Here?
Phonological Awareness

Students make initial sound substitutions during this fun-filled attendance song. At the beginning of the day, welcome each student by featuring his name in the song shown. To do this, lead students in inserting the child's name where indicated and replacing the initial sounds in the nonsense words with the initial sound of the child's name. What a "sound-sational" welcome!

Diane Rinehard
Cline Elementary School
Cold Spring, KY

House of Words
Word Families

Inside this house is a family—a family of words, that is! Write a chosen rime on the board. With student input, list several words that have the rime. Next, give each child an envelope and have her position it with the flap open as shown. Ask her to illustrate the envelope so that it resembles a house. Then give her several blank cards and have her write a different listed word on each card. After she practices reading her cards, encourage her to tuck them in her house for take-home reading practice.

Marzee Woodward
David Youree Elementary
Smyrna, TN

Bag Label

Use with "Picture This!" on page 116.

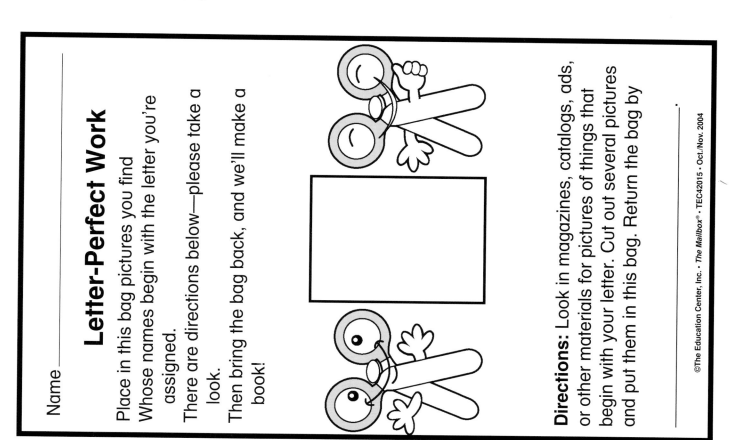

Letter-Perfect Work

Name _____

Place in this bag pictures you find whose names begin with the letter you're assigned.

There are directions below—please take a look.

Then bring the bag back, and we'll make a book!

Directions: Look in magazines, catalogs, ads, or other materials for pictures of things that begin with your letter. Cut out several pictures and put them in this bag. Return the bag by _____

Clapping Cards

Use with "Count the Claps" on page 116.

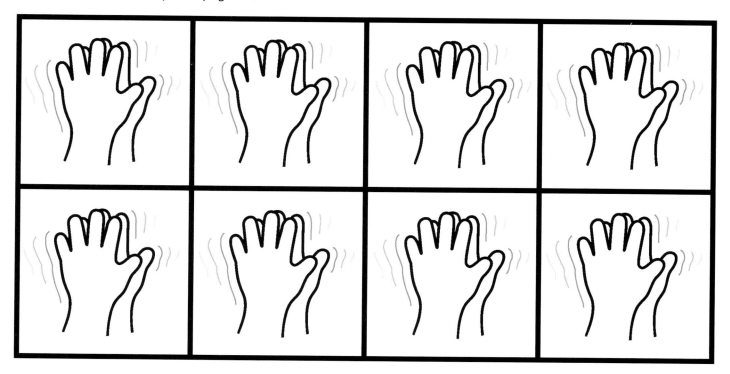

Popcorn Words

Name_____

Listen for directions.

Note to the teacher: Use with "Popcorn Words" on page 123.

©The Mailbox® • TEC42018 • April/May 2005

'Tis the Season

'Tis the Season

Speaking of Labor Day...

This Labor Day version of show-and-tell not only boosts language skills, but it also increases knowledge of community helpers. Send home a note requesting that each youngster bring in an item (or an illustration) that relates to the job of a parent or an adult friend. Plan for a few students to share their items each day until each youngster has had a turn. When a student takes a turn, have her show the class what she brought, tell what it is called, and name the job associated with it. Encourage her to explain how the item relates to the job. Then allow time for her to respond to a few comments or questions from her classmates.

Sue Lein, Wauwatosa, WI

Grand Art

An art project is twice as nice when it's shared with a grandparent! In honor of National Grandparents Day, have each student invite a grandparent or senior friend for a scheduled visit. (Make arrangements with volunteers or other adults as needed to ensure that each student has a special visitor.) On the designated day, have each youngster sit with his guest. Give each twosome a large sheet of white paper and glue. Also provide access to a supply of various precut geometric shapes.

Have each twosome position its paper horizontally and draw a line down the center of it. Ask the youngster to sign his name on one half and his guest to sign the other half. Then instruct each person to glue selected shapes on his half to create a desired picture. Showcase the completed artwork on a hallway wall and title the display "Grand Art."

Taryn Lynn Way, Los Molinos Elementary School, Los Molinos, CA

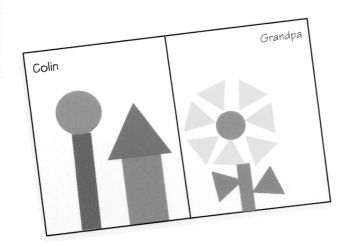

Tempting Survey

Whet students' appetites for math with this "apple-icious" idea! In advance, obtain apples and two toppings for your students to sample. Post a grid similar to the one shown that reflects the snack options; prepare a class supply of apple cutouts sized to fit on the grid. To begin, serve each youngster a few apple wedges and individual portions of the toppings. When a student finishes his snack, invite him to post a cutout on the grid to show which snack he prefers. After each student contributes to the grid, help youngsters count the cutouts in each row and compare the totals. Now that's a fresh look at data!

Shelly Kidd-Hamlett, Helena Elementary, Timberlake, NC

What Do You Like the Most?	
plain apples	🎃🎃
apples with cheese	🎃🎃🎃🎃🎃
apples with cinnamon and sugar	🎃🎃🎃🎃🎃🎃🎃

'Tis the Season

Spooky Sequence

Youngsters not only review story events with this activity, but practice ordinal numbers to boot! Make a class supply of page 135 plus one extra. Color the pictures on one copy and cut them out. For each child, fold two sheets of paper in half and staple them along the fold to make a booklet. Read aloud *The Little Old Lady Who Was Not Afraid of Anything* by Linda Williams. Then post a length of paper and have volunteers tape on the prepared pictures in story order. Refer to the display as you ask story-related questions with ordinal numbers.

To follow up, each youngster colors her patterns and cuts them out. On her booklet cover, she glues the title box and adds desired illustrations. She glues each picture on a separate page, using the front and back of the pages and referring to the displayed pictures for help with sequencing. She draws and colors a scarecrow on her last page and then labels her pictures. Now that's an idea sure to get each student's nod of approval!

Janet Witmer, Harrisburg, PA

Sizing Up Leaves

Students use nonstandard units with this "tree-mendous" idea. Prepare a recording sheet similar to the one shown. Give each child a copy of the recording sheet, a copy of the math mat (page 136), and a supply of Unifix cubes. Ask each student to sign his math mat and color the leaves. Have him use cubes to measure his leaves to the outer edges and then fill out his recording sheet. After students complete their work, prompt a class discussion to compare the measurements. Collect students' math mats for safekeeping, and plan to have youngsters repeat the activity with different types of manipulatives.

Sydna Daily, Oakland Heights Elementary School, Russellville, AR

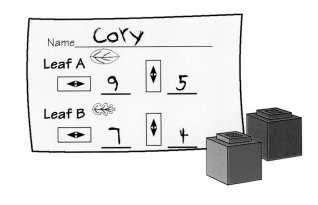

Heavier or Lighter?

A pumpkin is the only prop needed for these weighty comparisons! Display a medium-size pumpkin. Post a chart with two columns, one labeled "Heavier" and the other labeled "Lighter." Then have students name items that are heavier or lighter than the pumpkin, prompting discussion as appropriate. List each item in the correct column. Next, each youngster draws a line down the center of a sheet of drawing paper. On one side of the line, she illustrates something that is lighter than the pumpkin. On the other side, she shows something that is heavier than the pumpkin. She adds captions and then shares her comparison with a classmate.

Lin Attaya
Hodge Elementary School
Denton, TX

Sleepy Bears

Introduce probability with a cave of snoozing bears! In advance, cut off the top few inches of a white paper lunch bag. Illustrate a bear cave, several pawprints, and some snowflakes as shown. Then place in the bag ten teddy bear graham crackers—eight brown and two tan. Set aside some crackers for later student snacks.

To begin, display a recording sheet similar to the one shown. Ask a volunteer to remove a cracker from the bag at random. Use a tally mark to record the color and then have the youngster return the cracker to the bag. Repeat the process with nine more volunteers. After you total the tally marks, have students predict whether there are more brown or tan bears in the bag. Remove the bears to check their predictions.

Leelee Lewis, Matt Arthur Elementary School, Kathleen, GA

		Tally Marks	Total
tan		III	3
brown		IIII III	7

Picturing Kwanzaa

Here's a memorable Kwanzaa activity! Share a grade-appropriate book about the holiday, such as *Seven Candles for Kwanzaa* by Andrea Davis Pinkney. Then give each student a copy of the cards on page 138 and read them aloud. Ask each youngster to color her cards, cut them out, and then initial them. Next, pair students. Have the partners combine their cards to play a holiday version of Concentration. After a few rounds of play, give each student a 6" x 9" construction paper pocket. Invite her to personalize it as desired and then tuck her cards inside. Encourage her to take her cards home and tell her family how each illustration relates to Kwanzaa.

Hat Mix-Up

A flurry of skills practice awaits students at this interactive display. Prepare several paper doily snowpals similar to the one shown and an equal number of construction paper hats. Program the snowpals and hats to reinforce chosen skills. For example, label each hat with an uppercase letter and each snowpal with a lowercase letter. Or label each hat with a different rime and the snowpals with corresponding words. Display the snowpals within student reach on a prepared bulletin board. Stack the hats facedown nearby. Sit with a small group of students at the display. Have each student, in turn, take a hat, read it aloud, and then tack it to the corresponding snowpal. Continue until all of the hats are in place.

adapted from an idea by Maria Stipe
James E. Bacon Elementary
Jesup, GA

'Tis the Season

Special Delivery!

Your little postal workers are sure to have a red-letter day delivering this batch of addition problems. Label each of ten heart cutouts with a different addition combination. Write each sum on a separate house-shaped cutout. Place the cutouts in a Valentine's Day gift bag at a center. To use the center, a child spreads out the houses. Then she places each heart on a house with the corresponding sum. Knock, knock! It's a valentine delivery!

adapted from an idea by Tania Haynes
Webster Niblock School
Medicine Hat, Alberta, Canada

Rainbow Race

Students race leprechauns during this color-word game! Make two copies of the leprechaun game markers on page 139. Color the game markers and cut them out. Tape a short section of a cardboard tube to the back of each game marker to make it self-standing. Prepare a large rainbow gameboard similar to the one shown with six different-colored columns and a desired number of spaces. (Each space should be about 1½" x 2½".) Program a blank cube or a small paper-covered box with the corresponding color words to make a die.

Arrange for a small group of students to play. Have the students stand each leprechaun at a different starting place. To take a turn, a player rolls the die, reads the color word, and then moves the leprechaun in the corresponding column forward one space. The players take turns until one leprechaun reaches the end of the rainbow. Go green!

Tina Bellotti, G. A. Jackson Elementary School, Jericho, NY

"Egg-cellent" Vowels

A-tisket, a-tasket, it's a phonics-filled basket! In each of five classroom areas, post a large card labeled with a different short vowel. Copy the picture cards on page 139 so that there is one card per student. Cut out each card, fold it, and then place it in a plastic egg. Place the eggs in a basket.

To begin, distribute the eggs to students. Once each youngster has an egg, announce, "Hatch!" At this signal, each youngster opens his egg, softly names his picture, and then stands by the corresponding vowel card. After each student is in place, ask each group to announce its words; help the youngsters make any needed corrections. Then gather the eggs and picture cards for another round of "eggs-tra" special vowel practice.

Sandy Thrift, Virginia Beach Friends School, Virginia Beach, VA

Lots of Dots

With this small-group idea, you're sure to spot students enjoying addition! In advance, program a blank spinner with chosen addends. Give each student crayons and a copy of page 141. Then invite a student to spin the spinner and announce the number. Instruct each youngster to draw that many dots on the first wing of his first ladybug. Have a different student spin to determine the number for the second wing. After each student draws the appropriate number of dots, continue with the remaining ladybugs in the same manner. Ask each youngster to write the corresponding addition sentences and then color his ladybugs.

Kelly Finch, Vaughan Elementary, Powder Springs, GA

Amazing Changes

Use this "hand-some" project to explore the transformation from caterpillar to butterfly. Set out shallow containers of green, brown, and orange tempera paint. For each child, fold two 6" x 18" construction paper strips in half and then unfold them to make four sections. Staple them together end to end. To make a project, a student cuts apart a copy of the life cycle strips on page 142. He glues them on his construction paper in chronological order as shown. Then he illustrates his paper as indicated. After the paint is dry, he adds desired marker details. Impressive!

Roxanne LaBell Dearman
Western NC Early Intervention
*   Program for Children Who Are*
*   Deaf or Hard of Hearing*
Charlotte, NC

Illustrations
First section: Make a row of adjoining green fingerprints with a pinkie finger (small caterpillar).
Second section: Make a row of adjoining green thumbprints (large caterpillar).
Third section: Make a brown paint print with the edge of a fist (chrysalis).
Fourth section: Make two orange handprints as shown (butterfly).

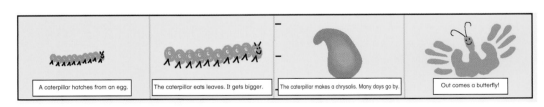

A caterpillar hatches from an egg. | The caterpillar eats leaves. It gets bigger. | The caterpillar makes a chrysalis. Many days go by. | Out comes a butterfly!

Drip, Drop, Raindrops

This writing activity is perfect for a rainy day! Have students listen to rain or a recording of rainy day sounds. Then prompt them to brainstorm a list of rain-related words, phrases, and activities. Next, give each student an enlarged copy of the raindrop pattern on page 142. Ask her to write about rain on her pattern and then sign her name. After she completes her writing, have her cut out her pattern and glue it onto a larger blue construction paper raindrop. Showcase students' completed work on a titled board decorated with clouds.

Stacey Helders-Pevan
Prince of Peace School
Milwaukee, WI

Rain is wet.
I like pudlz.
I war a rain
cote.
Jenna

'Tis the Season

Roll, Add, and Color!

Students create colorful butterfly pictures as they play this dice game. Divide students into small groups. Give each group crayons, two dice, and a copy of page 143 for each student. To take a turn, a player rolls the dice, announces the sum, and then colors one section on her paper that is labeled with that number. (If there isn't a corresponding section to be colored, her turn is over.) Players take turns until one player wins by coloring all of her numbered sections. At the game's conclusion, invite the players with incomplete pictures to finish their coloring before taking their papers home.

Tina Beeler
Lincoln Center Elementary
South St. Paul, MN

Think Summer!

What's in the cards? Thoughts of summer and literacy fun! Use the picture cards on page 144 with the ideas below.

Reading: Prepare several picture cards. For each summertime sight, write a sentence on a sentence strip, leaving a blank space for the card. Display the sentence strips and cards in a pocket chart. Then help students complete the sentences with the cards.

Writing: Give each student a blank booklet that has up to 12 pages. On each page, have her glue a different picture card and write a corresponding sentence.

ABC Order: Color a white construction paper copy of the picture cards. Cut the cards apart and then equally divide them among three resealable plastic bags. Place the bags at a center stocked with paper. A child chooses a bag, arranges the cards in ABC order, and then lists the words in order.

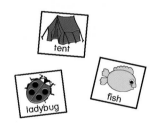
tent

ladybug

fish

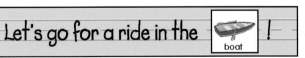
Let's go for a ride in the [boat]!

"Class-y" Welcome

With this look back, your students prepare a special welcome for youngsters who will be in your class next year. Help students recall several events from the past year. Then, as a class, write a letter explaining what your future students may look forward to. Next, give each student a sheet of drawing paper. Have him illustrate a fun activity, a memorable moment, or something that he has enjoyed about your classroom. After each youngster writes a caption, compile students' papers into a class book. No doubt your current students will be proud to know that their work will be shared with your upcoming class!

adapted from an idea by Deborah Patrick
Park Forest Elementary
State College, PA

The reading corner is cool!

Sum Tree!

 Cut.

Add. Use the apples to help you.

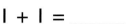

1 + 1 = _____   2 + 1 = _____

3 + 2 = _____   2 + 2 = _____

4 + 1 = _____   1 + 3 = _____

2 + 3 = _____   1 + 4 = _____

©The Education Center, Inc. • *The Mailbox*® • TEC42014 • Aug./Sept. 2004

The Little Old Lady Who Was Not Afraid of Anything

by Linda Williams

Sizing Up Leaves

Listen for directions.

A.

B.

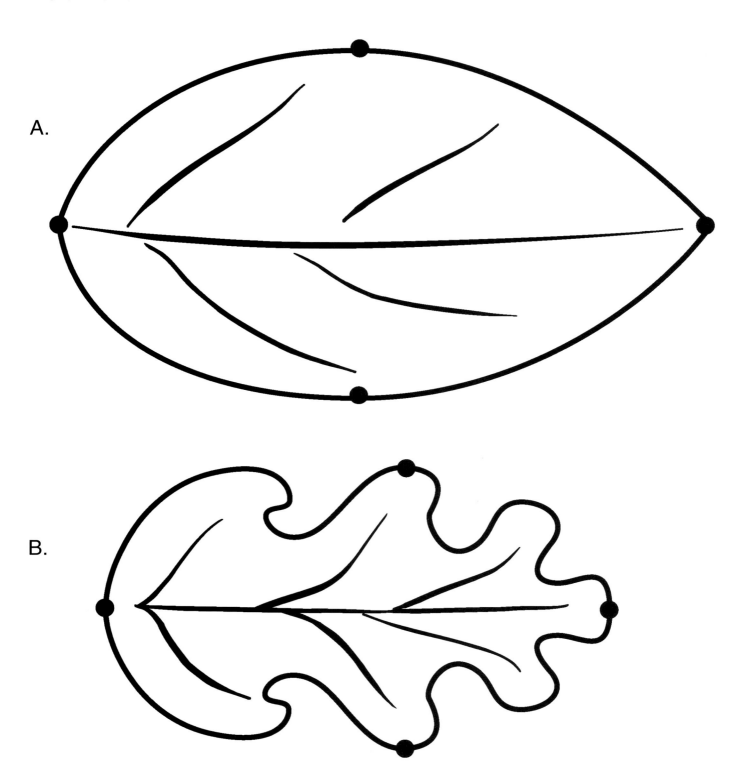

Note to the teacher: Use with "Sizing Up Leaves" on page 129.

Name —————

Slip and Slide!

✂️ Cut.

Glue to match the pictures and beginning letters.

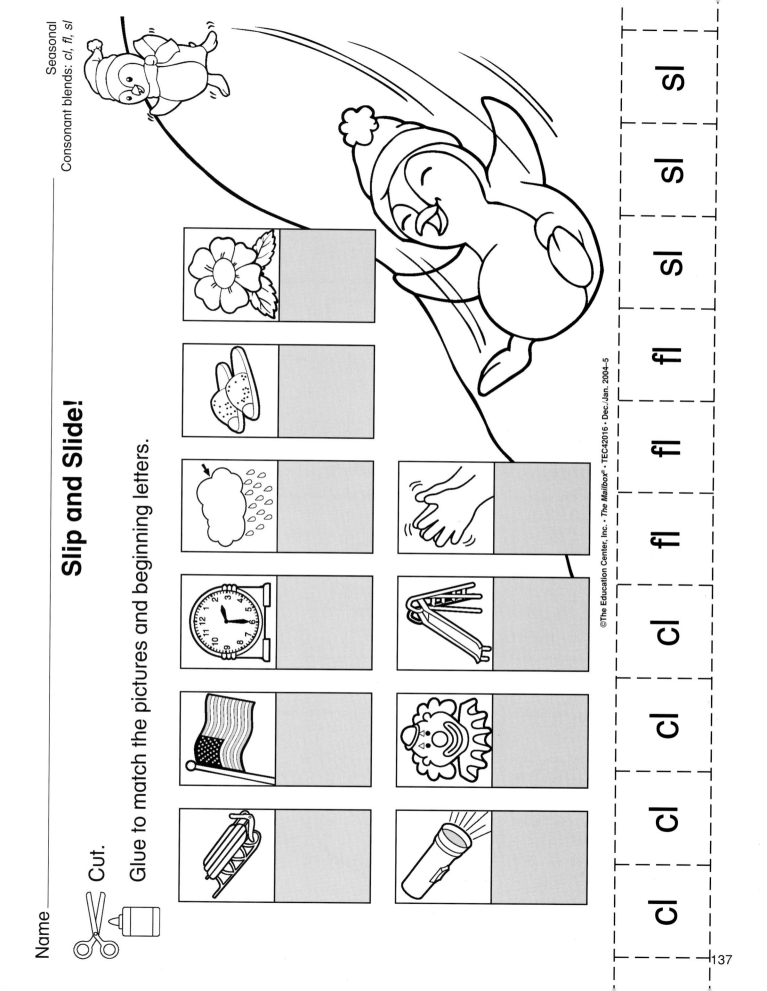

Picture Cards

Use with "Picturing Kwanzaa" on page 130.

one black candle

three red candles

three green candles

candleholder

seven days

unity cup

mat

gifts

corn

carrots

bananas

grapes

Picture Cards
Use with " 'Egg-cellent' Vowels" on page 131.

Name_____

Sweet Sums

 Cut. Glue to complete each fact.

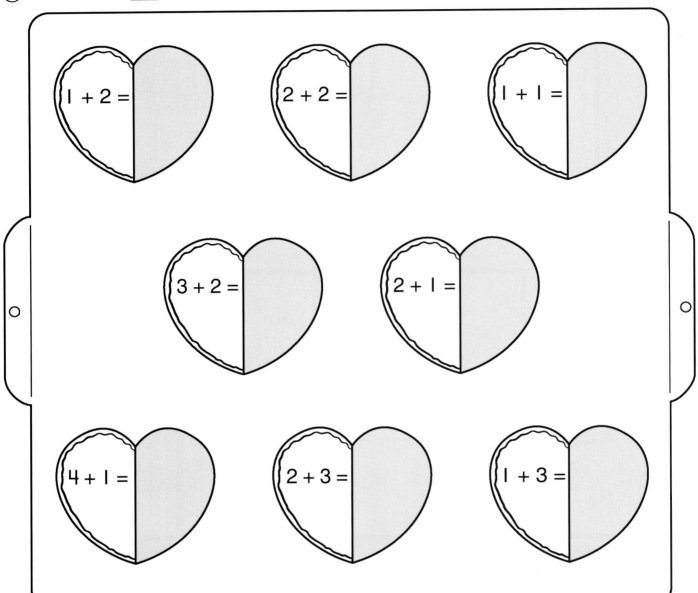

1 + 2 =

2 + 2 =

1 + 1 =

3 + 2 =

2 + 1 =

4 + 1 =

2 + 3 =

1 + 3 =

© The Mailbox® • TEC42017 • Feb./Mar. 2005

4   3   5   2   5   4   5   3

Note to the teacher: If desired, give each student five counters to use as manipulatives.

Lovely Ladybugs

Listen for directions.

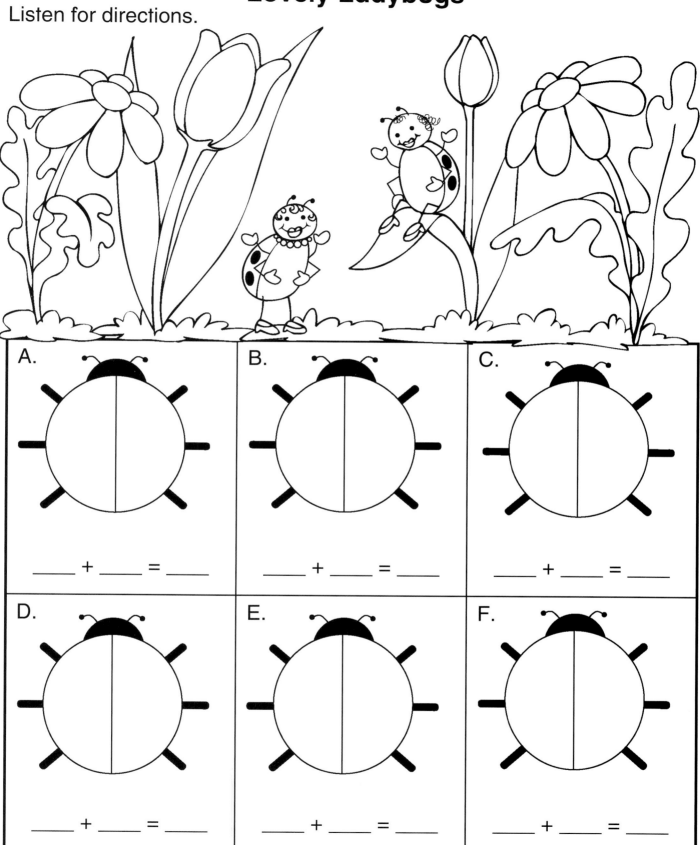

A. ____ + ____ = ____

B. ____ + ____ = ____

C. ____ + ____ = ____

D. ____ + ____ = ____

E. ____ + ____ = ____

F. ____ + ____ = ____

Note to the teacher: Use with "Lots of Dots" on page 132.

141

Raindrop Pattern

Use with "Drip, Drop, Raindrops" on page 132.

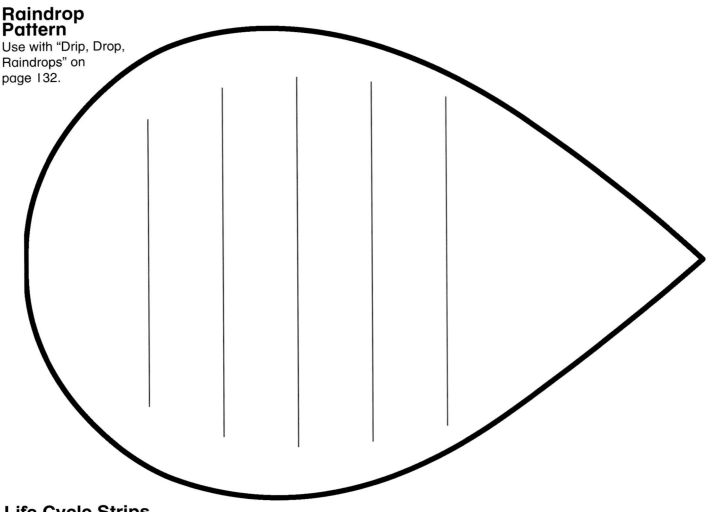

Life Cycle Strips

Use with "Amazing Changes" on page 132.

A caterpillar hatches from an egg.

The caterpillar eats leaves. It gets bigger.

The caterpillar makes a chrysalis. Many days go by.

Out comes a butterfly!

Colorful Sums

Listen and do.

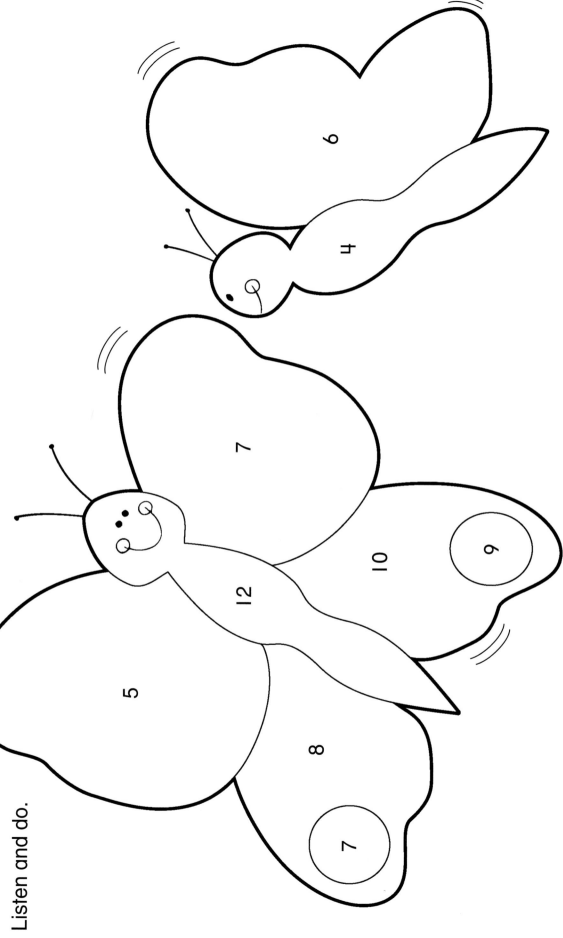

Note to the teacher: Use with "Roll, Add, and Color!" on page 133.

143

Picture Cards
Use with "Think Summer!" on page 133.

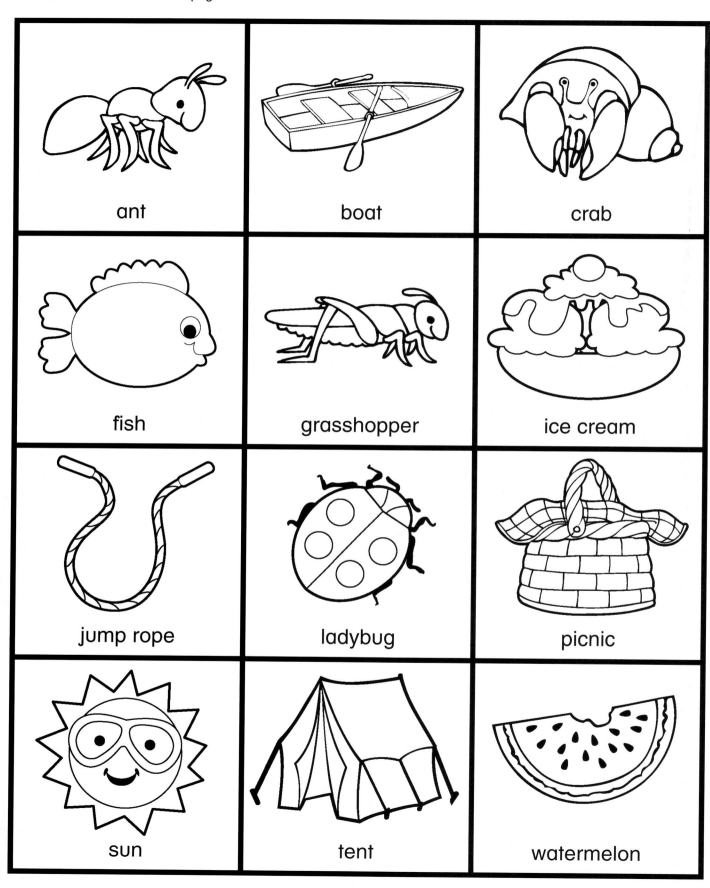

ant

boat

crab

fish

grasshopper

ice cream

jump rope

ladybug

picnic

sun

tent

watermelon

©The Mailbox® • TEC42019 • June/July 2005

WRITE ON!

Write On!

it is Sne

Everyone Writes!

Get every student involved in writing your morning messages! Before writing a day's message, give each youngster an individual chalkboard or whiteboard and writing supplies. As you write the message on a sheet of chart paper, periodically pause and ask students for their input. For example, ask what the first letter of a chosen word is or how to spell a familiar high-frequency word. Have each student write his response on his board and then hold it up. Scan the boards for accuracy and then use the correct response to continue the message on the chart paper. When the message is complete, pose a relevant question and have each youngster respond on his board. Ask volunteers to read their responses aloud. Now that's starting the day the "write" way!

Deborah Patrick, State College, PA

How Unique!

A classic picture book and one-of-a-kind artwork are the springboards for this caption-writing activity. Read aloud *The Big Orange Splot*, Daniel Manus Pinkwater's popular story of individuality. Then ask each youngster to consider what kind of house she would build on Mr. Plumbean's street. To share her ideas, she positions a 9" x 12" sheet of white paper vertically and then folds up the bottom three inches. She unfolds the paper and traces the crease. She illustrates a desired style of house above the line and writes a sentence about it below the line. Then she adds a splotch of orange paint to her house. Mr. Plumbean would be proud!

Betsy Chaplick, Booth Tarkington School #92, Indianapolis, IN

My house has flowers.

I Can Write!

by Drew

mom

I can write on an envelope. 3

Can-Do Booklet

This pride-boosting booklet project helps youngsters realize that they're writers! Give each student a copy of page 151 and read the sentences aloud. Next, ask each student to cut out his cover and pages. Help him sequence the pages behind his cover and staple the stack to make a booklet. On the cover, instruct the youngster to sign his name and color the illustration. On each page, invite him to write letters, words, or a sentence on the pictured item and then add any desired crayon details. After he practices reading his booklet, encourage the youngster to take it home and share it with his family.

Linda Rasmussen, Donner Springs Elementary, Reno, NV

Write On!

I saw a big cow with blak spots. It sed moo!

Destination? Anywhere!

Looking for a way to encourage youngsters to include details in their writing? Head to your carpet area! As you sit with students on the carpet, ask them to pretend that it is taking them on a trip to a chosen location, such as a farm, zoo, or fire station. Invite students to picture the location in their minds and describe what they see, hear, and feel. After plenty of discussion, have each child draw a relevant picture and write about her imagined experience. Your young writers will have such fun, they'll be eager to "travel" again soon!

Jeanne L. Ward, Hancock Elementary, Hancock, MD

Super Sentences
(sung to the tune of "London Bridge")

Capitalize the first word,
The first word, the first word.
Capitalize the first word
In each sentence.

(Use these sentences to compose additional verses.)
Put spaces between all the words in each sentence.

Use punctuation at the end of each sentence.

Writing Tune-Up

Use a toe-tapping tune to remind youngsters how to capitalize, space, and punctuate sentences. Write a morning message on your board, omitting some capitals at the beginning of sentences, spaces between words, and ending punctuation. After reading the message with students, suggest that the song shown can help them check your writing. Lead students in singing the first verse and then encourage them to identify and fix the capitalization error(s). Sing the additional verses to prompt corrections in spacing and punctuation. What a memorable way to tune up writing!

Ann Buhner, Kingsbury Elementary School, LaPorte, IN

We went to the pumpkin farm.

bus.

We t

Picture-Perfect Inspiration

Present familiar photographs, and your youngsters will be ready to write captions in a flash! Take photos during a field trip or special event. Or snap photos of classroom activities throughout a typical day. Choose several photos that show a sequence. Have students help you tape them in order on a length of paper, allowing ample space for captions. As you write student-generated captions, invite volunteers to contribute as appropriate for their abilities. For example, invite a child to add the final consonant to a word or have him write a familiar high-frequency word. Just watch those those writing skills develop!

Jan Messali, Canyon View Elementary, San Diego, CA

Write On!

Snowy Adventure

Imagine a snowpal that can join in on wintertime fun! That's what students do with this **sentence completion** idea. If desired, begin by sharing *The Snowman* by Raymond Briggs. Encourage students to imagine making a snowpal and seeing it come to life one night. Ask them to share their ideas about how they would spend their time with their wintry companions. Next, give each child a strip of paper that you have programmed with the sentence starter "My snowpal and I would _____." Have her complete the sentence (with assistance as needed) and then glue it at the bottom of a sheet of construction paper. Invite her to complete her work with an illustration of herself and her amazing snowpal.

Randalyn Larson, Chelsea, MI

Journal Watchword

Promote **conventional spelling** with this simple **journal** suggestion. Draw a large rectangle on the board and explain that it is a special word box. Each day write in the box a chosen grade-appropriate word as students observe. Read the word aloud and have each of several volunteers use it in an original sentence. Then ask each student to include the word in his journal entry for the day. Encourage him to underline the featured word and double-check its spelling. What a surefire way to build students' writing vocabularies!

Anita Busby, The Green Vale School, Old Brookville, NY

Vacation Snapshot

This **booklet project** is a picture-perfect follow-up to a school vacation! Copy the pattern on page 152 onto white construction paper to make a class supply of front booklet covers. Prepare for each child a camera-shaped booklet with a front cover, a desired number of white pages, and a construction paper back cover. When students return from a vacation, have each child personalize her front cover and decorate it as desired. Then ask her to write about her vacation in her booklet and add relevant illustrations. If desired, when a student takes time off from school for a family trip, have her take along a blank booklet and record highlights of her trip.

MarCella J. Watkins, Alderman Elementary School, Wilmington, NC

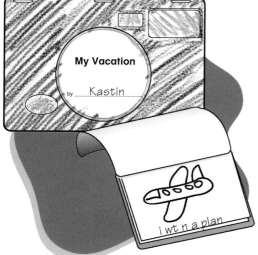

Write On!

Memorable Times

Inspire youngsters to **write about familiar experiences** with this ongoing project. Give each youngster a copy of page 153. Have him complete the sentence in the first box with the word *happy*. Ask him to title his paper to reflect a happy memory and write about it in the large box (or dictate the information for you to write). Then instruct him to draw an illustration in the oval. After he adds desired crayon details to his paper, have him cut along the bold lines. Store his completed paper in a personalized folder.

Periodically repeat the activity, having students write about various occasions, such as times when they were excited, silly, or proud. Then staple each youngster's work between construction paper covers to make a memory book. After he titles and decorates his front cover, encourage him to take the keepsake home to share with his family.

adapted from an idea by Stephanie Affinito—Reading Coordinator, Glens Falls, NY

Simple Sentences

Here's a surefire approach to writing **telling sentences**. Post the adjectives shown and two student-generated lists of nouns (animals or people) and action verbs that have been written on different-colored sheets of paper. Ask each child to choose one word from each list and then form a sentence with the words on provided paper. Encourage her to check her sentence for the appropriate capitalization and end mark and then illustrate her work. **For more advanced students,** post a second list of adjectives as well, and have each youngster include another describing word in her sentence.

Eleanor Stout, Windsor Elementary, Elyria, OH

Puzzling!

Spark students' imaginations at **journal time**! Place a class supply of stray puzzle pieces in a container. Have each child take a puzzle piece at random and then tape it to the corner of a blank journal page. Next, ask her to study her puzzle piece and imagine the type of scene it belongs in. Prompt her to think about various details that might be in the scene. Arrange for each student to show her puzzle piece to a neighboring classmate to generate additional ideas. Then ask each youngster to share her ideas in a journal entry. What a fitting way to promote creative writing!

Katie Zuehlke, Bendix Elementary, Annandale, MN

Write On!

Catapilrs are long and fuze.

Sentence Critters

This sentence-writing activity results in a cute bunch of caterpillars! Familiarize students with several facts about caterpillars. Then guide each youngster to write a sentence about the topic on provided paper. Encourage him to check his work for proper capitalization and punctuation. Next, have him draw a face on a 3½" x 4½" construction paper oval and glue on two construction paper antennae to make a caterpillar head. Instruct him to glue the head onto the left-hand end of a sentence strip. After he writes his edited sentence on the strip, ask him to glue on construction paper strips to resemble legs. Showcase students' completed critters on a hallway wall; then embellish the display with construction paper flowers and grass.

Linda Grenier, Frances Slocum School, Marion, IN

Kaylee
The flowers are purple. They have pointy leaves.

Signs of Spring

What better inspiration for using describing words than springtime observations? Accompany students on a walk outside, encouraging them to look for signs of spring. Take a snapshot of each seasonal sight that students spot. Later, display the photographs on a bulletin board. Prompt students to use describing words such as color, size, and number words as they write about the images. Have each child mount her completed writing onto colorful construction paper; then add students' work to the display. Welcome, spring!

Heather Keller, Valley Brook Country Day School, Long Valley, NJ

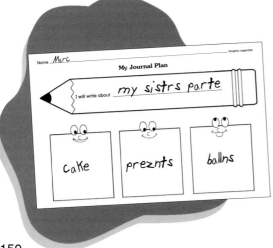

Name *Marc*   Graphic organizer

My Journal Plan

I will write about *my sistrs parte*

| caKe | preznts | ballns |

Journal Gem

Make prewriting a part of students' journal-writing time, and more well-developed entries are guaranteed! Display an overhead transparency of the graphic organizer on page 154. Complete the sentence with a student-generated topic. Then, with student input, write three words or thoughts about the topic in the provided boxes. Use this information to write three related sentences on a sheet of chart paper. Repeat the planning and writing process on several days. Once students understand how to use the graphic organizer, provide copies whenever it's time for journal writing. **For an easier version**, invite students to use the boxes on the graphic organizer for illustrations that they can refer to as they complete their journal entries.

Paula Segura, Linder Elementary, Austin, TX

1

I can write on paper.

3

I can write on an envelope.

I Can Write!

by _____

2

I can write on a card.

Booklet Cover

Use with "Vacation Snapshot" on page 148.

My Vacation

by _____

This page is about a time when I was very

_____ .

Graphic organizer

My Journal Plan

I will write about _____

Note to the teacher: Use with "Journal Gem" on page 150.

LITERACY UNITS

"A-peel-ing" Ideas for Young Writers

Whether your students write with random letters or understand the connection between letters and sounds, this bunch of ideas is certain to get them in the swing of writing!

ideas contributed by Marjorie Conrad, Kaysville, UT

Do you like cats or dogs more?

cats   I l'k dogs

SD6

The dar is bl

My Colorful Classroom
by Keshia

Ready Responses
Writing responses to questions

Sticky notes can make writing more fun than a barrel of monkeys! Every few days, write a question on a sentence strip, using a different-colored marker for key words and adding illustrations as desired. Early in the year you might present close-ended questions such as the one shown. Later, after students' skills have grown, you might ask more open-ended questions. Display the prepared question in an open area on a classroom wall. Next, give each student a large sticky note (2⅞" x 3⅞" or larger); then ask him to write a response on it. Invite him to read aloud his work before he posts it below the question. Wow! Writing is a fun way to share information!

Colorful Captions
Writing captions for illustrations

With this five-day crayon project, youngsters are sure to go bananas over writing captions! In advance, prepare a paper pocket for each student. To make one, position a 12" x 18" sheet of yellow construction paper vertically, fold up the bottom about seven inches, and then staple the sides. Ask each student to add crayon details to her pocket so that it resembles a crayon box. Then have her personalize it with a copy of the label on page 158. Tack the prepared pockets to a bulletin board.

On each of five days, announce a different color. Invite students to look for classroom objects that are the designated color, prompting them to tell about their finds with complete sentences. Next, give each child a copy of the crayon pattern on page 158. After the youngster colors the ends of her pattern with the designated color, ask her to illustrate a classroom object of the same color on the back of her pattern. Have her write a caption on the front. Then instruct her to cut out her crayon and tuck it into her displayed pocket. She'll soon have a pack of writing samples to share with her family!

Picture This!
Writing captions that match photographs

Spark bunches of writing ideas with a topic your students know best—themselves! Throughout the year, save photographs that you take of your students. To use a chosen photo for writing inspiration, place it in a resealable plastic bag to keep it free of fingerprints and then invite students to study the photo. After youngsters share their observations of it, have each student write a relevant caption on provided paper. Display students' writing with the photo as desired. A picture really is worth a thousand words!

Erin Green, Rosewood Elementary
Rock Hill, SC

Link by Link
Writing sentences

When a child contributes a sentence to this chain project, he's certain to feel like the top banana! To begin, prompt students to name things associated with fall. Then think aloud as you write "I like…" on a sheet of chart paper and complete the sentence with a favorite seasonal sight. With students' help, write a few more fall-related sentences in the same format.

To prepare a sentence chain, give each child a 2" x 18" strip of construction paper in his choice of fall colors. Have him use the modeled format and a crayon to write a sentence about fall. Staple students' strips together to form a chain as shown and then display it as desired to decorate your classroom. Repeat the activity throughout the year, varying the sentence starter to reflect your youngsters' abilities and to celebrate different seasons or holidays.

Spaced Out
Spacing words in sentences

As your students' writing skills develop, use this idea to point out the importance of spaces between words. While youngsters observe, write a sentence suitable for their reading abilities on a sheet of chart paper, leaving no space between the words. Lead students to realize that poor spacing makes the sentence difficult to read.

Next, suggest that a writing glove can help solve the problem. With great fanfare, place a colorful glove on your nondominant hand. Rewrite the sentence, using your gloved index finger as a space holder between words; then read the properly spaced sentence with students. Display the glove in a prominent classroom location for a handy spacing reminder. When it's time for students to write, encourage each youngster to don an imaginary writing glove!

157

Crayon Pattern and Label
Use with "Colorful Captions" on page 156.

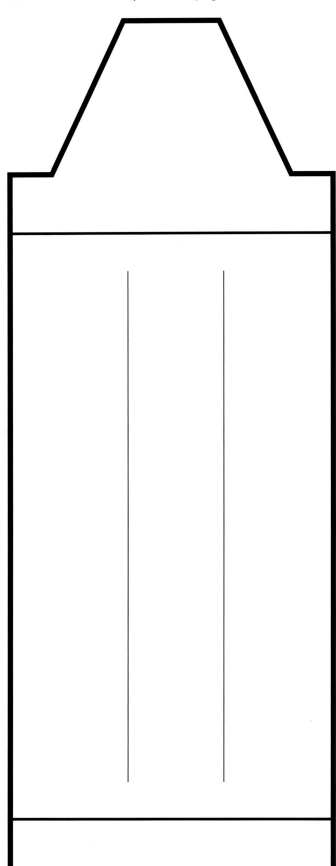

My Colorful Classroom

by _____

Alphabet Under Construction

Build your students' letter knowledge with the following ideas. They're just the right tools for engineering fun and constructive skills practice!

ideas by Ada Goren, Winston-Salem, NC

Namely, Bricks
Letters in students' names

Start with the letters that are bound to be the most important to your students—the ones in their names! Program red construction paper rectangles (bricks) with uppercase letters, one per brick, so that there are enough bricks to spell each student's first name. Use brown construction paper to prepare one blank brick per student. Scramble the red bricks and place them in a shallow box; place the brown bricks in another container. Set the bricks and reusable adhesive near an open wall space.

Arrange for each student, in turn, to visit the resulting construction area. The first student displays selected bricks in a row on the lower left-hand portion of the wall to spell her name. She secures a brown brick after her last letter to separate it from any name that will follow. Each remaining child adds her name and a blank brick to the right of a previously posted name, or she starts a new row of bricks (see the illustration). After the display is completed, use it to reinforce letter identification as desired. For a center-time variation, secure letter cards to wooden blocks and have students construct a three-dimensional name wall.

Nail It!
Upper- and lowercase letters, letter-sound relationships

This versatile letter activity is sure to be a hit with your young builders! Randomly display in a pocket chart several cards programmed with uppercase letters and the matching lowercase letters. Announce a chosen letter and then present a volunteer with a toy hammer. Have him use the hammer to tap the upper- and lowercase forms of the letter. Invite the child to tap and name any other letters that he recognizes. Then, in a similar manner, ask different students to point out certain letters. Repeat the activity to ensure that each youngster gets a turn.

When your students are ready to explore letter-sound relationships, modify the activity with picture cards. To take a turn, a student identifies a chosen picture and then taps the letter that corresponds with the beginning sound.

Kid Cranes
Letter-sound relationships

Help students pick up loads of letter-sound associations! In advance, tie one end of a length of string to a horseshoe magnet and the other end to a ruler. Obtain a set of magnetic letters (or prepare letter cards and slide a paper clip onto each one). Have students stand in a circle. Then spread out the letters magnet side up in the center of the circle.

Next, have one student imagine that he is a crane; ask him to hold the prepared ruler and use the magnet to pick up a desired letter. Instruct him to name the letter he gets and a word that begins with it, providing assistance as needed. Then have him return the letter. Encourage each student to take a turn in the same manner, challenging him not to repeat any previously named words.

Loads of Letters
Letter-sound relationships

Here's a center idea that gets phonics skills on the move. Make a copy of the picture strips on pages 162–164. Laminate the strips for durability and then cut them out. Set the strips at a center along with a toy dump truck containing a set of magnetic letters. A student takes two strips and dumps the letters from the truck. He softly names a chosen picture and places above it the letter that stands for the beginning sound. He continues pairing the letters and pictures as time allows. Then he reloads the letters for the next worker. For an easier version, limit the number of letters and strips.

Demolition Partners
Beginning consonants

Your students are sure to have a ball with this build-'em-up-and-knock-'em-down partner activity! Give each twosome several wooden blocks, a small rubber ball, and a paper lunch bag containing several consonant manipulatives.

To begin, two partners sit on the floor across from each other. Partner 1 uses the blocks to build a wall in front of herself. She takes a letter at random, without revealing it to her partner, and hides it behind her wall. Then she names a word that begins with the letter. Next, Partner 2 guesses the letter. To check her guess, she rolls the ball to knock down the wall and then removes the letter from the rubble. The partners trade roles and repeat the activity as time allows or until no more letters are in the bag.

160

ABC Delivery
Letter-sound relationships, alphabetical order
This small-group activity delivers practice with the order of the alphabet. To prepare, use large letters to write the alphabet across a length of adding machine tape. Use copies of the picture strips on pages 162–164 to make picture cards. Stack the cards facedown in the back of a toy dump truck. Lay the alphabet strip on the floor and set the truck near the letter *A*. A few feet away, have students sit side by side facing the strip.

To take a turn, a student turns over the top card and identifies it. After he names the letter for the beginning sound, he pushes the truck to the letter, places the card above it, and then returns the truck. The youngsters continue making letter-perfect deliveries as time allows or until all of the pictures are in place.

The "Write" Place
Letter formation
Set the foundation for proper letter formation at this partner center. Obtain a plastic trowel and a child's dress-up hard hat. Pour play sand in a shallow plastic container and dampen it slightly. Place several letter cards in the hat. Set the hat, sand, trowel, and an unsharpened pencil at a center. Arrange for students to visit the center in pairs.

Partner 1 takes a card and announces the letter without showing it to her partner. Partner 2 writes the letter in the sand with the pencil. After she uses the card to check her work, she smooths the sand with the trowel. Then the partners trade roles. The partners take turns until they have written several letters. Now that's "sand-sational" writing practice!

Building Booklets
Letter formation
Use this accordion-booklet project to show off students' letter knowledge in a big way! Give each student a copy of pages 162–164. Have him cut out the strips on the bold lines. Guide him to glue the strips together so that the cover is first and the remaining strips are in alphabetical order by picture. Help him accordion-fold the prepared strip as shown. Then invite him to personalize the cover of his resulting booklet.

Next, instruct each youngster to open his booklet so that the first two pages are revealed. For each picture, ask him to identify the corresponding beginning letter. Model the correct letter formation (upper- or lowercase) and have him write the letter above the picture. After students color their pictures, collect their booklets for safekeeping. Arrange for each student to complete his remaining pages over a few days. Then encourage him to take his long letter booklet home to share with his family.

My Long Book of Letters
by Max

Booklet Cover and Picture Strip

Use with "Building Booklets" on page 161. Also use the picture strip with "Loads of Letters" on page 160 and "ABC Delivery" on page 161.

©The Education Center, Inc. • *The Mailbox*® • TEC42014 • Aug./Sept. 2004

Use with "Loads of Letters" on page 160 and "ABC Delivery" and "Building Booklets" on page 161.

Picture Strips

Use with "Loads of Letters" on page 160 and "ABC Delivery" and "Building Booklets" on page 161.

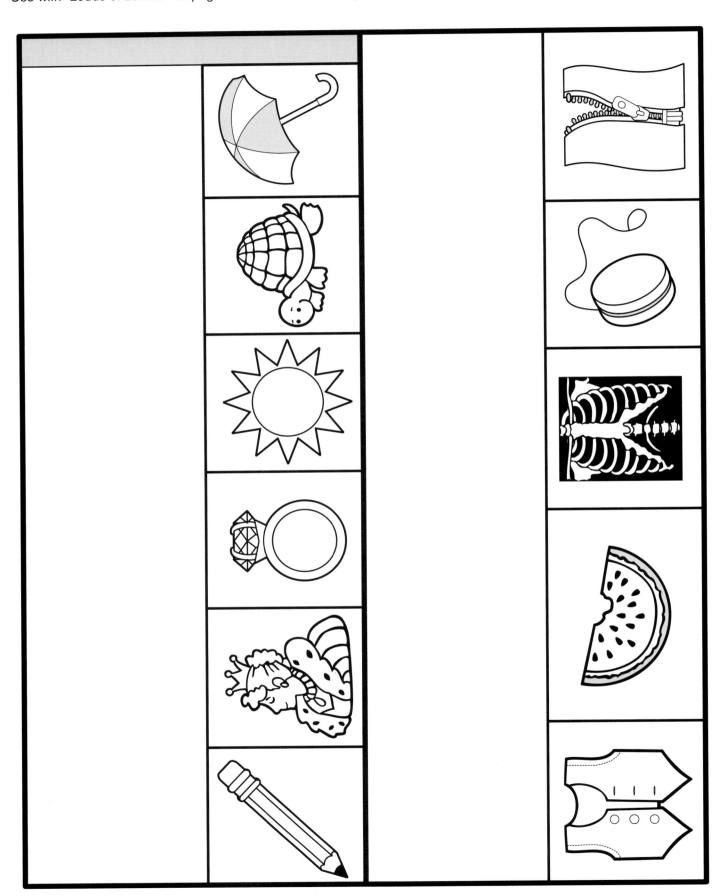

Stepping Ahead With Writing

Try these ideas on for size and you'll discover that no fancy footwork is needed to help your students improve a variety of writing skills!

ideas contributed by Stephanie Affinito—Reading Coordinator, Glens Falls, NY

A Week to Remember
Generating writing ideas

With this ongoing idea, students keep up-to-date with possible writing topics. On the first day of each full school week, make one copy of the graphic organizer on page 168. Fill in the appropriate dates. Then copy the paper to make a class supply, and prepare an overhead transparency of it. Display the transparency and comment that many things occur each week that could be interesting writing topics. Name examples such as visiting a friend and taking your dog for a walk in the snow. Then, in the first box on the transparency, use words and a simple illustration to record an event from the weekend.

Next, have each student record on a copy of the graphic organizer a weekend event that she may like to write about sometime. Ask her to store her paper in a personalized construction paper folder. Encourage her to record events throughout the week, and she'll have several memorable writing ideas!

Cultivating Topics
Generating writing ideas

Good ideas are sure to bloom when writers share their thoughts. And this garden project is a perfect way to do just that! Prompt a class discussion to generate a variety of writing ideas. If desired, spark ideas with photographs of school events and selected calendar or magazine pictures. Next, have each youngster illustrate and label a writing topic of his choice on a 4½-inch white construction paper circle (provide assistance as appropriate). Ask him to glue the circle on a six-inch construction paper blossom. Instruct him to color one side of a jumbo craft stick green and then write his initials on the other side. Have him use clear tape to secure the craft stick to the back of his blossom. If desired, invite him to glue on construction paper leaves. Set out blocks of floral foam and stand students' completed flowers in the foam. Whenever a student needs a writing idea, he simply picks a flower!

Dictation Station
Dictating brief narratives

What's a great first step in learning to write about familiar experiences? Telling about them! Place a blank cassette in a cassette player at a center. Demonstrate how to make a recording. (For easy management, color-code the buttons on the cassette player or have an adult monitor the center.) A student begins a recording by stating her name. Then she dictates a brief narrative about a recent experience. She removes the cassette and then places it in a designated location. Later, you or another adult transcribe the recording and then prepare the cassette so that other students may record on it. After the youngster illustrates her narrative and practices reading it, encourage her to share it with her family. The connection between oral and written language will be clear!

Dance class was fun. We got to do a new song. It was really fast! Mom took me for pizza after class.

by Lissa

Book Suggestions
Cookie's Week by Cindy Ward
Rosie's Walk by Pat Hutchins
Today Is Monday by Eric Carle

Fun With Favorites
Contributing to a story innovation

Something old becomes new again with this shared-writing project. Read aloud a brief story with a clear pattern or plot (see the list on this page). Then suggest a new version of the tale. For example, wonder aloud what would happen in *Cookie's Week* if the cat wasn't mischievous or if the main character was the class pet. Write a new version of the story on chart paper, incorporating students' written and oral contributions. Display the completed story on a hallway wall along with student illustrations. No doubt your young authors will want to model their independent writing after other favorite stories!

"Write" in Step!
Dictating and writing simple instructions

Help students organize their thoughts, step by step. Make several copies of the foot pattern on page 169 on light-colored paper and then cut out the patterns. Post a length of bulletin board paper. With student input, choose a simple task to write instructions for, such as pouring a glass of milk or sharpening a pencil. Write an appropriate title on the paper. Then guide students to dictate the instructions; write each step on a separate numbered cutout and tape it to the display in sequence. For additional reinforcement, place a supply of cutouts in a large shoebox at a center, and arrange for youngsters to prepare different instructions to display.

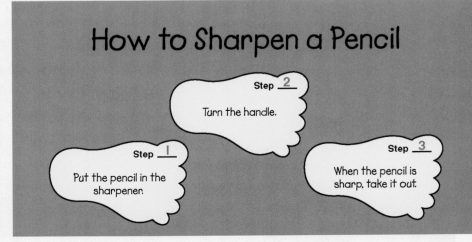

How to Sharpen a Pencil

Step 1
Put the pencil in the sharpener.

Step 2
Turn the handle.

Step 3
When the pencil is sharp, take it out.

Why did the turkey cross the road?

He didn't want to be chicken!

Learning From Riddles

Identifying appropriate capitalization and end marks

Are writing skills a laughing matter? Sure they are, when you use riddles to highlight capitalization and punctuation! Share a few grade-appropriate riddles with students. Then announce that students will make a class book of riddles. Invite volunteers to write original riddles or bring in their favorites.

To prepare a riddle for the book, write the question and answer on separate large sheets of paper, using students' writing assistance as appropriate for their abilities. As you prepare the riddle, prompt students to identify the proper capitalization and ending punctuation. After the writing is complete, ask students to circle the capital letters and end marks. Then have volunteers illustrate the resulting pages. Use metal rings to bind the pages between two construction paper covers, and plan to prepare additional pages during later writing sessions. Without question, your young authors will be eager to contribute!

Tarie Curtiss, Arthur Road Elementary School
Solon, OH

A Close Look at Words

Using describing words

With this idea, students take a fresh look at writing by using describing words. Obtain a pair of novelty sunglasses and conceal them from students' view. As students observe, write a simple, non–descriptive sentence on a sheet of chart paper. Read the sentence aloud. Next, announce that you have the perfect tool for making the sentence more interesting. Then don the sunglasses with great fanfare and suggest that they help you think about how each person, place, or thing mentioned in the sentence looks. Using appropriate describing words such as size, color, and/or shape words, rewrite the sentence to make it more descriptive. Then guide students to compare the original and revised sentences.

Repeat the activity with different sentences or a brief paragraph, inviting volunteers to take turns wearing the sunglasses as they brainstorm describing words. Then place at a center several pairs of novelty sunglasses (with lenses removed if needed for easy reading). Have youngsters wear the sunglasses during designated writing activities. Cool!

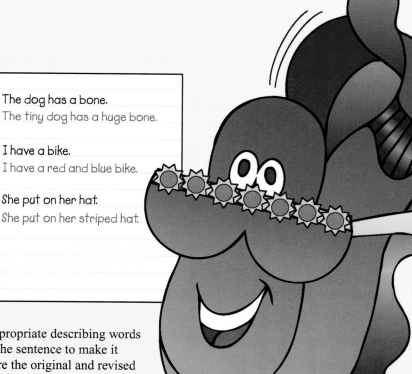

The dog has a bone.
The tiny dog has a huge bone.

I have a bike.
I have a red and blue bike.

She put on her hat.
She put on her striped hat.

Name _____

A Week to Remember

The Weekend

Dates
From _____
To _____

Monday

Friday

Thursday

Wednesday

Tuesday

©The Education Center, Inc. • *The Mailbox®* • TEC42016 • Dec./Jan. 2004–5

Note to the teacher: Use with "A Week to Remember" on page 165.

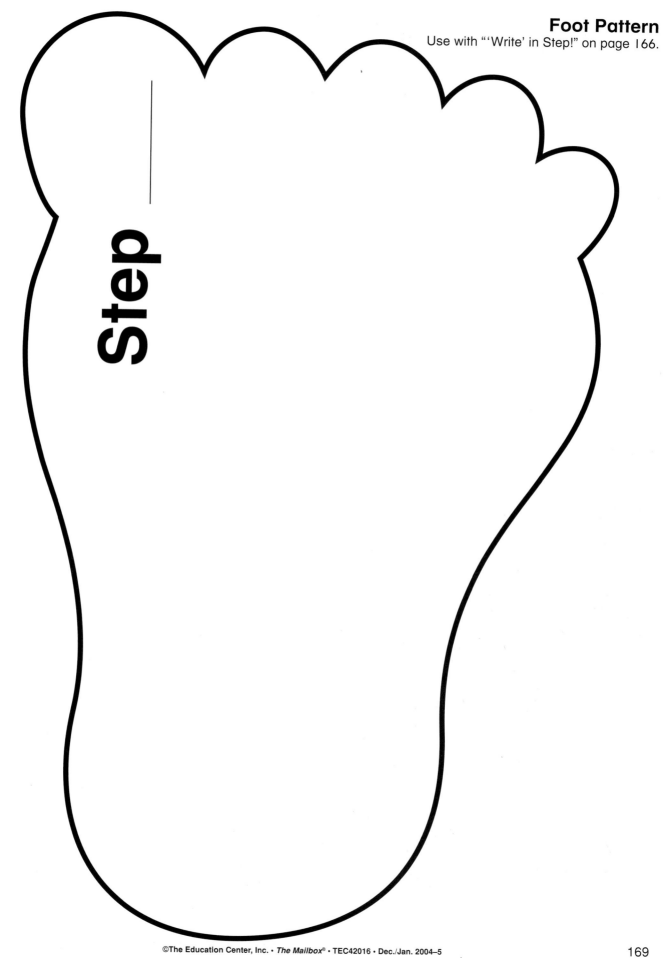

Foot Pattern

Use with "'Write' in Step!" on page 166.

Step

Falling for Number

Poke around this patch of ideas and you'll discover "unbe-leaf-ably" creative ways to help your students learn number words!

ideas contributed by Angie Kutzer
Garrett Elementary, Mebane, NC

Round and Round
Reading

Pass the pumpkin, please! The number word pumpkin, that is! In advance, prepare ten yellow construction paper seeds (approximately 4" x 6"). Use large letters to label each seed with a different number word. Place the seeds in a plastic pumpkin container.

To begin, sit with students in a circle and display the pumpkin. Remove each seed, in turn, and review the corresponding word with students. Then return the seeds to the pumpkin. Next, lead students in reciting the chant shown as they pass the pumpkin around the circle. The child who is holding the pumpkin at the end of the chant removes one seed at random. She shows her classmates the word and reads it aloud, enlisting their help as needed. After she announces a chosen type of action, such as clapping or winking, she leads students in performing the action the indicated number of times. Then she drops the seed back in the pumpkin. At this signal, students resume the chant for more reading practice fresh off the vine!

> Round and round the pumpkin goes.
> Number readers want to know—
> Who will pick a pumpkin seed?
> When we stop, it's time to read!

Pumpkin Pickin'
Matching numbers and words

This center activity is just "ripe" for pairing numbers and words! Prepare ten poster board pumpkins (approximately 4" x 5"). Use a craft knife to cut a slit at the top of each pumpkin large enough to hold a wooden ice-cream spoon as shown. Label the front of each pumpkin with a different number word from one to ten; write the number on the back of the pumpkin to make the activity self-checking. For each pumpkin, write the corresponding number on both sides of the large end of a wooden ice-cream spoon. Place the resulting stems and prepared pumpkins in a basket at a center.

A child spreads out the pumpkins, word side up. He inserts each stem into the matching pumpkin. He sequences the pumpkins in number word order and flips them to check his work. Then he removes the stems and returns the materials to the basket to prepare the center for the next visitor.

Words

Take Aim!
Reading

Reading and motor skills fall into place with this small-group activity! Prepare a jumbo seasonal cutout. Divide it into ten sections and label them with different number words. Place the cutout on the floor in an open area; ask youngsters to gather around it. Invite a child to toss a large pom-pom onto the cutout. As she announces the word in the section where the pom-pom lands, have each group member hold up the corresponding number of fingers. Then ask the child to retrieve the pom-pom and pass it to the next youngster. Continue until each student has had at least one turn taking aim at a word!

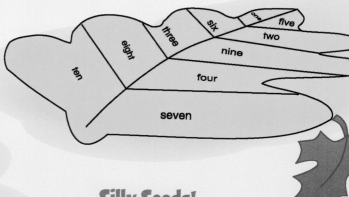

Silly Seeds!
Writing

Here's just the "write" way to culminate your number word study! In advance, prepare two construction paper pumpkins for each student, using a copy of a booklet page (page 172) as a pattern. To begin, instruct each youngster to cut out a copy of each booklet page (pages 172 and 173). Help her sequence her pages and staple them between her construction paper pumpkins. After each youngster's booklet is assembled, read the sentences aloud. Ask each student to fill in her blanks with the appropriate number words. Then have her title and personalize her front cover as desired.

Orderly Raking
Reading, sequencing

Raking isn't a chore with this partner activity; it's a heap of reading fun! Obtain two plastic toy rakes and prepare 20 construction paper leaves. Program the leaves with number words—one word per leaf—so that there are two leaves for each word. Laminate the leaves for durability if desired. Mix the leaves together in one pile. To introduce the center, explain that the goal is to collect ten leaves, each with a different number word. Demonstrate how to use the rake to carefully pull individual leaves toward you.

Have two students visit the center at a time. In turn, each partner rakes up one leaf and reads it aloud. If he already has a leaf with the word, he returns it to the pile. The partners continue until they each have ten leaves. Then each partner arranges his leaves in number word order. Rake on!

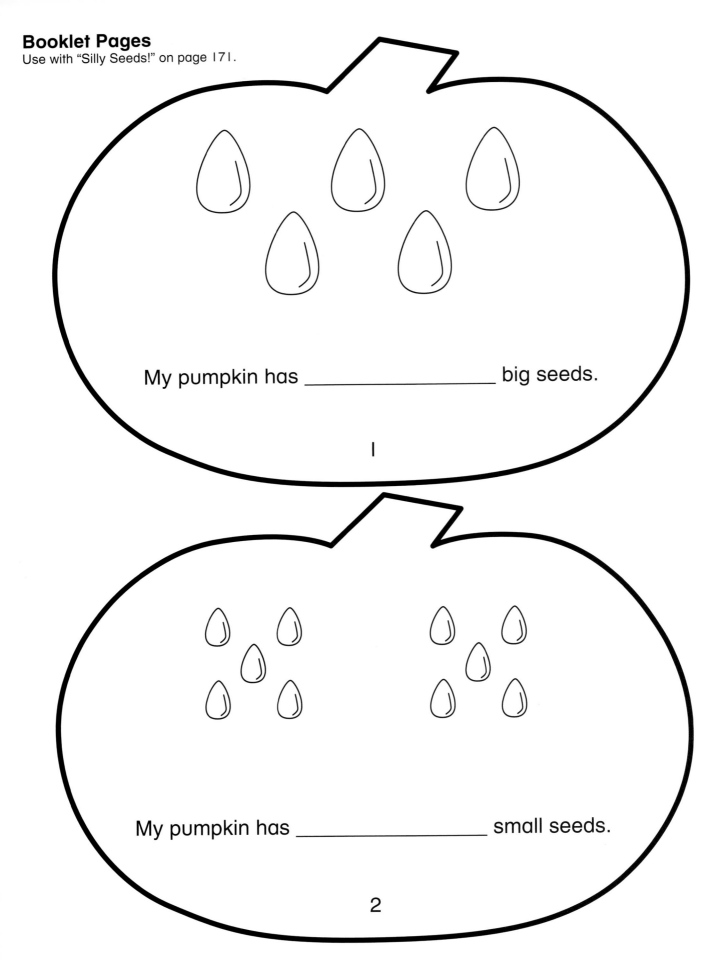

My pumpkin has _____ big seeds.

1

My pumpkin has _____ small seeds.

2

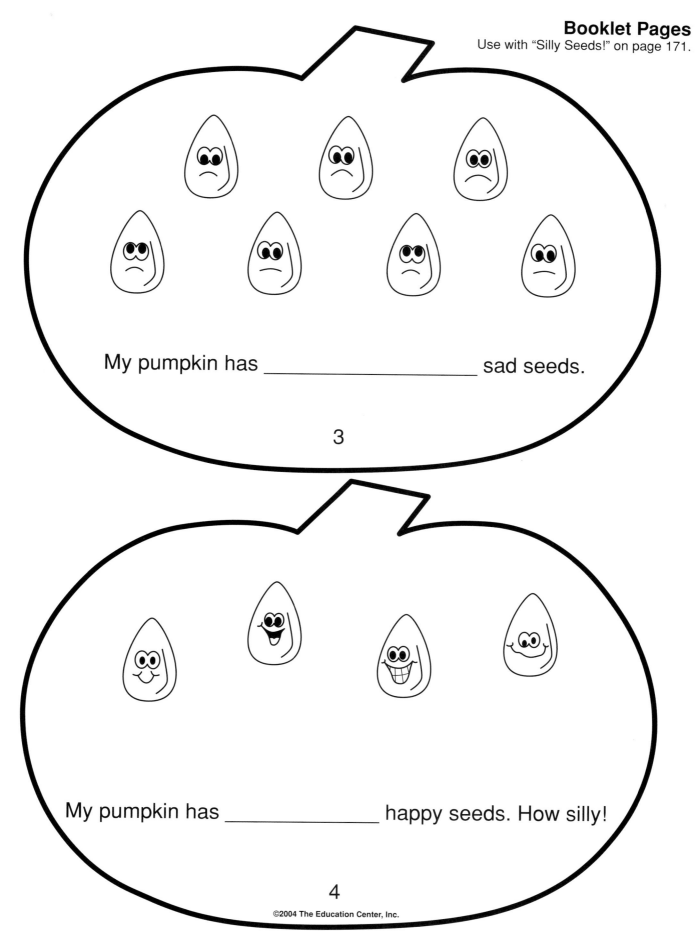

My pumpkin has _____ sad seeds.

3

My pumpkin has _____ happy seeds. How silly!

4

In Tune With Onsets and Rimes

This medley of ideas is composed of both oral and print activities to provide "sound-sational" practice with words!

ideas contributed by Julie Hays
Foothills Elementary, Maryville, TN

It's Song Time!

Recognizing words with the same rime

After a few verses of this lively tune, students are sure to have an ear for words that end alike! Lead students in the verse shown, inviting them to perform the appropriate actions. Repeat the song with different rimes, modifying the actions and examples (see the suggestions). If desired, post a student-generated list of words for each rime and vary the examples during later repetitions.

Listen and Do
(sung to the tune of "If You're Happy and You Know It")

If you hear a word with *-ap,* clap your hands.
If you hear a word with *-ap,* clap your hands.
If you hear a word with *-ap*—
Such as *nap,* or *snap,* or *tap*—
If you hear a word with *-ap,* clap your hands.

Suggestions for additional verses:
-all; stretch up tall; *ball, call, wall*
-in; show a grin; *fin, pin, spin*
-ip; swing your hips; *dip, ship, tip*
-op; hop two times; *mop, stop, top*

Chant
Listen, listen carefully.
One card doesn't fit, you see.
Which one is it? Do you know?
It's time to find out. Here we go!

Likely Trio?

Distinguishing rimes

With this group activity, careful listening is the key to making three of a kind. Copy onto white construction paper the picture cards on pages 177 and 178. Color the cards and cut them out. Have students sit in front of a pocket chart. In the top row of the chart, display three cards—two that represent words with the same rime and one that represents a word with a different rime. Place a desired number of the remaining cards in the lower rows.

To begin, say the chant shown as you lead students in patting their legs in a steady rhythm. Then stop and name the words for the three featured cards; have students repeat them with you. Next, have students tell which card does not belong and which card should replace it. Make the suggested change and then have students name the words for the correct trio of cards. Explore different sets of cards in a similar manner.

All Together Now!

Blending onsets and rimes

Step up youngsters' phonological awareness! To begin, march in place with students. Once a steady rhythm is established, announce a word, splitting it into its onset and rime as you keep the beat. (See the suggested words.) Have students say the word parts with you one or two times as they march. Then prompt students to stop and announce the word. Resume marching and explore another word in a similar manner. March on!

Words for Blending

f-it	s-ame
l-ip	sh-ell
m-eat	th-ing
n-ine	v-an
r-ing	w-est

Dog!

Stand Up, Please!

Blending onsets and rimes

When it comes to blending sounds, this fast-paced group activity will keep your youngsters on their toes! Copy the picture cards on pages 177 and 178 so that there is one card per student. (More than one student may have the same picture.) Jot down the corresponding words for your reference. Cut out the picture cards and distribute them. Have each youngster color his card and then glue it onto an index card for durability. Next, sit with students in a circle on the floor and ask each youngster to hold his card. Then announce a listed word, splitting the word into its onset and rime. Each student who has the word immediately stands, holds it up, and blends the sounds to say the word. As soon as he sits down, announce another segmented word. Continue until each student has had at least one turn.

Hooked With a Book

Reading words with familiar rimes

Here's a class book project that's guaranteed to prompt a few giggles and provide just-right reading practice. Read aloud *Hop on Pop* by Dr. Seuss. Revisit a few pages with students, pointing out the words that have the same rime. Next, write on the board a word with a familiar rime. After students read it aloud, list a few more words that have the rime and ask students to read them.

Next, invite students to say an original sentence that uses two or three of the words. Write the sentence near the bottom of a large sheet of paper, and write the words with the featured rime in the upper right-hand corner. Record on separate sheets of paper any other sentences students generate with the words. Then ask volunteers to add illustrations. Use metal rings to bind the completed paper(s) between two covers, and title the resulting book as desired. As students learn other rimes, create additional pages.

king
swing

The king likes to swing.

Word Worms
Forming words with onsets and rimes

Students mix and match these wriggly critters to form words! Copy the worm patterns (page 178) on construction paper so that there are four front sections and four back sections. Cut them out and then add colorful spots or stripes if desired. Program each front section with a different onset and each back section with a different rime (see the suggestions).

During a small-group time, arrange the worms face-down, grouping the front and back sections separately. Have one student take a front section and a different student take a back section. Ask the youngsters to assemble the worm. Once they announce the word, have each group member give a thumbs-up if it is a real word and a thumbs-down if it is not a real word. Confirm the correct response; then instruct the two students to return the worm sections. Continue the activity until each student has had at least two turns forming a word.

Onsets
c, p, r, t

Rimes
-an, -at, -est, -ot

Make It! Change It!
Adding and changing onsets

What's in a letter? Sometimes a whole new word! Make one copy of the picture cards on page 177 and then cut out the cards. Discard the cards for *clap* and *swing*. Color the remaining cards and then mount each one on a separate index card. Write the following onsets on a sentence strip, leaving a generous amount of space between them: *b, c, f, h, k, m, p, r.* Cut between the letters to make cards. Program a sentence strip length for each of these rimes: *-an, -ap, -at, -ing.*

To begin, have students sit with easy access to a pocket chart. Display the onsets in the lower rows; display the bat and *-at* cards above them. Name the picture and ask a volunteer to find the onset that will complete the word. After he sets the correct onset in place, read the word with students. Then announce, "Presto, chango, the bat is now a…" With great fanfare, place the hat card atop the bat card. Have students name the new picture. Then ask a volunteer to change the onset to match. Use a similar process to help students form words with the remaining rimes.

Picture Cards

Use with "Likely Trio?" on page 174 and "Stand Up, Please!" on page 175.

Worm Patterns

Use with "Word Worms" on page 176.

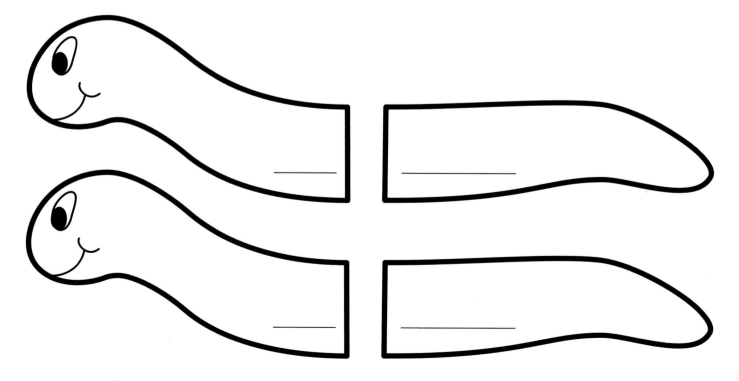

Sand, Surf, and Consonant Digraphs

Surf's up! Use these "sun-sational" ideas to help your students catch a wave of digraph practice!

ideas contributed by Stephanie Affinito
Reading Coordinator, Glens Falls, NY

What's Inside?
Sorting with ch *and* sh

Plenty of phonics fun is packed into this cool sorting activity! Bring in a small cooler and a beach towel. To prepare a class supply of items to be sorted, copy the *ch* and *sh* picture cards on page 181 so that there is one card per student. Mount the cards onto colorful rectangles. (Or prepare a combination of picture cards and real objects whose names begin with the digraphs.) Place the items in the cooler. Then label a separate blank card for each featured digraph.

To begin, gather students in a circle around the towel. Place the labeled cards on the towel, one near each end. Invite a youngster to remove an item from the cooler and name it. After the student sets the item near the corresponding digraph, have volunteers use the word in sentences. Continue with the remaining items in a similar manner. Then repack the cooler for independent sorting practice!

What a Catch!
Sorting with ch, sh, *and* th

Students reel in three digraphs at this partner center. Prepare a fishing pole by attaching one end of a length of yarn to an unsharpened pencil and tying the other end to a magnet. Decorate a large gift box with construction paper waves and label three plastic pails as shown. Make a copy of the picture cards on page 181 and then cut them out. Glue each card to a construction paper fish and attach a paper clip to each one. Then place the fish in the prepared box. Place the box, fishing pole, and pails at a center. Have partners take turns catching fish and placing them in the appropriate pails.

Fill the Pails!
Distinguishing digraphs

Invite your young beachcombers to dig into a phonics-related search! Divide students into groups of three. Give each student a pail cutout (about 8½ inches tall) and a construction paper shovel. Have each group member write a different digraph *(ch, sh,* or *th)* on her shovel. Give each group one set of precut picture cards (page 181) and instruct the students to arrange the cards facedown.

To take a turn, a student picks up a card. Then she names the picture and corresponding digraph. If it is her assigned digraph, she places the card on her pail. If it is not, she returns the card. Players take turns until all of the cards have been claimed. Next, each youngster glues her cards in place. She glues her pail and shovel onto a large sheet of paper and then draws a pail handle. **For more advanced students,** have youngsters write the word for each picture.

Beach Blanket Lotto
Reading words with digraphs

This class game makes reading seem like a day at the beach! In advance, invite each youngster to bring in a beach towel. Give each child a large paper plate on which you have drawn a tic-tac-toe grid. Post a list of 12 words that have digraphs. After each child programs his grid with nine of the listed words, invite the youngsters to sit on the towels. Provide Goldfish crackers or counters for game markers.

To play one round, announce a listed word and draw a checkmark beside it. Have each student who has the word mark it on his plate. Continue play until a student wins by marking three words in a row. Encourage youngsters to trade plates for another round of play!

Shell or Fish?
Distinguishing between beginning and ending sh

Help students listen to words from beginning to end! Write the words *shell* and *fish* on the board to create column headings. Underline the digraphs and illustrate the words. Have each youngster write and illustrate the same words on separate blank cards. Next, announce a word that either begins or ends with *sh.* If the word begins with *sh,* each student holds up her shell card. If it ends with *sh,* she holds up her fish card. After you confirm the correct response, invite a volunteer to write the word in the correct column on the board. Continue in this manner with several other words. Then have students read the lists.

A Shower of Word Family Fun

With this easy-to-adapt unit, the forecast is improved reading and spelling skills. Now that's just ducky!

ideas by Stephanie Affinito, Glens Falls, NY

Simple Signals
Distinguishing rimes

Dive into new word families with this "sound-sational" idea! Select a word from a chosen word family that can be easily represented by a cutout. For example, you might choose *rain* from the *-ain* word family and plan to make raindrop cutouts. Make a class supply of cutouts labeled with the word.

To begin, give each student a cutout. Familiarize youngsters with the word and have them underline the rime. Next, announce the word and one other word. If the words have the same rime, each youngster holds up his cutout. If they do not, he sets his cutout facedown. Write the words on the board and confirm the correct response. Continue the activity with several different word pairs. Then have each youngster store his cutout in a resealable plastic bag. Repeat the activity with different word families, and have him add each newly acquired cutout to his bag for later reference.

All Aboard!
Sorting words

This class activity is just the ticket for increasing students' reading vocabularies! From construction paper, cut one train engine and a supply of train cars. Label the engine with a chosen rime and an illustration of a word that has the rime. Program several cars with words that have the rime and the remaining cars with words that do not. Secure a piece of magnetic tape to the back of the engine and each car. Display the engine on a magnetic board. Draw a large box and label it "Station."

Next, hold up a train car and ask a volunteer to tell whether it has the featured rime. If it does, the youngster posts it next to the engine. If it does not, she places it at the station. After students sort the remaining cars in a similar manner, have them read the trainload of words. **For more advanced students,** display three engines with different rimes and have youngsters add corresponding train cars.

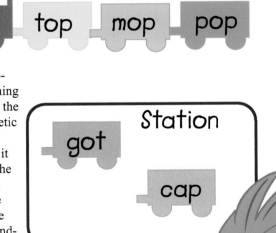

Stick Sort
Sorting and writing words

Birds of a feather flock together and so do words in the same word family! Cover two canisters with colorful paper and then label each one with a different rime. Program each of several jumbo craft sticks with a different word that has one of the rimes. Then place the sticks in a small gift bag. Set the canisters and sticks at a center stocked with paper. Arrange for students to visit the center in pairs.

Each student, in turn, takes a stick at random, reads it aloud, and then places it in the appropriate canister. The students continue alternating turns until all of the sticks are sorted. Then each youngster removes the sticks from one of the canisters. After he lists the words on a sheet of paper, he presents his work for teacher approval.

Family Portraits
Reading word families

Welcome students to the family—the word family, that is! Choose several word families to reinforce. Prepare a class set of word cards so that there are two to five words from each word family. Randomly distribute the cards to students. Next, have a volunteer stand at the front of the class and read her card aloud. Invite each student with a word in the same word family to announce her word and stand with the volunteer. When the group is complete, lead the class in reading the words. Snap a photo of the group, taking care that the word cards are in clear view. Continue with the remaining word families in the same manner. Display the photos on a bulletin board titled "Family Portraits" to create a picture-perfect word reference.

House of Words
Reading word families

Build reading confidence with this class book project. Prepare a large house-shaped book that has a cover similar to the one shown and several blank pages. Complete the pages with students over several days. To complete a page, title it with a chosen rime. Add an illustration of a word that has the rime and write the word. List several additional words that have the rime, pausing for students to read each one and for you to underline the rime. When you present unfamiliar words, point out that students can use words they know with the same rime to help them figure out the new words.

183

Notable Words
Blending onsets and rimes

Sticky notes make this small-group activity a kid-pleasing way to explore words. List the same rime several times on a sheet of chart paper. Program an equal number of sticky notes with onsets that form words with the rime. Adhere the sticky notes to the bottom of the paper and then post the paper within student reach. Next, invite a student to select an onset, secure it to the paper to form a word, and then read the word aloud. Continue in this way with the remaining sticky notes. For additional reinforcement, return the sticky notes to the bottom of the paper and offer the activity as a partner center.

Clip It!
Forming and writing words

What's in the cards? A surefire approach to forming words! Label each of several white index cards with rimes and an equal number of colorful rectangles with onsets as shown. Place the cards and a supply of clothespins at a center stocked with paper. A student clips each onset to a rime to form a word. When all of the onsets and rimes are paired, she lists the words on her paper. Then she writes sentences with two of the words.

Take Two!
Identifying real and nonsense words

Is it real or nonsense? That's the question students answer with this partner activity! For every two students, program eight white cards with the same rime. Program eight colorful cards with onsets, ensuring that some onsets form real words with the rime and some do not. Give each twosome a set of onsets, a set of rimes, and a sheet of paper.

To begin, one partner divides the paper into two columns. She labels one column with a happy face and one column with a sad face. The youngsters stack each set of cards facedown. To take a turn, a child flips over one card of each color. She tells whether the cards form a real or nonsense word. Her partner writes the word below the happy face if it is a real word and below the sad face if it is a nonsense word. Then the partners set the two cards aside. The partners alternate roles until they have formed and written all of the words.

Name _____

Pitter, Patter!

 Cut.

Glue to match.

-an

-at

Name _____

A Rainy Day

✏ Write **-ake** or **-ail**.

✂ Cut.   🧴 Glue to match.

				 **-ake**
sn ___	l ___	r ___	c ___	
sn ___	n ___	t ___	p ___	**-ail**

©The Mailbox® • TEC42018 • April/May 2005

Pocketing LEARNING Fun

Use this stash of pocket chart activities to help students' literacy skills grow by leaps and bounds!

Animal Sightings
Word recognition, sentence formation

Count on this "bear-y" simple idea to strengthen a range of literacy skills. In advance, attach a bear cutout to one end of a pointer. Share with students Bill Martin Jr.'s *Brown Bear, Brown Bear, What Do You See?* Then display in a pocket chart the first sentence shown. Next, invite students to name various animals and their colors. Use students' suggestions and the format shown to prepare sentences for the amounts one through four or more. Then add the last sentence to the pocket chart. Read the sentences with students, using the pointer to direct attention to each word. After students are familiar with the sentences, choose from the ideas below to reinforce selected skills.

- **Recognizing words:** On each sentence strip, add a visual clue for each number, color, or animal word. Name several of the words and have volunteers point them out.

- **Matching words:** Prepare separate word cards (with or without visual clues) for the number, color, and animal words. Have volunteers place each card atop the matching word in the pocket chart.

- **Forming sentences:** Cut apart the words in selected sentences. Return them to their pockets in scrambled order and then have volunteers unscramble them.

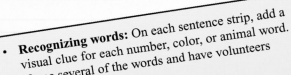

Cool Consonants
Initial or final consonants

Sorting practice is in season with this small-group activity, which can be used for either initial or final consonants! Color a copy of the snowpal and picture cards on page 189. Cut out the cards and then mount them on tagboard cards for durability. Place the snowpal cards in separate rows of a pocket chart. (If you choose to focus on final consonants, set aside the *B* snowpal.) Shuffle the picture cards and then stack them facedown. In turn, have a student take a picture card, identify the corresponding initial (final) consonant, and then place the card in the correct row. Continue in this manner until all of the cards are sorted.

Jackie Wright
Summerhill Children's House
Enid, OK

187

More From the Morning Message
Concepts of print, word recognition

Here's a way to reinforce several skills with just one morning message. Prompt students to dictate a brief message about the day. Use a different-colored marker to write each sentence on a separate sentence strip. Then display the sentences in a pocket chart. Guide students to track the print as they read the message.

Next, help students count the sentences and words. Cut between the words in a chosen sentence; display the words in random order nearby. To reassemble the sentence, announce each word in order, pausing for a volunteer to find it and set it in place. For later reinforcement, cut apart the remaining sentences and return the words to their pockets in scrambled order. Invite students to reassemble the sentences during center time.

Whose Names?
Spelling

This kid-pleasing center features some of the words your students know best—their names! Write the letters in each of several students' names on separate blank cards. Place in random order each group of letters in a separate pocket of a pocket chart. Mount photos of the children on blank cards; place them nearby.

To complete the activity, a student studies the photos. He arranges the groups of letters to spell the appropriate names and then adds the corresponding photos beside them. **To make the activity easier,** label the photos with the corresponding names and place them in the correct pockets for students to use as models. Change the names periodically to give each student a turn in the spotlight!

Jennifer Schear
Cedar Falls, IA

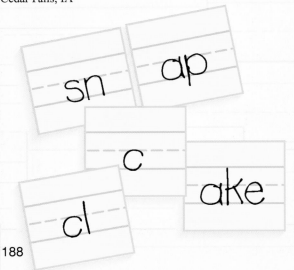

Mix and Match!
Onsets and rimes

Loads of word-forming possibilities await students at this partner center! Write a different rime on each of two blank cards. Prepare several onset cards that can be used to form a word with one or both rimes. Place the cards in a pocket chart and provide a clipboard stocked with paper. Partner 1 forms a word with a chosen onset and rime and then reads it aloud. Partner 2 writes the word on the clipboard. Then the partners trade roles. They continue taking turns as time allows or until they form a designated number of words.

Beverly Wells, Hopkins Road Elementary, Richmond, VA

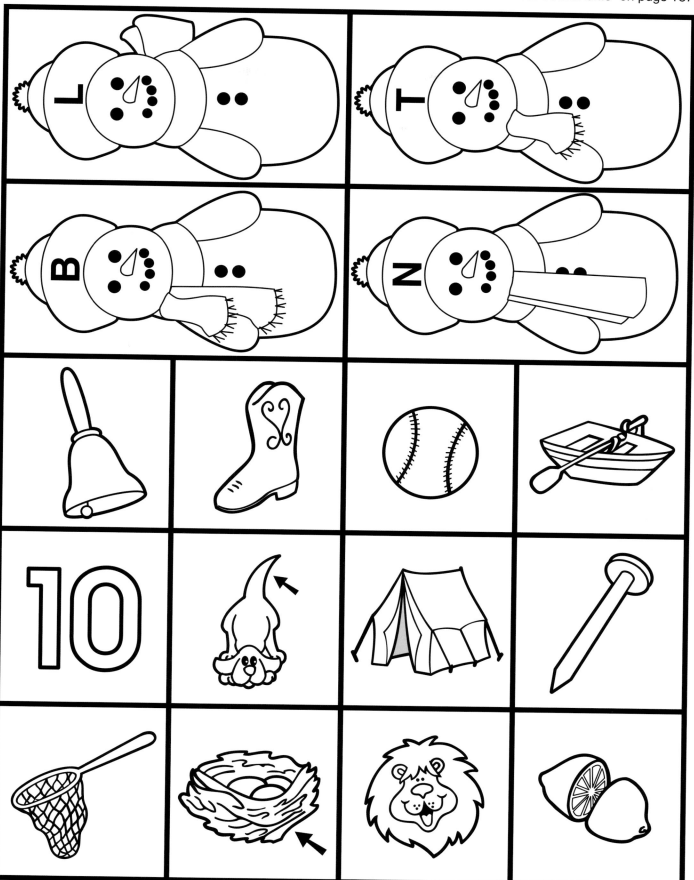

It's a Reading and Writing Picnic!

This summery unit is packed with fun ways to review and celebrate literacy skills!

ideas contributed by Beth Marquardt
St. Paul's School of Early Learning, Muskego, WI

Pass the Plates

Serve up a lively **word review** with this kid-pleasing idea. Obtain a class supply of small paper plates. Use large letters to program each plate with a familiar high-frequency word. Then spread a large checkered tablecloth on the floor and have students sit around it. Give each student a prepared paper plate. To begin, play some lively music and ask the students to pass their plates around the group. Stop the music after a few minutes. At this signal, have the youngsters stop passing the plates. Go around the group, asking each student to read the plate he holds and to show the word to his classmates. Resume the music to continue the activity.

For an alphabet letter version, program the plates with various letters. When you go around the group, ask each student to hold up his plate and read his letter aloud. Then name chosen words and have students tell who has the corresponding initial letters.

Other!

with

other

Icy Sort

Here's a refreshing center activity for **word families.** Vertically position three 5" x 9" yellow construction paper rectangles and then trim the sides to make the rectangles resemble tall glasses of lemonade. Label each glass with a different rime as shown. Then glue a construction paper strip (straw) to each glass. To prepare ice cubes, cut 12 or more 1¾" white squares. For each glass, program each of several ice cubes with a different word that has the corresponding rime. Place all of the ice cubes in a resealable plastic bag. Set the glasses and bag at a center.

A student arranges the glasses on a work surface. Then she sorts the ice cubes by placing them on the appropriate glasses. **For more advanced students,** provide paper ruled into three columns and have each youngster list each group of words in a different column on her paper.

-in	-op	-est
pin	shop	nest
thin	mop	best
grin	top	est
chin	st	-est

-in	-op	-est
pin	shop	nest
thin	mop	best
grin	top	rest
chin	stop	test

How Cool!

Promote reading and writing with a cooler? Sure! Simply stock an empty cooler with read-alouds or books that your students read this past year. Encourage youngsters to revisit the selections. Or place a lidded cooler in your group-time area and designate it a Cool Stool. Invite student authors to sit on the stool and read samples of their writing to the class.

Nancy Dembkowski, Rhodes School, River Grove, IL

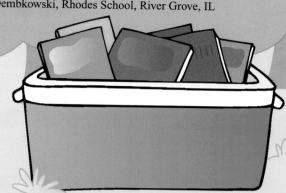

Sentence Slices

Sharpen students' **punctuation skills** with this mouthwatering center idea. To prepare, make several watermelon slices similar to the one shown by gluing together red and green semicircles. Prepare an equal number of large construction paper seeds. Program each slice of watermelon with an unpunctuated sentence so that there are questions, exclamations, and statements. Program the seeds with corresponding end marks. Place the seeds and watermelon slices at a center stocked with paper.

A student takes a watermelon slice and reads the sentence. After he uses a seed to correctly punctuate the sentence, he writes the punctuated sentence on his paper. Then he helps himself to another slice of watermelon!

Do you like picnics

Ants, Ants, Ants!

Wherever there's a picnic, you're sure to see ants. And with this **rhyming** activity, students see them all over! Color a copy of the picture cards on page 193 and then cut them out. Display in a pocket chart the four sentences shown, leaving a blank space for each picture card. Set aside the picture of the shoe and display the remaining cards in an empty row.

To begin, read the first sentence with students. Have a volunteer place a chosen picture card in the first blank. Guide students to identify the picture that completes the rhyme and then ask a volunteer to set it in place. Complete the next two sentences in a similar manner. Then set the shoe card in the first space in the last sentence. After a volunteer completes the sentence, lead youngsters in reading the chart from beginning to end. **For more advanced students,** follow up by helping youngsters write different ant-themed rhymes.

I see ants on the [ ] and ants on the [ ] .
I see ants on the [ ] and ants on the [ ] .
I see ants on the [ ] and ants on the [ ] .
I see ants on my [ ] and ants on [ ]

Basket Booklets

Invite your young authors to show off their writing with this nifty **publishing** idea. For each student, staple several half sheets of white paper between two 6" x 9" pieces of construction paper to make a booklet. Round the two bottom corners as shown. To begin, give each student a sheet of writing paper and have her write about the best picnic ever (real or imagined). Encourage her to check her work with a copy of the writing checklist on page 194. Write the youngster's edited story in a prepared booklet and then have her illustrate it.

To complete her booklet, each youngster glues on a construction paper handle. She colors a red-and-white checkered pattern on a 4" x 8" piece of white paper. She cuts a triangular shape from the paper and then glues the top of it to her booklet as shown. **For an easier version,** have each student illustrate a summer sight on each booklet page and then add captions.

Picnic Plans

Whether you have a picnic **celebration** indoors or outdoors, it's a perfect way to celebrate reading, writing, and the end of the year! Fill out a copy of the invitation on page 194 and then duplicate it to make a class supply. Have each student color an invitation, cut it out, and then take it home to his family. On the day of the event, decorate your picnic site with balloons. Provide picnic blankets for students and their invited guests to sit on. Use the ideas below, and serve a snack such as lemonade and cookies or watermelon. What fun!

Proud Readers: Set out familiar books in picnic baskets and coolers. Have students read selections to (or with) their guests.

Fun Favorites: Lead students in reading poems or singing songs that they learned during the past year.

Awesome Authors: Encourage students to read aloud their writing from "Basket Booklets" on this page. Display previously made class books for students to share as well.

Top Ten: Have the students present ten posters that they made earlier to highlight the ten most memorable events of the year.

Field Day

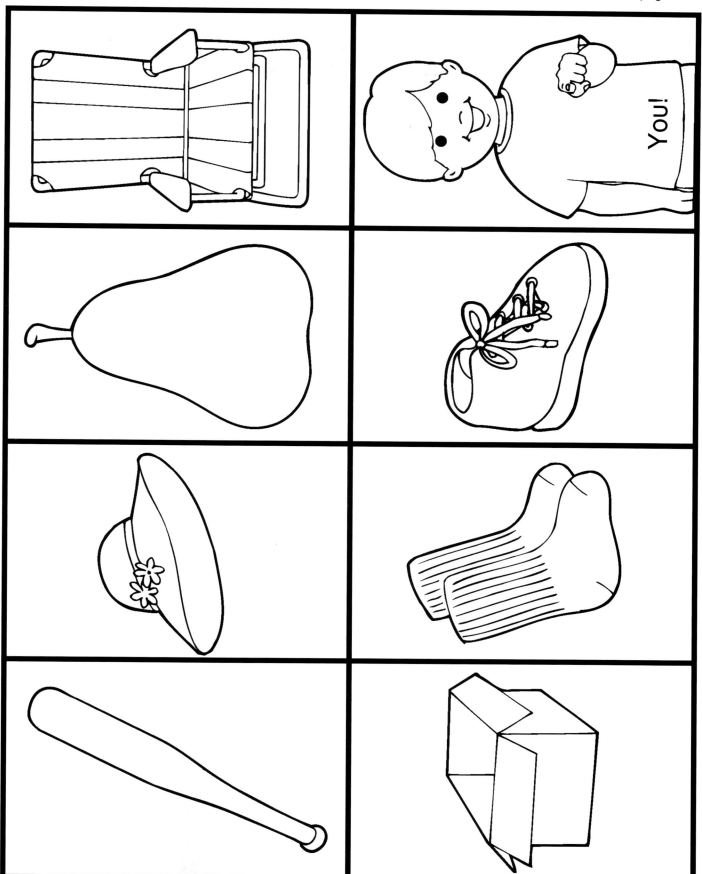

You!

Writing Checklist

Use with "Basket Booklets" on page 192.

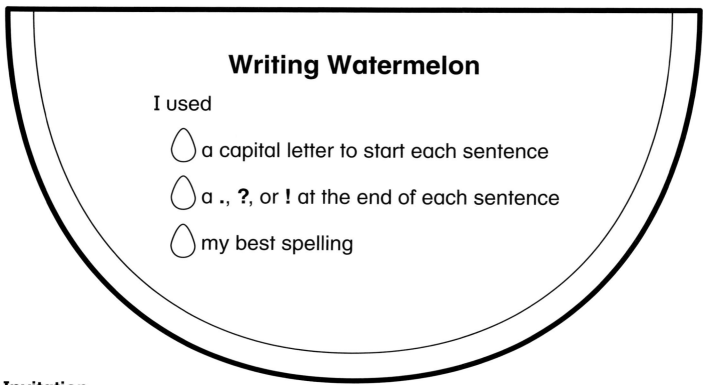

Writing Watermelon

I used

◯ a capital letter to start each sentence

◯ a **.**, **?**, or **!** at the end of each sentence

◯ my best spelling

Invitation

Use with "Picnic Plans" on page 192.

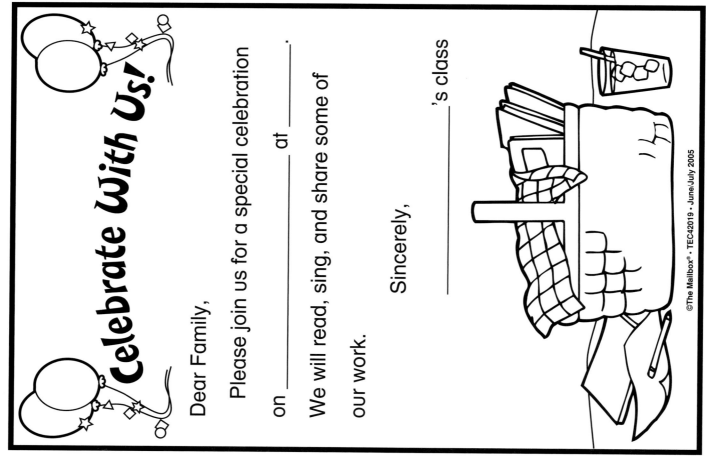

Celebrate With Us!

Dear Family,

Please join us for a special celebration

on _____ at _____ .

We will read, sing, and share some of

our work.

Sincerely,

_____'s class

LITERATURE UNITS

Hattie and the Fox

Written by Mem Fox • Illustrated by Patricia Mullins

When a nose pokes through nearby bushes, Hattie alerts her uninterested farm friends. As the hidden animal slowly reveals itself, Hattie becomes increasingly agitated, but her friends continue to disregard the situation—that is until Hattie declares that the animal is a fox!

ideas by Stephanie Affinito—Reading Specialist
Craig Elementary School, Niskayuna, NY

What Could It Be?
Making predictions

Hattie doesn't know what kind of animal is lurking in the bushes until it completely reveals itself. But no doubt your students have some ideas! Before reading the book, tell students that the story includes an animal that is hiding. Encourage youngsters to predict what kind of animal will be revealed. Then explain that since the animal is revealed a little at a time, it is difficult to identify at first.

To explore how the clues may be pieced together, give each student a sheet of drawing paper. Comment that a nose is the first part seen and have each youngster draw an animal nose. Announce each later sight (eyes, ears, legs, body, tail), one at a time, and ask each student to add it to his drawing. After the drawings are complete, invite youngsters to confirm or change their predictions. Have them settle in for a reading of the book to check their ideas.

Participating With Puppets
Participating in a read-aloud

Even though Hattie's friends seem unconcerned, they have quite a bit to say! After a first reading, bring the critters' exchanges to life with the help of your students and these easy-to-prepare puppets. To make a Hattie puppet, color a copy of the hen pattern (page 198), cut it out, and then tape a craft stick to the back of it. Next, ask each child to color a copy of an animal pattern (pages 198 and 199) other than the hen and fox. Then have her cut it out and tape on a craft stick to make a puppet.

Instruct each youngster to hold her puppet as you group students in your storytime area in this order: geese, pigs, sheep, horses, and cows. Help the students practice reciting the appropriate dialogue while animating their puppets. (Plan to provide the dialogue for any animals not represented.) Then, as you read the book aloud, use your puppet to dramatize Hattie's dialogue and prompt the students in each group to join in with their lines.

Critter Comments
Contributing to a story innovation

The farm animals respond to Hattie's concerns in the same way throughout the story until the very end. Have youngsters add variety to the exchanges by substituting their own responses during a unique rereading! First, encourage children to brainstorm different remarks the animals might make as you write their suggestions on chart paper. Then write five chosen remarks on a fresh sheet of chart paper to replace the characters' repeated remarks. After children practice reading the new dialogue with expression, reread the story, pausing for students to make the substitutions.

"Yikes!" said the goose.

"No way!" said the pig.

"Wow!" said the sheep.

"I don't believe it!" said the horse.

"Big deal!" said the cow.

Add Some Drama!
Retelling a story with props

After students are familiar with the book, have them dramatize a retelling of the story with this center idea. At a center, place a cassette player, a blank cassette tape, and at least one copy of the book. Also provide a small plastic animal to represent each character in the story. Or, to make the props, color white construction paper copies of the animal and scenery patterns (pages 198 and 199) and cut them out; then glue a section of a cardboard tube to the back of each one to make a stand. Arrange for students to visit the center in pairs. To use the center, the youngsters retell the story with the props, referring to the book as needed. Once they are comfortable with the task, invite them to record their retelling for you to review later.

That was close!

Speechless!
Extending a story

The animals are at a loss for words after the fox leaps from the bushes, but this imaginative follow-up gives voice to their thoughts! Show students the illustration of the silent animals at the book's conclusion and encourage them to suggest what the animals might say if they shared their thoughts. After several suggestions, invite each child to color a farm animal other than the fox from a copy of page 198 or 199. Then ask her to cut it out. Give each child a construction paper speech bubble and have her write what the animal might say (or have each child dictate the comments for you to write). Showcase each student's speech bubble with her animal on a bulletin board. Then title the display "Let's Talk About It!"

Animal Patterns
Use with "Participating With Puppets" on page 196 and "Add Some Drama!" and "Speechless!" on page 197.

Pig and Goose Patterns

Use with "Participating With Puppets" on page 196 and "Add Some Drama!" and "Speechless!" on page 197.

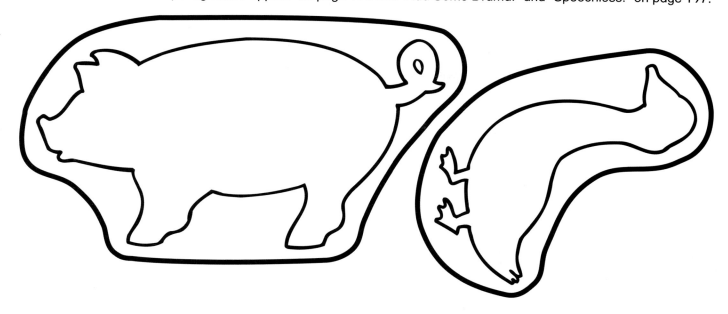

Fox and Scenery Patterns

Use with "Add Some Drama!" on page 197.

Letter-Perfect Literature

With the featured books and accompanying ideas, strengthening literacy skills is as easy as A, B, C!

*ideas by Lucia Kemp Henry
Fallon, NV*

Old Black Fly

Written by Jim Aylesworth • Illustrated by Stephen Gammell

A pesky fly creates an alphabetical trail of mayhem as it buzzes around in this rollicking rhyming tale.

Word Pairs

pie—cry
sack—back
dog—cat
sink—wink
door—store
bed—head
eggs—milk
heat—feet
milk—noodles
lap—flap

What's the Buzz?
Rhyming words

Old Black Fly's mischievous deeds provide plenty of opportunities for identifying rhymes. After reading the book for students' listening enjoyment, reread selected pairs of pages and have students identify the rhyming words. Next, ask students to listen carefully as you announce a rhyming or nonrhyming word pair (see the suggestions). If the words rhyme, the youngsters say, "Buzz!" If the words do not rhyme, they say, "Shoo, fly!" Pause to confirm the correct response, repeating the words to emphasize the ending sounds. Then explore a desired number of additional word pairs in a similar manner. Rhyming skills are bound to be off to a flying start!

Out of Place
Alphabet sequence

The pesky fly causes quite a mess, but it keeps its route in order—ABC order, that is! Challenge your youngsters to create their own alphabetical lineups with this class activity. In advance, prepare a large letter card for each letter of the alphabet. To begin, have five volunteers stand side by side facing the class. Select six alphabetically sequenced cards. Secretly remove one of the middle cards at random and set it aside. Distribute the remaining cards to the volunteers in order and ask them to hold the letters in clear view. Lead the seated students in reading the letters aloud.

Next, present the reserved letter to an additional volunteer. To determine where the letter belongs in the sequence, prompt students to say or sing the alphabet. After verifying where the letter belongs, invite the cardholder to imitate a fly buzzing as he positions himself in the line. Then have students read the entire letter sequence. Repeat the activity with different students and letters as desired. To keep your youngsters' alphabet skills buzzing along, have each student complete a copy of page 203.

I belong right after C!

by JANE BAYER • pictures by STEVEN KELLOGG

A My Name Is Alice

Written by Jane Bayer • Illustrated by Steven Kellogg

This picture book version of the popular jump rope rhyme features an alphabetical assortment of animals. The comical critters come from all over the world and sell various wares, from ants to zippers!

Grade A Shopping List
Letter-sound relationships

There's no question about it, the enterprising characters sell an intriguing collection of wares! Help students take stock of the merchandise with this follow-up activity. Post a large sheet of paper and title it as shown. Then revisit each page in order, asking students to name the letter and corresponding merchandise. Write the letter and word, repeating the word to emphasize its beginning sound. When you reach the page for *X*, point out that few English words start with *X*. Add the letter and featured ware to the list and then draw a box around the word to remind students that it is made up.

Later, use the completed list to explore letter-sound relationships in a variety of ways. For example, announce, "I need some [listed type of merchandise]," emphasizing the beginning sound of the word. Then ask students to name the "letter store" you should visit, such as the *B* store for balloons or the *D* store for dust. Youngsters are sure to buy into the unique phonics practice!

ABC Shopping List
A ants
B balloons
C cakes
D dust
E eggs

Classy Catalog
Letter-sound relationships

What's a perfect way for the characters to advertise their wares? Why, in an alphabetical catalog, of course! Invite your young entrepreneurs to advertise their own letter-themed shopping suggestions with this catalog project. For each youngster, prepare a die-cut letter, omitting less frequently used letters and repeating letters as necessary. Mark the back of the letter to indicate on which side the student should later apply glue. Confirm that each youngster can identify her letter and the sound it represents.

Have each student glue her letter in the upper right-hand corner of a horizontally positioned sheet of drawing paper. Near the bottom of her paper, help her write a chosen store item that begins with her letter (or have her dictate the word for you to write). After each student illustrates her work, alphabetize students' pages and bind them between two construction paper covers. The resulting book is guaranteed to suit young readers to a T!

TOOT & PUDDLE

Puddle's ABC

by HOLLY HOBBIE

Toot & Puddle: Puddle's ABC

Written and illustrated by Holly Hobbie

When Puddle takes it upon himself to teach his friend Otto how to spell his own name, he decides to teach him the alphabet as well. A creative combination of narrative and alliterative text brings the charming story to life.

What's in a Name?

Letters in context

Once Otto learns the alphabet, he realizes that some words have a lot in common. No doubt this name investigation will help your youngsters reach a similar conclusion. After sharing the book with students, return to the page where Otto comments that his name is *Toot* spelled inside out. Guide students to compare the letters in the two names.

Next, have each youngster write his name on a sentence strip length. After each student completes his writing, announce a letter. At this signal, each student whose name either starts or ends with the letter stands at the front of the classroom with his name strip. (If only one student has a name that meets the criteria, announce a different letter and have each corresponding student join the youngster.) Have students tell whether the names begin or end alike and then guide them to identify any other letter-related similarities. Then ask the name-holders to return to their seats. Announce different letters to continue exploring students' names in this manner. After each student has had at least one turn at the front of the classroom, collect the name strips for use in the next activity.

Tomas

We both have an *o*!

Trenton

At the Beginning

Letter-sound relationships, using picture cues

Puddle's paintings and captions are not only entertaining, but are also a perfect tool for letter-sound reinforcement! Reread selected captions to students, guiding them to notice the words that begin with the same letters and sounds. Then give each student her name strip from the previous activity. Have her glue her strip at the bottom of a vertically positioned sheet of drawing paper. Ask her to illustrate herself and an action or object that begins with the same letter as her name. As students work, help each youngster, in turn, label a sentence strip length with her chosen word. Use a hole puncher and large paper clip to display the word below her name as shown.

After students complete their work, collect the projects. On each of several days, post a few projects that feature different beginning letters. Unclip the word strips and scramble them. Have volunteers clip each word to the correct project. Then model how to use the picture and letter cues as you lead students in reading the captions.

Jill

jUmps

Name _____

Letter Search

✂ Cut.   🧴 Glue.

| A | B | | D | E | F | G | | I |

| J | | L | M | N | | P | Q | R | S |

| T | | V | W | X | | Z |

K   Y   C   O   H   U

Bonus Box: Look at each letter. If it is in your first name, use a crayon to draw a line below it.

©The Education Center, Inc. • *The Mailbox*® • TEC42014 • Aug./Sept. 2004

Note to the teacher: Use with "Out of Place" on page 200.

203

The Pick of dePaola

Tomie dePaola's flair for spellbinding stories is certain to make his books favorites among your students! Use the ideas below with any book by this talented author-illustrator and the activities on the next two pages with two of his most popular selections.

ideas contributed by Lucia Kemp Henry, Fallon, NV

Finding Favorites
Forming opinions

No doubt your youngsters delight in listening to many of dePaola's tales. But what do they enjoy most about the selections? The memorable characters? The humorous situations? Or something else? Help youngsters identify some of their favorite story details with this notable idea. Display a selection of the author's works. Over several days, read aloud each book and invite students to share their thoughts about the stories and illustrations. After students are familiar with the books, set out a supply of large sticky notes. Encourage each youngster to revisit his favorite book during an independent-reading time. Ask him to write on a sticky note a detail that he likes about the book and sign his name. Then have him adhere the sticky note to the inside front cover or a relevant page. What a simple way to get students thinking about books!

Big Anthony is funny.

Carlos

I lk the PKSHrz.

Kevin

All About a Book!
Identifying story elements

What's almost as fun as sharing a Tomie dePaola book? Why, recapping the story, of course! Review the story elements of a chosen book with this booklet project. In advance, make one copy of page 207 and write the book title in the blank. Copy the programmed page onto light-colored paper to make a class supply. Instruct each student to cut her labels apart. Then have her use a glue stick to glue each label near the top of a separate sheet of white paper. Ask her to stack the resulting pages in order, placing the title page on top. Help her staple the stack across the top.

To begin, read the book aloud. Then ask each student to illustrate her booklet's title page. After students complete their artwork, collect their booklets for safe-keeping. The next day, redistribute the booklets and read aloud the page labels. Ask students to listen for the corresponding story details as you reread the book. Then have each youngster write the information on her labels and add illustrations below them.

The Characters
1
a lamb family

The Art Lesson
by Tomie dePaola

Tommy loves to draw! He eagerly anticipates his first real art lesson at school only to find that it involves copying—a task that falls far short of his expectations. But Tommy and his art teacher discuss his disappointment and come up with a solution that reflects the art of compromise!

I like to go camping. Brianna

I like to dans.   Rosine

How Unique!
Making personal connections

Just as Tommy and his friends enjoy a wide variety of activities, your youngsters surely have favorite pastimes, too! After reminding students of the characters' diverse interests, give each youngster a sentence strip. Have her write a sentence about one of her favorite activities and sign her name. After students complete their writing, ask each youngster, in turn, to read her sentence aloud and tell the class any additional information that she would like to share. If desired, invite each student to bring an item from home that relates to her interest for later sharing. Post the sentence strips on a hallway wall and title the display "Favorite Ways to Have Fun."

Totally Tomie
Writing in response to literature

With careful attention to story details, youngsters can learn a lot about Tomie dePaola as a young boy. Tell students that the book is based on the author-illustrator's childhood. Ask them to listen carefully for details that tell about the main character as you read the book aloud. Afterward, ask students to recall what they learned about Tomie as you list the information on a sheet of chart paper.

Next, give each child a sheet of white construction paper. Add writing lines if desired. Have him write something he learned about Tomie and draw a matching illustration. Bind students' completed work into a class book and title it as shown. Ask one or two volunteers to add a cover illustration. As you share the finished book with the class, invite each child to come forward and read his page. Who knows? One of them might become an author-illustrator just like Tomie!

When Tomie dePaola Was a Young Boy

Strega Nona

retold and illustrated by Tomie dePaola

When Big Anthony disregards Strega Nona's directions and uses her magic pasta pot, he inadvertently causes a large pasta problem! Fortunately, Strega Nona returns just in time to save everyone from harm. Plus, she has a fitting (and humorous!) solution for dealing with the flood of pasta.

Before Reading

It cooks all by itself.
It changes everything into pasta.
It never stops cooking.

During Reading

The pasta will push Big Anthony out of the town.
After a while, it will just stop.
They'll call for help.

Interesting "Pasta-bilities"
Making predictions

Ask a question before and one during a reading of this classic book, and your youngsters will bubble over with story predictions! Post two jumbo pasta pot cutouts titled as shown. Explain that there is a magic pasta pot in the story you're about to read. Ask students to predict what magical qualities the pot possesses, and write their thoughts on the "Before Reading" cutout. Begin reading the book, encouraging students to listen carefully and study the illustrations to check their predictions. Stop at the point when the pasta bubbles out of Strega Nona's house. Ask students what they think will happen and write their predictions on the "During Reading" cutout. Then finish reading the story to reveal the actual story events.

What Would You Do?
Writing a response to a question

Big Anthony tries shouting at the pot, lifting it, and sitting on it to stop the flood of pasta. But nothing he tries works. Use this follow-up activity to explore some pasta-stopping tactics Big Anthony hasn't tried! First, ask students what they would do if they were faced with the overflowing pasta pot and didn't know the magic words. Encourage creativity as you take several suggestions. Then have each child explain her favorite solution on provided paper. Post each child's writing around a large cooking pot cutout that you have tacked to a bulletin board. Add the title "Pasta Pot Solutions."

To embellish the display, work with a few students at a time. Give each youngster several lengths of white yarn and a ten-inch square of aluminum foil. Ask him to dip a length of yarn into a pan of liquid starch. Have him slide the yarn between two fingers to remove the excess starch and then randomly place the yarn on his foil. Ask him to repeat the process with the remaining yarn, overlapping it so that it resembles tangled pasta. After the yarn dries for at least 48 hours, peel it off the foil and staple it to the display.

All About

_____

by Tomie dePaola

1 **The Characters**

2 **The Setting**

3 **What Happens**

STORY AND PICTURES BY MAURICE SENDAK

Written and Illustrated by Maurice Sendak
In this Caldecott Medal book, a mischievous boy named Max is sent to his room. Soon afterward, his room transforms into a forest and Max "travels" to the land where the wild things are. Much to Max's delight, he is named king, and he has a grand time cavorting with the creatures. But in the end, Max is lonely and returns home—the place where he is loved best of all!

ideas contributed by Stephanie Affinito—Reading Coordinator
Glens Falls, NY

Fantastic?
Distinguishing between reality and fantasy

A blend of reality and fantasy results when Max visits the land of the wild things. Use this prereading activity to bring the distinction between real and fantastic into focus. In advance, color a copy of the picture cards (page 211) and cut them out. Post within student reach a two-column chart titled as shown. To begin, hold up a chosen card. Have students name the picture and categorize it as real or pretend. Then invite a child to tape the card in the correct column. Continue in a similar way with each remaining picture. If desired, ask students to name other real or pretend things for you to list on the chart. Explain that the story has both real and pretend elements. Then have students settle in for an enchanting read-aloud!

Real	Pretend
school	talking animals
table	unicorns
principal	

My fet cnt tch the grnd.

This is fun!

Look at mi scre teeth

A Wordless Rumpus
Responding to a story through writing

No words are spoken as Max and the wild things frolic during the rumpus. But no doubt the characters are thinking a variety of wild thoughts! After a first reading, direct students' attention to the word-less pages. Welcome students' ideas about why the author-illustrator designed the pages so that there is no text and the illustrations are full size. Then explain that students will give voice to the characters' thoughts.

Place the book and a supply of large sticky notes at a center. When a child visits the center, she studies the wordless pages. She writes on a sticky note what a chosen character might be thinking and then places her sticky note on the appropriate page. Near the end of each day, remove the labeled notes and display them on a poster. Return the book to the center for more thought-provoking responses!

A Tale in a Tree

Identifying the beginning, middle, and end

Explore the beginning, middle, and end of the story with these projects, which would remind any wild thing of home! For each child, fold a 12" x 18" sheet of tan construction paper into thirds (to 6" x 12"). Unfold the paper and label each section with the headings shown.

As you discuss the story with students, guide them to identify the beginning, middle, and end of the story. Next, give each child a prepared paper and have him trace the fold lines. Ask him to draw and label a picture in each section to represent the corresponding part of the story. Then have him refold his paper and glue on torn-paper leaves to resemble foliage as shown. Finally, have him write the book title on the trunk and sign his name. Encourage youngsters to take their "tree-mendous" projects home and use them to tell their families about the story from beginning to end!

From Wild to Happy!

Contributing to a story innovation

As the story begins, Max acts like a wild thing. So it seems fitting that his adventure takes him to where the wild things are. But what if he were a happy thing? Use this mural idea to help students speculate about the possibility. Lightly tape a length of bulletin board paper to a tabletop for easy management. Encourage youngsters to imagine that Max visits the land of the happy things. Invite each child to use drawing paper and provided arts-and-crafts materials to design a happy thing. Have volunteers fashion trees and vines from construction paper. Then help students glue their artwork onto the prepared paper. After the scene is complete, display the resulting mural on a wall.

Next, post a sheet of chart paper titled as shown. Prompt students to tell a brief story about Max and the happy things; write their tale on the paper. Then display the completed story near the mural.

Where the Happy Things Are
Once there was a land where everyone was happy. The creatures laughed and smiled all the time. There were parties every day and the creatures were never sad. Max visited the land of happy things and had lots of fun. One day he was sad because he missed his mom. Then he went home.

Furry, Bumpy, and Scaly
Responding to a story through art

These masks not only have the trademark luminous eyes of the wild things, but they also have the textured look of the creatures! Invite each student to study the illustrations of the wild things and comment on the details that she notices. Then give each child a 12-inch white construction paper circle, crayons, and access to various textured materials, such as cork, sandpaper, and corrugated cardboard. Have her completely cover her circle with crayon rubbings of desired materials.

Next, assist each student in cutting eyeholes in her mask. On the back of her mask, have her tape a piece of yellow cellophane over the eyeholes. Ask her to glue on cut-paper teeth, horns, and any other desired features. Finally, have her tape a jumbo craft stick to the back of her mask to make a handle. What a perfect prop for a wild rumpus!

Boo!

If I were a wild thing, I would
__sa boo and wv mi arms__ .

Scare Tactics
Responding to a writing prompt

From roaring their terrible roars to rolling their terrible eyes, the wild things react to Max's arrival and departure in exactly the same way. Perhaps they could spice up their repertoire of actions with suggestions from your youngsters! Revisit the book with students and review the wild things' response to Max when he arrives and leaves. Then give each student a 12" x 18" sheet of drawing paper and a copy of the prompt shown.

Ask each youngster to complete his sentence to tell how he would act fiercely if he were a wild thing. Have him glue his sentence near the bottom of his paper and draw a picture of this wild thing in action. Then invite students to share their wild ideas!

Fruity Things

With this simple snack suggestion, youngsters can make their own wild things and then eat them all up! To make her snack, a child spreads strawberry cream cheese or jam on an English muffin half. Then she arranges various fruits (see the suggestions) on top to make a wild thing face. When a desired effect is achieved, she digs in to her snack!

Suggested fruits: pineapple tidbits, banana slices, halved strawberries, blueberries, mandarin orange segments, peach slices, halved maraschino cherries

Allison Pratt
Winona, MN

Hats Off to Dr. Seuss!

Mark your calendars! March 2 is the anniversary of Dr. Seuss's birthday, and there's no better time to celebrate reading! Try the ideas below to set the stage for Seuss-style fun, and use the activities that follow to complement two beloved Seuss classics.

Hooray for Books!
Reading motivation

Part of the fun of reading great books is sharing them, so why not invite guest readers to do exactly that? Designate a guest reader week. For each corresponding school day, arrange for a different community member or school staff member to read aloud a Dr. Seuss book to your students. To set a festive tone for the visits, decorate the classroom doorway and your group reading area with red and white streamers and, if desired, balloons. Display a poster with the rhyme shown and post a jumbo red-and-white-striped hat cutout that students have signed. During each visit, snap a few photos of the guest as he reads and invite him to add his signature to the hat. Later, thank each guest with a note from the class and a photo of his special visit!

Whether there's rain
Or plenty of sun,
We think reading is lots of fun!

Rhymes? Where?
Rhyming, word recognition

This word wall idea features rhymes from here to there! Display on a bulletin board a jumbo signpost labeled as shown. Nearby, set out a supply of large blank cards, markers, and a collection of Dr. Seuss books. Tack a manila envelope to the board within student reach.

Over several days, ask each youngster to prepare at least one card for display. To do this, a youngster chooses from a book a rhyming word pair that is not yet displayed. She draws a line down the center of a card, writes each word on a separate half, and then deposits her card in the envelope. (As an alternative, have students identify rhyming words during read-aloud sessions; then prepare word cards with students' help.) Each day, add any newly prepared cards to the display and lead students in reading all of the rhymes!

Pat Bedi, South Amboy Elementary School
South Amboy, NJ

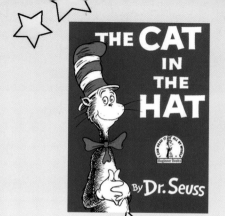

The Cat in the Hat
by Dr. Seuss

One cold, wet day, Sally and her brother have nothing to do—that is, until the Cat in the Hat arrives. The mischievous feline conjures up all kinds of zany ways to pass the time, making it a day the twosome will never forget!

I play on the computer. It's fun!

Pitter, Patter
Art, writing

When it comes to thinking of rainy day activities, Sally and her brother are at a loss. They can think of nothing to do but sit! Invite your students to share some of their rainy day pastimes with this writing project. In advance, use 6" x 9" tagboard rectangles to prepare several house-shaped templates for students to share. After sharing the book with students, instruct each youngster to fold a 9" x 12" sheet of white construction paper in half to 6" x 9". Then have her trace a template on it as shown. Ask her to cut out the tracing, leaving the fold intact.

To complete her project, the student adds desired crayon details to the front of her house and then unfolds her paper. She illustrates a rainy day activity on the left-hand side of her paper and writes about it on the right-hand side. The Cat in the Hat is right—there are lots of ways to have fun on rainy days!

Silly Sights
Rhyming, spelling

A cat in a hat is quite a sight! Bring several other silly sights into view with this rhyme-filled class activity. Make an enlarged copy of the picture cards on page 215. Color the cards and then cut them out. Use loops of tape to display the cards on the board, leaving a generous amount of space between them. Give each student an individual chalkboard or whiteboard and writing supplies.

To begin, ask a volunteer to choose a card and identify the two pictured rhyming words with a sentence that begins with "I spy." For example, he might say, "I spy a fox on a box." Write the first rhyming word near the card. Have each student write the second rhyming word on his board and then display it for you to see. Scan the responses and write the correct spelling. After each student erases his board, continue with the remaining cards. **For an easier version,** announce a pictured word and have students name the corresponding rhyme; write both words on the board with student input.

adapted from an idea by Kim Parker
Christian Heritage School, Longview, TX

bug
rug

The Cat in the Hat Comes Back
by Dr. Seuss

The Cat in the Hat is back! This time he causes a huge, colorful mess that spreads out into the yard. To clean it up, the cat enlists the help of an alphabetical lineup of friends. But it's not until the tiniest friend comes on the scene that the cleanup efforts succeed.

Cat Problems
Problem solving

The Cat in the Hat and his friends have some unusual problem-solving strategies! Encourage students to put their own problem-solving skills to use with this math journal idea. For each student, prepare a hat-shaped journal with several blank pages similar to the one shown. After reading the book aloud, have students recall how the characters try to clean up the spots. Point out that some strategies are unsafe, and caution students not to imitate them.

Next, have each student sign his journal cover and color it as desired. Then present a story-related problem (see the example). To solve the problem, each youngster draws a picture on his first page and writes the corresponding number sentence. After confirming the correct answer, collect the journals for safekeeping. Over the next few days, present different problems for students to solve on their remaining journal pages.

Deborah Furtado, Betsey B. Winslow School, New Bedford, MA

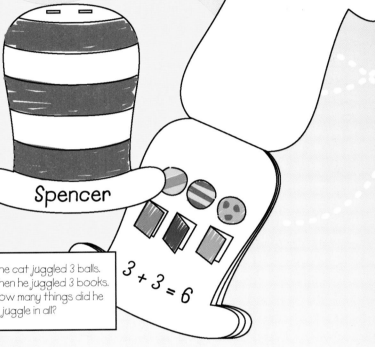

Spencer

The cat juggled 3 balls. Then he juggled 3 books. How many things did he juggle in all?

3 + 3 = 6

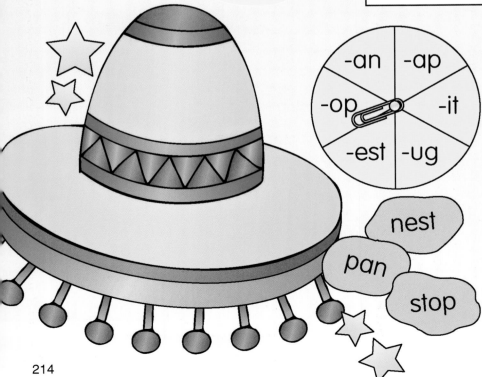

-an	-ap
-op	-it
-est	-ug

nest

pan

stop

Clean Up the Spots!
Word families

With this partner game, students use their reading skills to clear away spots. Divide a five-inch tagboard circle into six sections. Program each section with a different rime. Secure a metal brad and a large paper clip to the circle to make a spinner as shown. Prepare 12 pink construction paper spots. Program each spot with a word that includes a featured rime so that there are two words for each rime. Place the spots in a container.

Each player takes six spots at random and spreads them out on a work surface. To take a turn, a player spins. If she has a word with the rime, she announces, "Clean up"; reads the word aloud; and returns the spot to the container. If she does not have a word with a rime, her turn is over. Players alternate turns. The first player to return all of her spots wins.

Just Junie B. Jones

Junie B.'s unique way of viewing the world is sure to tickle your students' funny bones! Plus, her irrepressible behavior is a perfect springboard for discussions about making good choices. Use the following ideas with any books in the popular series by Barbara Park.

Meet Junie B.
Listening for story details

There's no doubt about it—Junie B. is definitely one of a kind! Invite students to share what they learn about the quirky character with this simple display idea. During one or more read-aloud sessions, encourage students to listen carefully for details about Junie B. Then post a sheet of chart paper labeled with the character's name and the book title. Have students recall what they know about the character and name words that describe her; list the information. Display the list in an open area of a classroom wall.

Next, have each youngster create a captioned illustration of the character on provided paper. Showcase students' completed work around the posted list. Revisit the display after later reading sessions to add any newly learned information.

Lucille is Junie B.'s best friend.

Junie B. is the same age as me!

Model Behavior?
Evaluating a character's actions

Does Junie B.'s behavior make the grade? Find out what your students think with this report card activity. In advance, write the title of a chosen book on a copy of the report card form on page 218. Copy the form to make a class supply. Read the book aloud to a preselected point and then ask each child to sign his name on a prepared form. Have him color a face in each row of the chart to rate Junie B.'s behavior. Then ask him to write a relevant comment on the provided lines. Instruct him to cut out his form, fold it in half (with the programming to the inside), and add a school-related illustration to the resulting front cover.

After each student completes his work, invite volunteers to tell how they rated the character's behavior and why. Guide students to identify times when Junie B. made poor choices and to suggest how she might improve her behavior. Now that's a Grade A strategy for promoting critical thinking!

Jasmine

Junie B. Jones

Journals About Junie B.

Responding to writing prompts

Junie B.'s middle initial is pretty important to her, so she'd certainly appreciate a letter-perfect journal! To prepare a journal, a student staples several sheets of paper in a construction paper folder. She glues a die-cut *B* in the middle of her front cover and completes the character's name as shown. Then she personalizes the cover as desired. After each of several read-aloud sessions, give each youngster a paper strip programmed with a prompt (see the examples shown). Have her glue it to a blank journal page and then write a response.

Supersimple Ideas

- **Prediction Pals** After the first read-aloud session for a chosen book, help students recap the story before you resume reading it. Then have each youngster tell a neighboring classmate what he predicts will happen. *Making predictions*

- **A Way With Words** As you read aloud a book about Junie B.'s kindergarten year, use sticky notes to flag pages where she misuses a word or makes one up. Later, write selected examples on the board or a sheet of chart paper and have students correct them. *Exploring word usage*

best
"I have two ~~bestest~~ friends at that place."

- **Remember the *B*!** Have each student use colorful markers to write her initials on a large blank card and add desired decorations. Display the prepared cards and then have students study them. Do any students share an initial with Junie B.? Does anyone have the same initial for their first and last names just as Junie B. does? To wrap up the activity, ask volunteers to tell what they like most about their names. *Making personal connections*

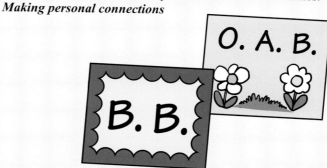

- **Helpful Handbook** Have students brainstorm school rules and manners that would be good for Junie B. to keep in mind. Then help them create a class book of reminders. *Responding to literature*

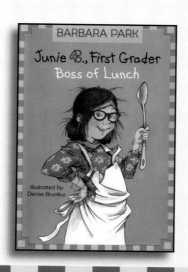

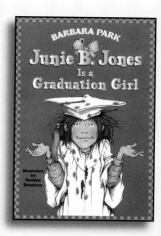

Report Card Form
Use with "Model Behavior?" on page 216.

Story Report Card

Character: Junie B. Jones   **Report by** _____

Book: _____

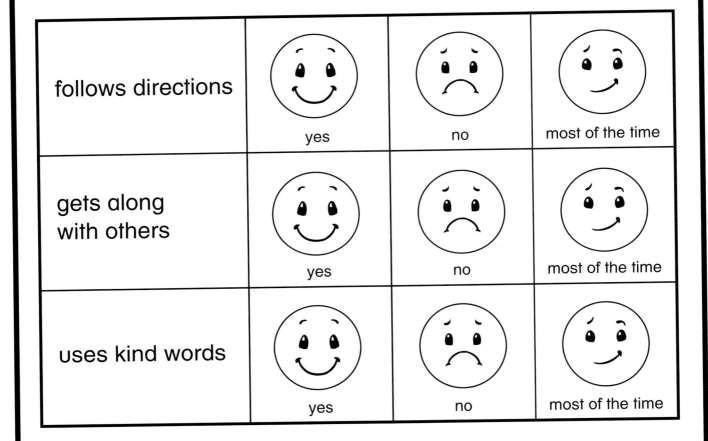

follows directions	😊 yes	🙁 no	🙂 most of the time
gets along with others	😊 yes	🙁 no	🙂 most of the time
uses kind words	😊 yes	🙁 no	🙂 most of the time

Junie B. _____

_____

_____

An Arthur Extravaganza

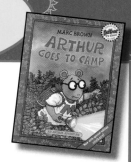

Delight students with two summertime stories about the beloved aardvark Arthur! Use the ideas below with both featured books, or delve into the stories separately with the ideas on the following pages.

ideas contributed by Julie Hays
Foothills Elementary, Maryville, TN

Get Ready!
Using prior knowledge

Spark interest in Arthur's vacation adventures with a suitcase packed with props! Place in a small suitcase several items that relate to one of the featured books. For example, for *Arthur's Family Vacation,* you might pack a bottle of suntan lotion, a toy camera, a beach towel, and some postcards. For *Arthur Goes to Camp,* you might pack a flashlight, a bottle of mosquito repellent, a sweatshirt, and some comic books. Present the suitcase to students and open it with great fanfare. Invite students to help you unpack the suitcase. Then ask youngsters to share their thoughts about the type of trip for which the suitcase was packed. After discussing students' ideas, present the book and announce where the characters are headed!

A Journey Journal
Writing in response to literature

What better place to write about Arthur's trips than in a suitcase-shaped journal? To make a journal, staple several sheets of paper inside a 9" x 12" construction paper folder. Trim the corners of the journal to resemble a suitcase. Then glue on two construction paper handles and a personalized luggage tag.

After sharing a featured book with students, pose a story-related question (see the suggestions below). Then have each youngster write a response in his journal. Invite him to add an illustration if desired. Arrange for him to make entries on his remaining journal pages on the following days. When his journal is complete, it will be just the ticket to prompt book-related discussions at home!

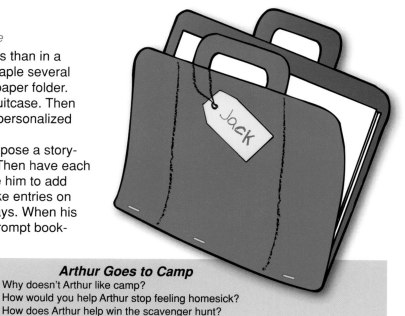

Arthur's Family Vacation
Why doesn't Arthur want to go on a family vacation?
What helps Arthur enjoy his vacation?
How do you have fun on rainy days?

Arthur Goes to Camp
Why doesn't Arthur like camp?
How would you help Arthur stop feeling homesick?
How does Arthur help win the scavenger hunt?

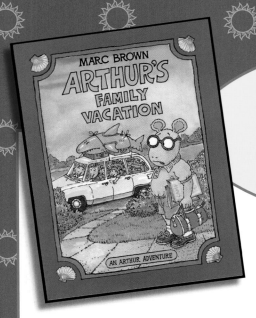

Arthur's Family Vacation

by Marc Brown

Arthur's summer trip with his family doesn't get off to a good start. He misses his friend, the motel pool is smaller than a bathtub, and the weather is horrible. But just when D. W. declares the vacation a disaster, Arthur thinks of a way to transform it into a raging success!

Banish the Blues!

Exploring a story's problem and solution

The family vacation lacks a very important element—fun! That is until Arthur comes up with some entertaining ideas. Invite your students to suggest other creative solutions with this follow-up activity. First, confirm that students recognize the main problem in the story and its solution. Then ask youngsters to brainstorm different ways that Arthur and his family could solve their problem. After youngsters share several ideas, give each student a construction paper raindrop and have her write or illustrate her favorite solution on it. To showcase students' shower of advice, post a titled cloud cutout on a prepared bulletin board. Then display students' completed raindrops below it.

Solutions for Rainy Day Blues

Splash in the puddles.

On a Roll

Retelling story events

Students are sure to have a ball with this approach to reviewing the story! After a second reading of the book, have students sit in a circle on the floor. Take a beach ball and join the group. As you hold the ball, recall the first story event. For example, you might say, "Arthur has a test on the last day of school." Then toss the ball to a child. Prompt him to name the next event and then toss the ball to a classmate. After this student tells what happens next, have him toss the ball to a youngster who has not had a turn. Continue the retelling in this manner until the entire story is told.

Arthur Goes to Camp

by Marc Brown

Frogs in bed, bad food, and scary sounds at night—summer camp is terrible, just as Arthur suspected! The reluctant camper sneaks away just as a scavenger hunt begins. As he heads home, though, he inadvertently helps his team win and decides that camp isn't such a bad place after all!

Mail Call!

Writing a letter

Writing letters is a perfect way for Arthur to tell his family about camp. It's also a great way for your students to tell their families about the story! After reading aloud the book, explain that students will tell their families about the story on jumbo postcards. Give each student a white construction paper copy of the postcard on page 222. Have her cut it out and then complete the letter. After the youngster checks her work, instruct her to write the names of the intended recipients where indicated. Invite the youngster to color the illustrations as desired. Then have her turn the postcard over and decorate the front of it with a story-related illustration. **To adapt the activity for more advanced students,** ask each youngster to write the appropriate mailing address on her postcard.

Remember When?

Story recall, writing captions

During Arthur's stay at camp, there are lots of memorable moments. Invite students to showcase their favorites with a picture-perfect display. Read aloud the book a second time, encouraging students to listen closely to the story details. Then give each student two white photo-size rectangles. Invite him to illustrate the rectangles to resemble photographs of two favorite moments in the story. Instruct him to arrange his photos on a 12" x 18" sheet of construction paper as desired and then glue them in place. After he adds captions, have him embellish his paper with camp-related materials, such as small twigs, leaf cutouts, frog stickers, and letter *M* cutouts (for Meadowcroak). Display students' completed work around the classroom. Ah, what great memories!

Postcard Pattern
Use with "Mail Call!" on page 221.

To:

_____

_____

_____

_____

Dear _____,

We read Arthur Goes to Camp.

_____

_____

_____

Love,

_____

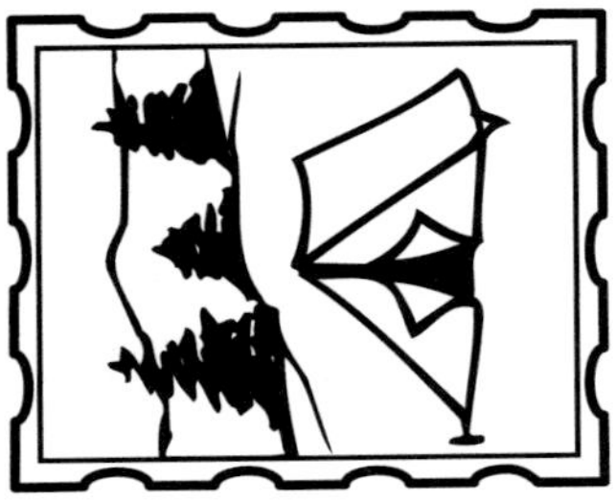

Camp Meadowcroak

Tent 3

MATH UNITS

Math to Start the Day

Students' math skills are sure to shine when you incorporate the following ideas into your morning routine. Now that's something to crow about!

ideas contributed by Angie Kutzer
Garrett Elementary, Mebane, NC

Day: Monday
How Many? 19

Sign-In Savvy
Counting, comparing numbers

No doubt students will enjoy being in attendance for this daily activity. Prepare an 11" x 17" sign-in sheet, similar to the one shown, with a space beside each student's name. Before school, label a copy of the sheet with the current day; place the sheet, a small rubber stamp, and an ink pad on a table. As each student arrives, have her stamp an image beside her name.

During your morning group time, display the stamped sheet. Lead students in counting the stamps and then write the total. Collect the attendance information in the same manner throughout the school week, adding each stamped sheet to the display. At the week's end, prompt youngsters to use the words *more, less,* and *the same* as they compare the totals. What a fun way to size up attendance!

Name That Number!
Counting, naming numbers

Bring number skills up to date with a supply of sticky notes and a monthly wall calendar! In advance, cover two or more dates with sticky notes. Point to each calendar space as you lead students in reading the dates shown. When you reach a sticky note, pause for students to name the hidden number. Remove the note to check their responses. Later in the year, use notes labeled with individual students' names and have the corresponding children identify the hidden numbers.

Dear Class,
 Today is Tuesday. After music class, we will read a farm book!
 Sincerely,
 Mr. Roost

Count on Messages!
Estimating, counting

Round out your morning message time with an idea that increases number sense as well as print awareness. Ask students to estimate the number of words in the day's message. After several volunteers share their thoughts, have students count as you underline each word. Compare the total with students' estimates. Repeat the activity with several days' messages. As students' skills develop, pose different questions such as "How many *A*s are there?" The math possibilities are countless!

Timely Tune

Using yesterday, today, *and* tomorrow

Get youngsters singing and moving with calendar vocabulary! Write each day of the week on a separate blank card. Also program a different card for each of the following words: *yesterday, today,* and *tomorrow.* Within student reach, sequence the days in a row on a bulletin board. Secure the hook side of a Velcro dot above each day and the loop side to the back of each word card.

To begin, ask a volunteer to secure the today card above the correct day. Then lead students in singing the first verse of the song shown. Slowly read aloud the days as you point to them, prompting students to stand when you reach the name of the previous day. After confirming the correct day, have a student secure the yesterday card above it. Invite youngsters to recall what they did during the day. Next, lead students in the second verse, asking them to signal the day that tomorrow will be by sitting at the appropriate time. Then ask a volunteer to label the day with the corresponding card.

Yesterday and Tomorrow
(sung to the tune of "If You're Happy and You Know It")

When I point to yesterday, stand up tall.
When I point to yesterday, stand up tall.
What did you do yesterday?
Did you run and jump and play?
When I point to yesterday, stand up tall.

When I point to tomorrow, please sit down.
When I point to tomorrow, please sit down.
When tomorrow comes along,
We'll stand again and sing this song.
When I point to tomorrow, please sit down.

●	Yesterday	Today	Tomorrow	●	●	●
Sunday	Monday	Tuesday	Wednesday	Thursday	Friday	Saturday

Which Month?

Understanding ordinal numbers

Line up ordinal number practice, month by month! Write each month of the year on a large tagboard strip. If desired, decorate each resulting sign to reflect special observances or holidays. Have 12 children stand shoulder to shoulder, and distribute the signs to them in order. As you recite the months with students, point to the signs. Next, ask a month-related question that includes an ordinal number, such as "Which month is third?" or "Who has a birthday in the first month of the year?" When a student supplies the correct answer, have her point out the corresponding month. After youngsters answer several questions, collect the signs for later use with different sign holders.

Lunch Plans
Displaying and interpreting data

Use the daily lunch count to whet students' appetites for collecting data! To prepare, laminate a wallet-size photo of each student and attach a magnetic strip to the back of it. Place the photos in a basket or lunchbox. Use masking tape to divide a large, horizontally positioned cookie sheet into one row for each lunch choice and a column for row labels. (See the illustration.) Color a copy of page 227 as desired and then laminate it. Cut out the cards and attach a magnetic strip to the back of each one. Prepare additional cards, as needed, to represent any other lunch choices. Store the cards in a resealable plastic bag.

Each day, use selected cards to label the rows with the appropriate food choices. Instruct each child to indicate his selection by placing his photo in the correct row. Next, have students count each set of photos as a designated student lunch helper displays the cookie sheet. Prompt a class discussion to explore the totals. After lunch, have the helper clear the sheet to prepare it for the next day's count.

Student Sets
Comparing numbers

All sorts of number comparisons are possible with this activity, and no manipulatives are required! Help students sort themselves into two groups based on whether they are wearing shoes with or without laces. Then have each group count its members and announce the total. Write the two numbers on the board and ask students to compare them. For additional practice, explore different categories such as the ones listed on this page. Or announce three categories at a time to set up more challenging comparisons.

Suggested Categories
Children who
- ride/do not ride the bus
- are wearing clothing with/without buttons
- like/do not like apples
- like/do not like rainy weather

Totally Equal
Exploring addition

This introduction to addition is a simple way to take comparing sets a step further. Count with your youngsters the number of boys and the number of girls present. If the totals are unequal, arrange the boys and girls in lines to check the one-to-one correspondence between the two groups. Help students use the resulting visual cue to determine how many more boys or girls are needed to make the groups equal. For example, if there are ten girls and eight boys, two more boys are needed to make equal groups. Then, with student input, write on the board the corresponding addition sentence.

Emily Porter
Garth Elementary
Georgetown, KY

$8 + 2 = 10$

Lunch From Home

Pizza

Hamburger

Taco

Spaghetti

Hot Dog

Sandwich

Chicken Nuggets

Ravioli

Turkey

Salad

Sloppy Joe

A 100th Day Rodeo

Rustle up excitement for the 100th day of school
with these rootin'-tootin' math ideas!

Count On It!

Get the day's festivities off to a rip-roarin' start
with an **estimating and counting** challenge. Post
the rhyme shown. Before reading it, ask students
to estimate how many letters it has; write their estimates on the board. Read the rhyme aloud and then
lead students in counting the letters. So that's what
100 looks like!

Lucille Iscaro, PS 257, Bronx, NY

...98, 99, 100!

One hundred takes a while to count—
It is such a large amount!
But I know you'll take the time,
To count the letters in this rhyme!

Hats With 100

Counting by tens can play a role in outfitting your
young wranglers! Make a slightly enlarged copy of the hat
pattern on page 230. Give each student a tan construction
paper copy of the enlarged pattern and access to stamper
markers. Have each youngster stamp ten images in each
section of her hat. Then guide her to count the images by
tens. After she cuts out her hat, staple it to a three-inch-wide
construction paper strip. Size the strip to her head and staple
the ends. Invite her to wear her hat throughout the day. For
added fun, present each youngster with a construction paper
badge similar to the one shown. Hooray for 100!

adapted from an idea by Barbara Cohen
Horace Mann School, Cherry Hill, NJ

Saddlebag Shuffle

This versatile idea is packed with ways to **explore the concept of 100.**
In advance, obtain a leather bag to represent a saddlebag. (Or cut two bag
shapes and a long strip from a brown paper grocery bag; add desired marker
details, glue the strip to resemble a handle, and then staple the shapes
together as shown.) Ask youngsters to name several activities that can be done
100 times or for 100 seconds. For example, students might suggest writing
numbers or names, swinging an imaginary lasso in the air, or trotting like a
pony. Write each activity on a separate blank card and tuck it in the saddlebag.
Periodically throughout the day, have a young cowpoke remove a card and
then lead his classmates in the activity. Yee-haw!

Kelly A. Lu, Berlyn School, Ontario, Canada

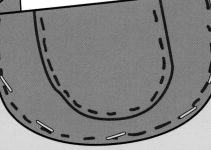

Swing an
imaginary lasso
100 times.

Write numbers
for 100 seconds.

Lasso the Loot

Spur students on to **counting pennies!** Use money stampers to show ten pennies on each of nine white 5" x 7" cards and a dollar bill on a colorful 5" x 7" card. Arrange a large rope lasso on the floor and then place the dollar card in it. Sit with students around the lasso. Distribute the loot cards to the first nine students beside you and help them count off by tens. Next, as you lead students in singing the song shown, direct each cardholder, in turn, to raise his card. During the last line of the song, prompt each cardholder to place his card in the lasso; then remove the dollar card and hold it up. Repeat the song with different cardholders until each child has had at least one turn holding some loot.

Marjorie Davis, Kingsville, TX

100 Pennies
(sung to the tune of "Ten Little Indians")

10 little, 20 little, 30 little pennies,
40 little, 50 little, 60 little pennies,
70 little, 80 little, 90 little pennies,
100 pennies make one dollar!

Trains With Tens

Use this group activity to keep your students' **number sense** skills chugging along. Give each child ten interlocking manipulatives that are the same color (give students a variety of colors). Have her link her manipulatives together to represent a train car. Then prompt students to count the manipulatives by tens to 100 and form a train with the corresponding train cars. Ask students to count any remaining manipulatives and form a second train with them. Next, instruct students to break apart each train after a train car of a chosen color. Ask them to determine the number of manipulatives in each resulting set. Write each pair of numbers on the board and guide students to compare them. After students reassemble the trains, continue with additional number comparisons as desired. Chug-a, chug-a, choo-choo!

Alyssa Weller, South School, Glencoe, IL

Rope 'em Back!

Don't stop the counting fun on the 100th day of school. **Count backward!** Post a hundred chart within student reach. Underline the number on the chart that tells how many days are left in the school year. Each following day, ask a child to use a marker to "lasso" the next smaller number. Help youngsters count backward from the underlined number to the newly circled number. Or have students count backward from the circled number to the number 1. What clever cowhands!

Megan Mathers
Glenn Dale Elementary
Glenn Dale, MD

1	2	3	4	5	6	7	8	9	10
11	12	13	14	15	16	17	18	19	20
21	22	23	24	25	26	27	28	29	30
31	32	33	34	35	36	37	38	39	40
41	42	43	44	45	46	47	48	49	50
51	52	53	54	55	56	57	58	59	60
61	62	63	64	65	66	67	68	69	70
71	72	73	74	75	76	77	78	79	80
81	82	83	84	85	86	87			90
91	92	93	94	95	96				

Hat Pattern
Use with "Hats With 100" on page 228.

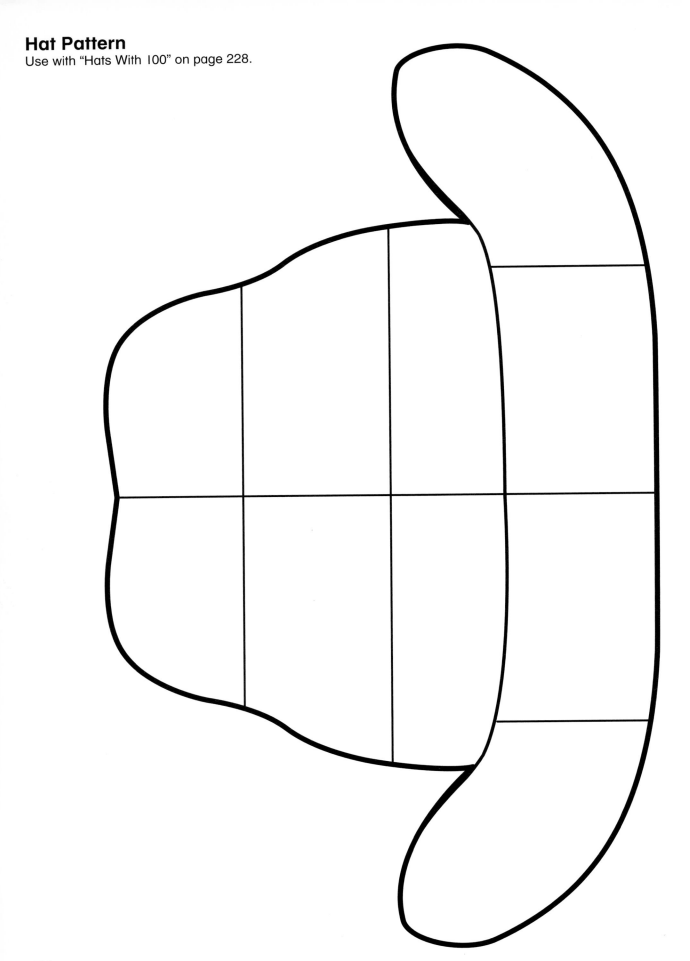

Bouncing Into Number Patterns

Your students are sure to hop, skip, and jump their way through this pouchful of ideas for exploring number patterns!

Tens Are the Tops!
Counting by tens

Here's a display project that provides skip-counting practice by the bushel! Read aloud *Ten Apples Up on Top!* by Theo. LeSieg. As you read the story, pause on selected pages that show stacks of ten apples and lead students in counting the apples by tens. Next, have each youngster create a self-likeness on a four-inch construction paper circle. Ask her to glue the circle at the bottom of a 1" x 12" white paper strip as shown. Then instruct her to adhere colorful dot stickers to the strip to resemble a stack of apples. After she adds any desired crayon details, have her trim the excess paper.

To promote counting by tens to various numbers, arrange students' completed projects in different-size groups on a classroom wall. Help students post number cards to label the projects in each group by tens. The result will be a top-notch counting reference!

Janet S. Witmer, Harrisburg, PA

Hives of Fives
Counting by fives

Use this honey of an idea to help youngsters count by fives. In advance, obtain a supply of Honey Nut Cheerios cereal. For each student, cut a large beehive shape from a 9" x 12" sheet of construction paper. Divide it into five sections as shown. Give each student a hive, 25 pieces of cereal, and glue. (Put aside individual servings of the cereal for later student snacks.) On the left-hand side of each hive section, have the youngster glue five pieces of cereal. Encourage him to practice counting the resulting sets by fives.

After the glue dries, arrange for students to sit with their hives in groups of four. Have the youngsters in each group count their cereal pieces by fives as they point to each corresponding set. To follow up, ask students to number their hives from 5 to 25 as shown. Guide them to identify the resulting number pattern, and no doubt they'll be abuzz about their discovery!

Jennifer Weimann, Dover Children's Center, Dover, NH

A Full Plate

Counting by twos

Make counting by twos as easy as pie! Type the rhyme shown (leaving the lines blank) and then copy it to make a class supply. For each student, stack six six-inch white circles. Staple the stack to an eight-inch construction paper circle, as shown, to make a booklet.

To complete his booklet, a student writes his name and the correct pronoun on the blanks in his rhyme. Then he glues the rhyme to his cover. Next, he numbers the front and back of his pages by twos from 2 to 20. He makes the corresponding number of red ink fingerprints (cherries) on each page. Then he draws stems to pair the cherries as shown. Finally, he writes "Yum!" on the large circle and decorates it to resemble a plate. What a fresh way to sharpen students' skip-counting skills!

Erin Inghram, The Colorado Springs School
Colorado Springs, CO

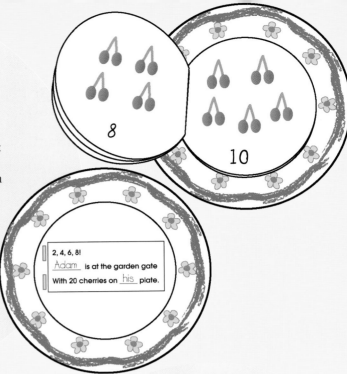

2, 4, 6, 8!
Adam is at the garden gate
With 20 cherries on his plate.

Pair Up!

Identifying odd and even numbers

The difference between odd and even numbers is clear with this class activity! Number ten cards from 1 to 10 and then place them in a paper bag. Draw a two-column chart on the board. Label it as shown. To begin, invite a student to take a card and read the number. Then call that number of students to the front of the class. Explain that if each student has a partner, the number is *even*. If any student does not have a partner, the number is *odd*. Have the students pair up. After youngsters tell whether the modeled number is odd or even, have the cardholder tape the card in the appropriate column of the chart. Continue in this manner with the remaining number cards, arranging for each youngster to help model a number.

For additional reinforcement, circle each number in the odd column with a colorful marker. Then arrange all of the cards in number order and help students identify the pattern.

We're even!

Even	Odd
6	5
8	7

Memorable March

Reciting odd and even numbers

Step up to a review of odd and even numbers! Invite students to march in place and have them echo you after each line of the chant shown. In no time at all, they'll know the number pattern by heart!

Brenda Saunders, Beale Elementary, Gallipolis Ferry, WV

2, 4, 6, 8, 10!
Even numbers are our friends!

1, 3, 5, 7, 9!
Odd numbers are really fine!

Jumping Joeys

Count by fives. Write the missing numbers.

A.

5   10   _____ _____ _____ _____   35

B.

15   20   _____ _____ _____   40   _____

C.

35   _____   45   _____ _____ _____   65

D.

70   75   _____ _____ _____ _____   100

Bonus Box: Use a red crayon to circle the even numbers. Use a blue crayon to circle the odd numbers.

Digging In to Addition and Subtraction

Use this colossal collection of ideas to help students work with sets in a big way, and they'll unearth a solid understanding of addition and subtraction!

ideas contributed by Jamie Dunk Beckman—Joel School Clinton, CT

Prehistoric Performances
Role-playing addition and subtraction

Set the stage for addition and subtraction with prehistoric playacting! To begin, sketch on the board several large, leafy trees and any other desired details to create a simple backdrop. Nearby, place on the floor a large plastic hoop or a large circular piece of blue paper to represent a swamp. Ask students to imagine that it's the time of the dinosaurs. Then present a dinosaur-related scenario that reflects addition or subtraction and have volunteers act it out. For example, ask students to show that three brontosauruses are by the swamp and two horned dinosaurs are by the trees; then the horned dinosaurs stomp over to the swamp. Guide students to identify the corresponding math concept (three dinosaurs and two more dinosaurs make five dinosaurs in all). After exploring several scenarios in this manner, give the dinosaur actors a round of applause!

$5 + 1 = 6$

$4 + 1 = 5$

$2 + 1 = 3$

On the Scene
Modeling addition and subtraction

Count on students to delight in math practice when it involves these prehistoric pals and workmats. Give each student a copy of page 237. Have him sign his name, color the illustrations, and cut along the dotted lines. Give him a personalized resealable snack bag for storing his dinosaurs and a construction paper folder for holding his workmat when not in use. On each of several days, have students use their workmats and dinosaurs to practice addition and subtraction as desired (see the suggestions below).

- **Adding one or two:** Have one student roll a large die and announce the number. After each student puts this many dinosaurs on his workmat, ask him to add one (or two). Write the corresponding addition sentence with students' input.
- **Combining sets:** Pair students. Have one student display two sets of dinosaurs on his workmat. Ask his partner to determine how many there are all together. Then instruct the partners to trade roles.
- **Subtracting:** Announce that a certain number of dinosaurs are in a swamp; invite a volunteer to suggest how many dinosaurs went away and why. Ask students to model and write the corresponding subtraction sentence.

The Same Sum
Identifying combinations for sums

When it comes to investigating sums, this idea has "dino-mite" possibilities! In advance, prepare a supply of green and brown one-inch squares (each student needs four squares of each color). Tell students that no one knows what color dinosaurs were but to imagine that they were green and brown. Then have students pretend that four baby dinosaurs just hatched. Wonder aloud how many dinosaurs of each color there could be.

To find out, have each student use green and brown squares to identify various combinations of four. Ask him to record each combination on provided paper. For a greater challenge, have students identify all possible combinations. After students complete their work, list on chart paper each different answer and then add any other possible combinations.

2 + 2

3 + 1

1 + 3

2 + 5 = 7

Totally "Eggs-traordinary"
Combining sets

Hatch addition practice with this partner activity! To make cards, divide a sheet of paper into a 2 x 4 grid. Label two boxes for each number from 2 to 5, writing each number in a box corner. Give each student a copy and have her illustrate a corresponding set of dinosaur eggs in each box. Then ask her to cut her boxes apart and write her initials on the back of each resulting card.

Next, pair students and give each youngster a sheet of paper. Have each student stack her cards facedown. In each twosome, the partners display their top cards at the same time. After they determine the total number of eggs, they write the corresponding addition sentence and set the two cards aside. They use their remaining cards to create more "egg-cellent" addition sentences!

Lots of Dots!
Writing addition sentences

This center idea makes writing number sentences a "hole" lot easier for students! Copy the dinosaur cards on page 238 to make 12 construction paper cards. Label two cards for each of the numbers 1–6. Laminate the cards, cut them out, and then punch a corresponding number of holes in each one (see the illustration). Place the cards in a decorated envelope at a center stocked with paper, crayons, and pencils.

A student places a chosen card on a sheet of paper, colors in the holes to make dots, and then removes the card. He writes the corresponding number below the dots and then writes a plus sign after it. He uses a second card to make another set of dots as shown and again writes the corresponding number. Then he completes the addition sentence. He continues with different pairs of cards as time allows.

5 + 4 = 9

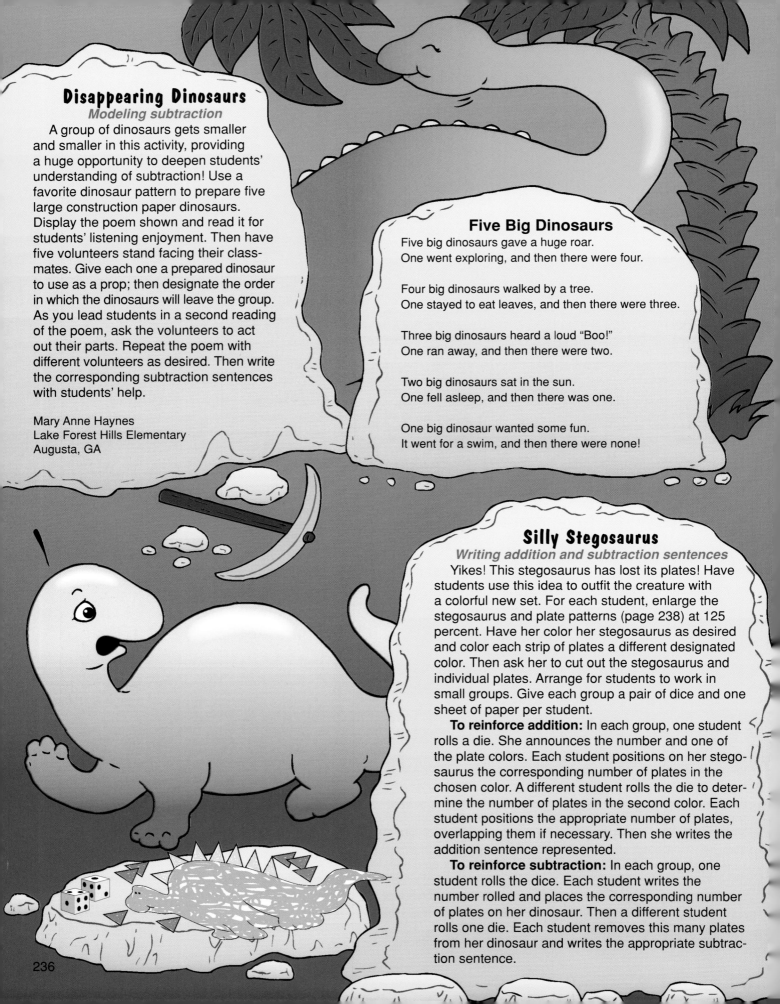

Disappearing Dinosaurs
Modeling subtraction

A group of dinosaurs gets smaller and smaller in this activity, providing a huge opportunity to deepen students' understanding of subtraction! Use a favorite dinosaur pattern to prepare five large construction paper dinosaurs. Display the poem shown and read it for students' listening enjoyment. Then have five volunteers stand facing their classmates. Give each one a prepared dinosaur to use as a prop; then designate the order in which the dinosaurs will leave the group. As you lead students in a second reading of the poem, ask the volunteers to act out their parts. Repeat the poem with different volunteers as desired. Then write the corresponding subtraction sentences with students' help.

Mary Anne Haynes
Lake Forest Hills Elementary
Augusta, GA

Five Big Dinosaurs

Five big dinosaurs gave a huge roar.
One went exploring, and then there were four.

Four big dinosaurs walked by a tree.
One stayed to eat leaves, and then there were three.

Three big dinosaurs heard a loud "Boo!"
One ran away, and then there were two.

Two big dinosaurs sat in the sun.
One fell asleep, and then there was one.

One big dinosaur wanted some fun.
It went for a swim, and then there were none!

Silly Stegosaurus
Writing addition and subtraction sentences

Yikes! This stegosaurus has lost its plates! Have students use this idea to outfit the creature with a colorful new set. For each student, enlarge the stegosaurus and plate patterns (page 238) at 125 percent. Have her color her stegosaurus as desired and color each strip of plates a different designated color. Then ask her to cut out the stegosaurus and individual plates. Arrange for students to work in small groups. Give each group a pair of dice and one sheet of paper per student.

To reinforce addition: In each group, one student rolls a die. She announces the number and one of the plate colors. Each student positions on her stegosaurus the corresponding number of plates in the chosen color. A different student rolls the die to determine the number of plates in the second color. Each student positions the appropriate number of plates, overlapping them if necessary. Then she writes the addition sentence represented.

To reinforce subtraction: In each group, one student rolls the dice. Each student writes the number rolled and places the corresponding number of plates on her dinosaur. Then a different student rolls one die. Each student removes this many plates from her dinosaur and writes the appropriate subtraction sentence.

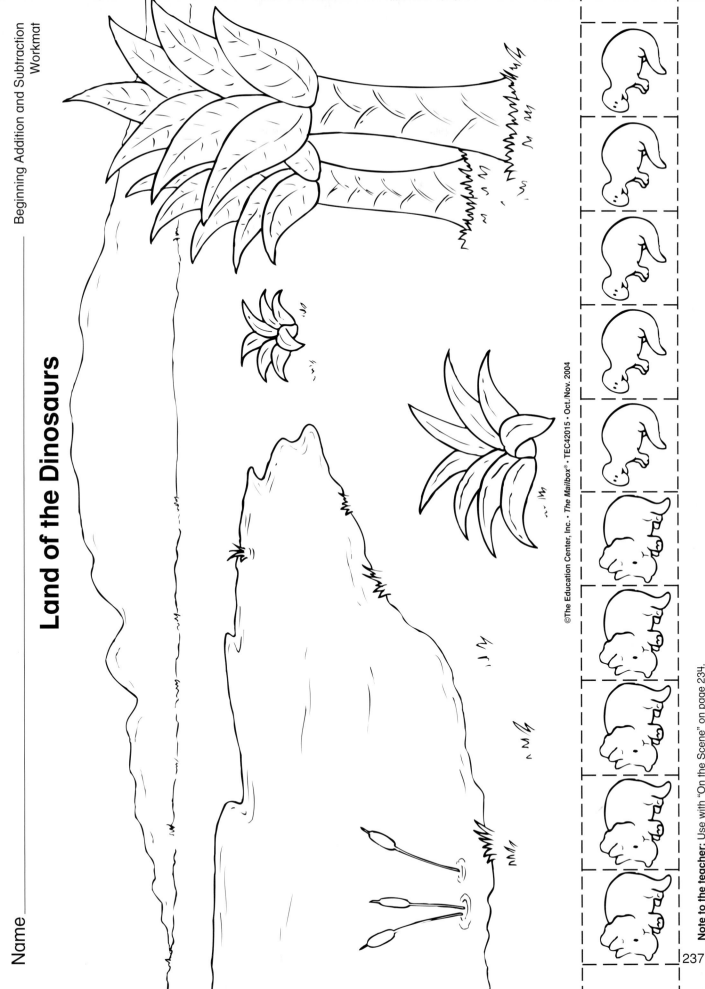

Name

Land of the Dinosaurs

Note to the teacher: Use with "On the Scene" on page 234.

237

Dinosaur Cards
Use with "Lots of Dots!" on page 235.

Stegosaurus and Plate Patterns
Use with "Silly Stegosaurus" on page 236.

"Toad-ally" Terrific Addition

Make a splash with these kid-pleasing addition activities.
They're sure to help your students leap ahead in math!

Lynn C. Mode, Antioch Elementary, Indian Trail, NC

Flies for the Frog
Modeling addition

Count on this workmat idea to create a buzz about addition. Give each student a small resealable plastic bag and a copy of the workmat and fly counters on page 241. Have him color the workmat and counters, cut them out, and then put the counters in the bag.

Next, pair students and have one student in each twosome put his workmat and counters aside. Give each twosome a sheet of paper and a die. To begin, Partner 1 rolls the die and places this many counters to the left of the cattail. Partner 2 rolls and places this many counters to the right of the cattail. Then the partners write the corresponding addition sentence. They model and write several addition sentences in this manner. To follow up, present problems for each youngster to solve with his own workmat and counters.

$3 + 4 = 7$

Ready, Set, Hop!
Adding with or without manipulatives

Two frogs and a pond add up to learning fun at this partner center! On a 12" x 18" sheet of paper, prepare a grid similar to the one shown. Color a reduced copy of the frog patterns on page 242 and then cut them out. On each of 14 blank cards, write a different addition problem; write the sum on the back of the card. Then, to indicate how many grid spaces to move, write "1" or "2" in a corner of each card and circle it. Place the grid, frogs, and cards at a center. Provide manipulatives for students if desired.

Each partner places a frog on Start. One partner stacks the cards faceup. To take a turn, a partner draws a card and announces the sum. Then she flips the card over to check her answer. If it is correct, she moves her frog the number of spaces indicated. If it is incorrect, she places the card at the bottom of the stack, and her turn is over. The partners alternate turns and continue play until both frogs reach the pond!

$9 + 7$

Start

16 ①

239

"Sum" Flies
Recalling addition facts

Try this "ribbit-ing" review of math facts. Program nine blank cards with different addition combinations and a copy of the fly cards on page 242 with the sums. Cut out the fly cards and then glue them onto a paper pond, leaving space between them. Attach a frog cutout (patterns on page 242) to a clean flyswatter.

To begin, display the pond in front of a small group of students and give a volunteer the flyswatter. Next, read aloud an addition card. As the group announces the sum, the volunteer swats the corresponding fly. Then all of the students state the addition fact. Continue in a similar manner, reusing the cards as needed, until each student has swatted a fly!

Problems at the Pond
Solving word problems

Problems at the pond are the topic of these math journals! To prepare a journal, each student folds a 9" x 12" sheet of paper in half lengthwise. With the fold at the top, he adds crayon details to resemble a log. He folds a few sheets of white paper in half lengthwise and then staples them inside the log. He colors a copy of a frog pattern on page 242, cuts it out, and then glues it to his log.

On each of several days, present an addition word problem for students to solve in their journals. After students solve the problem, discuss their strategies and confirm the correct answer.

A frog hops 2 times.
A toad hops 3 times.
How many hops are
there in all?

Orderly Lily Pads
Adding two or three addends

With this easy-to-adapt idea, students learn that numbers can be added in any order. Program several construction paper lily pads with chosen numbers. Add the corresponding number of dots to each lily pad if desired. Lead students in creating and solving several problems as described below, prompting them to notice that changing the order of the numbers does not change the sum.

For addition with two addends, invite two volunteers to tape two lily pads to the board and form a problem as shown. After students solve the problem, change the order of the lily pads to create a new problem.

For addition with three addends, have students create problems with three lily pads at a time and help them explore adding the numbers in different orders.

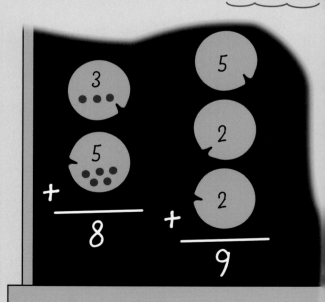

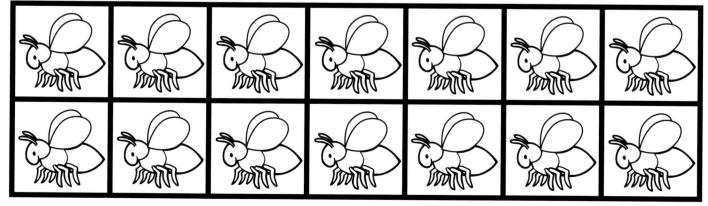

Frog Patterns

Use with "Ready, Set, Hop!" on page 239 and "'Sum' Flies" and "Problems at the Pond" on page 240.

Fly Cards

Use with "'Sum' Flies" on page 240.

Name _____

Leap!

Add.
Color the lily pads by the code.

Color Code
even—yellow
odd—green

A.
$$\begin{array}{r} 9 \\ +5 \\ \hline \end{array}$$

B.
$$\begin{array}{r} 8 \\ +8 \\ \hline \end{array}$$

C.
$$\begin{array}{r} 9 \\ +8 \\ \hline \end{array}$$

D.
$$\begin{array}{r} 5 \\ +9 \\ \hline \end{array}$$

E.
$$\begin{array}{r} 6 \\ +7 \\ \hline \end{array}$$

F.
$$\begin{array}{r} 10 \\ +5 \\ \hline \end{array}$$

G.
$$\begin{array}{r} 9 \\ +9 \\ \hline \end{array}$$

H.
$$\begin{array}{r} 7 \\ +8 \\ \hline \end{array}$$

I.
$$\begin{array}{r} 9 \\ +3 \\ \hline \end{array}$$

J.
$$\begin{array}{r} 7 \\ +7 \\ \hline \end{array}$$

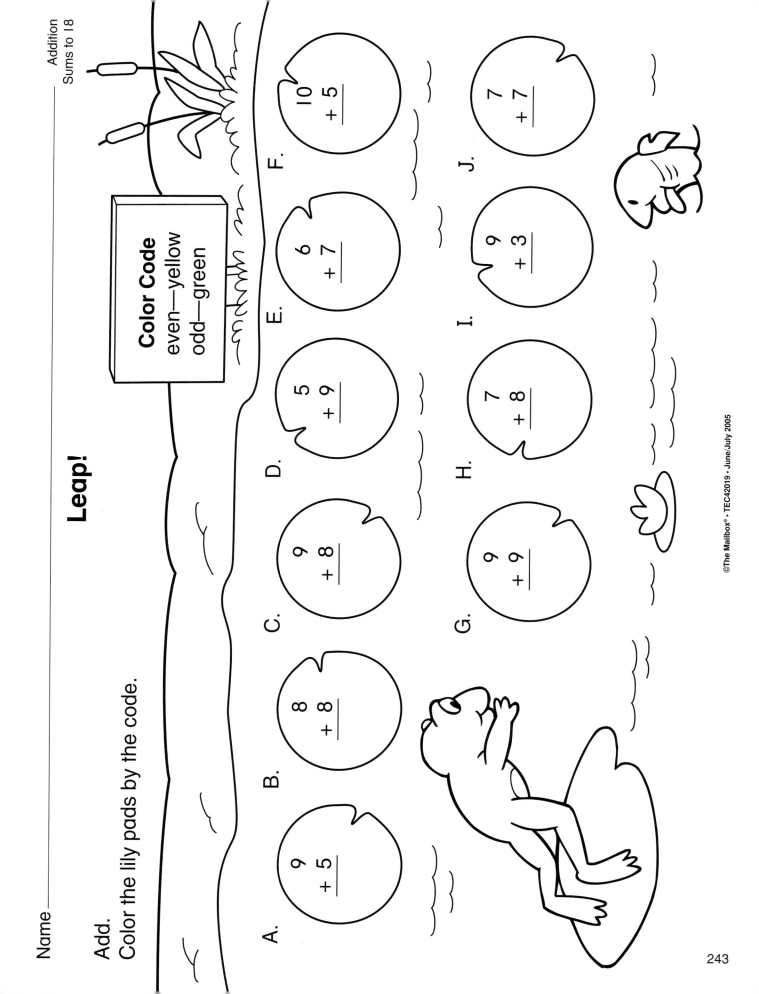

Winning Ideas for Telling Time

Clock Close-Up
Identifying the parts of a clock
Warm up youngsters' time-telling skills with this toe-tapping approach. Familiarize students with the numbers, hour hand, and minute hand on a demonstration clock. Then lead students in singing the song shown, displaying a different time on the clock during each verse and pausing for the group to announce the time. Ticktock!

(sung to the tune of "The Mulberry Bush")
The clock has the numbers one through 12,
One through 12, one through 12.
The clock has the numbers one through 12.
Who can tell what time it is?

The short hand is the hour hand,
The hour hand, the hour hand.
The short hand is the hour hand.
Who can tell what time it is?

The long hand is the minute hand,
The minute hand, the minute hand.
The long hand is the minute hand.
Who can tell what time it is?

Kathy Brand, Cornerstone Christian School, New City, NY

Use these first-rate clock ideas to help your students race ahead to math success!

Schedule Savvy
Exploring the times of everyday events
Invite students to take a timely look at each day's schedule. Display two or more manipulative clocks on a magnetic board. Program blank cards with the digital times of various school activities and then adhere a piece of magnetic tape to the back of each card. Each day, manipulate the clocks to show the times of selected school activities. Write the names of the activities to the left of the clocks and have volunteers post the corresponding cards to the right of the clocks. As students' skills progress, trade tasks—post the appropriate cards and have youngsters manipulate the clocks to match.

Kelley Lagana, Blessed Sacrament School, Burlington, NC

"Write" on Time!
Writing times
The skill sheet on page 246 gives practice writing times in not just one way but two! To introduce the activity, read aloud your favorite version of *The Tortoise and the Hare.* After discussing the story with students, suggest that Hare needs help keeping track of time. Then have each youngster complete a copy of the skill sheet.

race — 9:00
snack — 10:00

Hooray Hare!

It's Time!
Reading an analog clock

Here's a way to check students' time-telling skills lickety-split! Give each youngster a mini chalkboard or whiteboard and writing supplies. Place a transparency of an analog clockface on an overhead projector that is turned off. Draw clock hands to show a chosen time. Then announce, "It's time!" and turn the projector on. At this signal, each student writes the corresponding digital time on his board and holds it up for your approval. Scan the responses and announce the correct answer. Explore several additional times in this manner. For added fun, invite students to take turns at the overhead projector!

Andrea M. Singleton
Waynesville Elementary
Waynesville, OH

Partner Search
Reading analog clocks and digital times

With this class activity, students pair up like clockwork. For every two students, prepare a clockface card that shows a different time. For each clock card, program a blank card with the matching digital time. (If you have an odd number of students, program two cards for one of the clocks.)

To pair students, randomly distribute the cards. Have each youngster search for the classmate with the card that matches her own. When she finds the student, the two youngsters sit together. After all of the students are paired, confirm each twosome's match. Collect the cards and redistribute them for additional practice. Try this pairing strategy whenever you need to partner students for an activity, and youngsters will be buddied up in no time at all!

Sheila Criqui-Kelley, Lebo Elementary, Lebo, KS

Hickory, Dickory, Booklets
Modeling times

This adorable booklet project puts a skill-boosting twist on a traditional rhyme! Make one copy of page 247 and program the blanks on the booklet pages with chosen times. To begin, review the rhyme "Hickory, Dickory, Dock!" with students. Then give each student a copy of the programmed paper, scissors, and a construction paper copy of the clock and clock hands on page 248.

Next, have each youngster sign his booklet cover. Instruct him to color his patterns and cut them out. Ask him to stack the pages in order behind the cover and then help him staple the stack to his clock as shown. Hole-punch the clock hands and then attach them to the clockface with a brad. As the youngster reads his completed booklet, encourage him to move the clock hands to match each page.

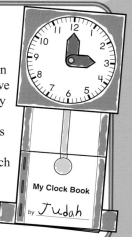

adapted from an idea by Lisa Wilkinson, Loveville School, Loveville, MD

Watch the Time!

Read each clock.

 Write each time two ways.

Go Tortoise!

1.

___ o'clock

____ : ____

2.
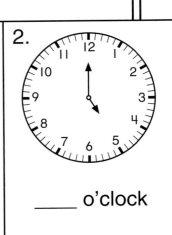

___ o'clock

____ : ____

3.
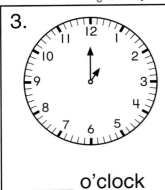

___ o'clock

____ : ____

4.

___ o'clock

____ : ____

5.

___ o'clock

____ : ____

6.
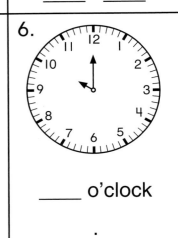

___ o'clock

____ : ____

7.

___ o'clock

____ : ____

8.

___ o'clock

____ : ____

Bonus Box: Hare takes a nap at 9:00. He sleeps for 2 hours. What time does he wake up? ____ : ____

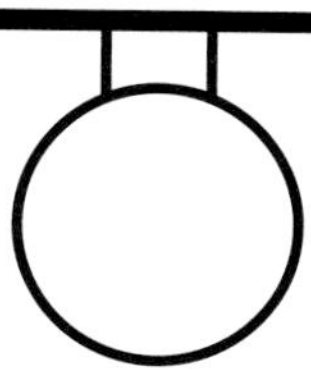

My Clock Book

by _____

Hickory, dickory, dock!
It is time to read
the clock!

1

It is ___ : ___.

2

It is ___ : ___.

3

It is ___ : ___.

4

It is ___ : ___.

5

Clock and Clock Hands
Use with "Hickory, Dickory, Booklets" on page 245.

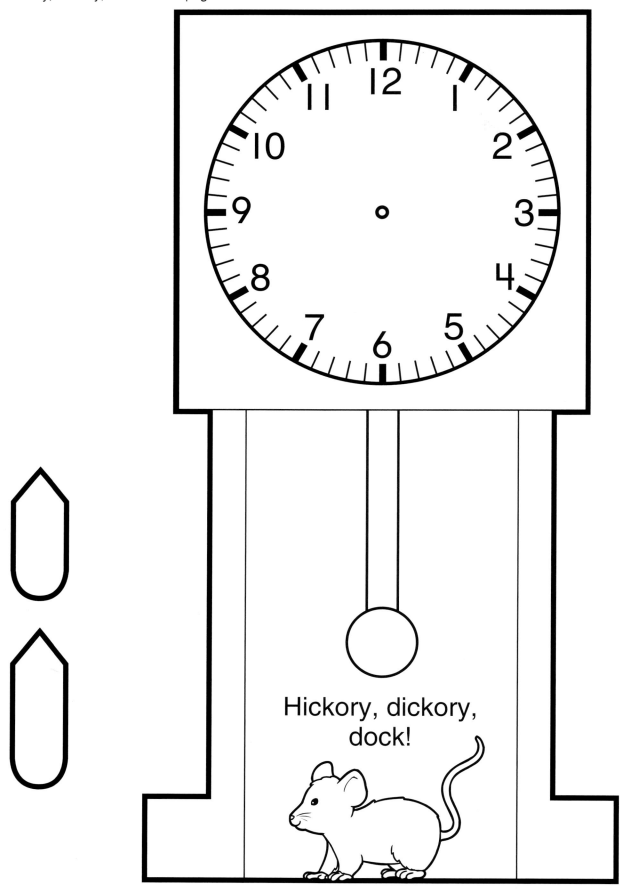

Hickory, dickory, dock!

"¢ent-sational" Math Ideas

Provide valuable learning experiences for your students with this stash of coin activities!

Valuable Sights
Identifying coins and values

Here's a skill-boosting song that's right on the money. Enlarge the coins on page 252. Copy the coins on construction paper to make a class supply and then cut them out. Stand with students in a circle and give each student a construction paper coin. Confirm that each student can identify her coin and its value. Next, lead students in the song below, prompting each youngster who has a penny to respond and hold the coin up during the second and fourth lines. Substitute the appropriate coin names and values as you repeat the song for each remaining type of coin. Then redistribute the coins for another profitable round!

(sung to the tune of "Where Is Thumbkin?")

Teacher and students: Where are the [pennies]? Where are the [pennies]?
Students with featured coin: Here they are. Here they are.
Teacher and students: How much are they worth?
Students with featured coin: They are each [one cent].
Teacher and all students: Let's save them. Let's save them.

Jennifer Schmidt
Jefferson Elementary
Beaver Dam, WI

Money Moves
Identifying coin value

Warm up students' money skills at group time! Make two copies of the coin patterns on page 252 and then cut them out. Secure six of the coins to a small, empty box to make a coin die. (You may use two coins of the same denomination.) Discard the remaining coins.

To begin, sit with students in a circle. Have a volunteer roll the die and then announce the coin and its value. Ask a different student to name an action for students to perform the corresponding number of times. For example, students may clap, nod, or hop five times if a nickel is rolled. After students perform the action, invite a different student to roll the die. Continue as described to keep your students' math skills rolling along!

Helaine Donnelly
Washington School
Plainfield, NJ

Looking for coin-sorting fun? Check out the Presidents' Day skill sheet on page 269.

Race to the Bank!
Identifying coin value

Where might a trail of coins lead? Why, to the bank, of course! Cut out a construction paper copy of the spinner on page 252. Secure a large paper clip to it with a brad as shown. Place the spinner, a copy of the gameboard on page 253, and two different-colored counters at a center. Arrange for two students to visit the center at one time.

Each player places a counter on the space marked "Start." To take a turn, a player spins and moves his counter to the first space with the corresponding coin. If there is no space to which he may advance, his turn is over. Players alternate turns until one player reaches the piggy bank.

Tina Bellotti
G. A. Jackson Elementary School
Jericho, NY

Money Socks
Comparing money amounts

Sock away some money and improve students' math skills in the process! Obtain one small sock for every two students. If desired, roll down the cuff for easier handling. In each sock, place several imitation coins of various denominations. Give each twosome a prepared sock, and give each student a piggy bank recording sheet with six boxes (see the illustration to the right).

In each student pair, each player removes two coins at random and then announces the amount. The player with the greater amount draws an X in a box on his bank. If the amounts are equal, neither player draws an X. The players return their coins to the sock. The game continues until one player has an X in each of his boxes. The first player to fill his bank wins!

adapted from an idea by Pam Dunham
Franklin Elementary School
Creston, IA

Heads or Tails?
Comparing money amounts

No doubt students will flip over this approach to counting coins. Pair students. Give each twosome one penny, nickel, or dime; an appropriately titled recording sheet similar to the one shown; and a box (or box lid). Partner 1 tosses the coin into the box and announces whether it lands on heads or tails. Partner 2 colors one space in the appropriate column. Then the partners switch roles. The partners continue in this manner until one column is completely colored. Next, they count the boxes in each column by ones, fives, or tens according to the coin denomination. They write the amounts on the provided lines and circle the greater amount.

Andrea Esposito
Brooklyn, NY

Coin Canisters
Determining money amounts

Provide a wealth of coin-counting practice with the help of film canisters! To prepare this small-group activity, sequentially number several lidded film canisters. Place in each canister a different assortment of real or imitation coins.

To begin, give each group member a numbered paper and a canister. Then instruct her to gently spill the coins from the canister, determine the money amount, and write it beside the corresponding number on her paper. After you check her work and she returns her coins, present her with a different canister. Continue as time allows or until each student has determined the amount in each canister.

Sheila Criqui-Kelly
Lebo Elementary
Lebo, KS

Daily Change
Modeling money amounts

Help students improve their money skills day by day. Laminate a large poster board piggy bank cutout and then secure 31 loop sides of self-adhesive Velcro fastener to it. Obtain 31 plastic coins and adhere the hook side of a Velcro fastener to each coin. Display the cutout near your calendar. Each day, have a volunteer secure one or more coins to the cutout so that the money amount is equal to the date.

For more advanced students, set out coin stampers and blank paper after your calendar time on selected dates. Arrange for each youngster to use the materials to show a different way to model the amount.

Heather Dusich
Clearview Elementary
Hanover, PA

Perfect Purchases
Modeling money amounts

Your young shoppers are sure to buy in to this small-group math activity! Obtain several magazine or newspaper pictures that relate to a chosen topic, such as pets, toys, or food. Glue each picture to a separate blank card and use an adhesive dot to label it with a grade-appropriate price. Sit with a small group of students and display the cards. Give each youngster an assortment of coins and a form similar to the one shown.

Next, ask each youngster to silently choose one item and count out coins that equal the corresponding price. When she is satisfied with her coin selection, have her identify her purchase and count her coins aloud. After making any needed corrections, ask her to record the information on her sheet (see the illustration). Then invite her to "shop" some more!

Janis M. Smith
W. C. Britt Elementary
Snellville, GA

Katie Zuehlke
Bendix Elementary
Annandale, MN

251

Coin Patterns
Use with "Valuable Sights" and "Money Moves" on page 249.

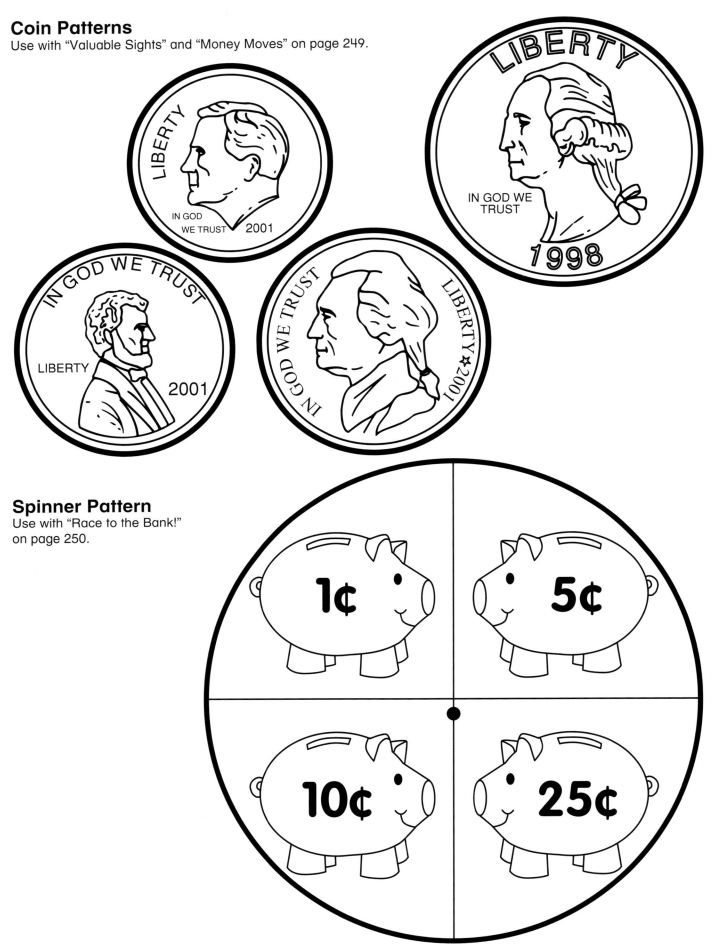

Spinner Pattern
Use with "Race to the Bank!"
on page 250.

Race to the Bank!

Start

©The Mailbox®. TEC42017 • Feb./Mar. 2005

Note to the teacher: Use with "Race to the Bank!" on page 250.

All Aboard With Pattern Blocks!

Anchors aweigh! Use the following pattern block ideas to chart a course for improved math skills!

ideas contributed by Angie Kutzer
Garrett Elementary, Mebane, NC

Which Shape?
Identifying and describing shapes

What better way to launch your pattern block unit than with a review of shapes? Post several different-colored shape cutouts. Then, pantomime looking through a telescope at the display. Suggest that your special telescope helps you examine the shapes. Encourage students to study the shapes in a similar manner.

Next, secretly choose one shape and announce the number of sides it has. Invite students to tell which shape(s) it could be. Announce the number of corners and ask students to confirm or change their guesses. Then name the color of the shape. After students correctly identify the shape, review the three clues that describe it. Repeat the activity with different sets of clues to help students develop shipshape geometry skills!

The hexagon is the biggest!

Chant
Pattern blocks, pattern blocks
Heading your way;
When you take one,
What will you say?

Pass the Pattern Blocks!
Describing, naming, and sorting shapes

Once your youngsters are familiar with the attributes of various shapes, bring pattern blocks on deck! Place in an opaque bag a class supply of pattern blocks plus several extra. Sit with students in a circle on the floor. Remove from the bag one pattern block of each type. Spread out the chosen pattern blocks on the floor and name each shape. Next, lead students in the chant shown as they pass the bag around the circle. At the conclusion of the chant, have the student who is holding the bag remove one pattern block at random. Ask her to show it to the group and make a statement about it. For example, she might name the shape, tell the number of sides, or comment on its size. Ask her to place the pattern block with the matching block in the circle and then pass the bag to the next student. Resume the chant for more sorting fun.

Shapely Combinations

Representing equivalent forms of the same number

This partner center sets students' sights on number combinations. Label a box with a chosen number from 5 to 10 and place a supply of pattern blocks in it. Set the box at a center stocked with crayons and sheets of drawing paper. One partner writes the designated number near the top of the paper and then circles it. Without looking in the box, the partners take turns removing blocks, one at a time, until they have the indicated quantity. Next, they sort the blocks on their paper by shape. They trace around each block, remove it, and then color the tracing to match the block. After all of the tracings are colored, the twosome writes the corresponding addition combination.

Fishy Problems

Solving addition and subtraction problems

Make number sentences the catch of the day with these math journals! Give each student a 6" x 9" construction paper booklet with several white pages. Have him trace several pattern blocks on his front cover to resemble fish. Ask him to add desired crayon details and sign his name. Each day, arrange for students to sit in small groups with their math journals. Provide each group with a supply of pattern blocks and glue sticks. Give each youngster a strip of paper programmed with a fish-related problem similar to the one shown. Have him glue the problem on his first blank journal page. Ask him to solve the problem with pattern blocks and then write the corresponding number sentence. Present a different problem on each of several days to hook students on problem solving!

There are 10 fish. 2 fish swim away.

$$10 - 2 = 8$$

Alec

A Sizable Fleet

Estimating, measuring with nonstandard units

Invite your young shipmates to size up a fleet of ships! Prepare four different-size ship cutouts. Use a colorful marker to draw a thick line along the base of each ship to indicate the length students should measure. Letter the ships from A to D. Set the ships, a supply of square pattern blocks, and copies of the recording sheet (page 257) at a center. A student estimates the length of a ship to the nearest block, writes his estimate, and then determines the actual measurement. He sizes up the remaining ships in the same manner, using the size of each previously measured ship as a benchmark for his estimates.

The Right Place
Describing and identifying locations

Forming pattern block designs is a perfect way to navigate position words! Have each student color a copy of the pattern blocks on page 257 and cut them out. Display an overhead pattern block on an overhead projector. (Or use Sticky-Tac to display a pattern block on a piece of cardboard.) Add three or four different pattern blocks to the display, one at a time, to create a desired arrangement. Each time you add a block, prompt students to describe its relative position with words such as left, right, above, and below. After your pattern block arrangement is complete, ask each youngster to make the same arrangement with her pattern blocks.

For a greater challenge, create a pattern block arrangement without showing it to students. Describe the location of each block, allowing time for students to arrange their blocks accordingly. Then display your pattern blocks and have students check their work.

Fill the Ship!
Visual-spatial reasoning

This hands-on activity delivers a boatload of problem-solving possibilities. Give each child a copy of page 258 and access to a supply of pattern blocks. Then ask him to fill in the ship with chosen blocks. When he is satisfied with his work, have him write how many blocks of each type he used. Instruct him to trace the blocks and then color the tracings or replace the blocks with construction paper pattern blocks that he glues in place. Ask students to display their completed papers on their desks or tables and invite youngsters to view their classmates' work by walking along an established classroom path. Wow! There are a lot of different ways to fill the ship!

How Many Triangles Did We Use?		
less than 2		
2		
more than 2		

Totally Triangles
Graphing

Combine graphing and number comparisons with this follow-up to "Fill the Ship!" on this page. Prepare a graph with three rows and label them as shown. Also prepare a class supply of green construction paper triangles. Ask each youngster to determine how many triangles she used to fill her ship. Then have her use a loop of tape to post a triangle in the appropriate row on the graph. Once each student contributes to the graph, prompt a class discussion about the displayed data.

Name _____

Measurement
Recording sheet

How Long Are the Ships?

Ship A
guess _____ blocks
check _____ blocks

Ship B
guess _____ blocks
check _____ blocks

Ship C
guess _____ blocks
check _____ blocks

Ship D
guess _____ blocks
check _____ blocks

©The Education Center, Inc. • *The Mailbox*® • TEC42016 • Dec./Jan. 2004–5

Pattern Block Patterns
Use with "The Right Place" on page 256.

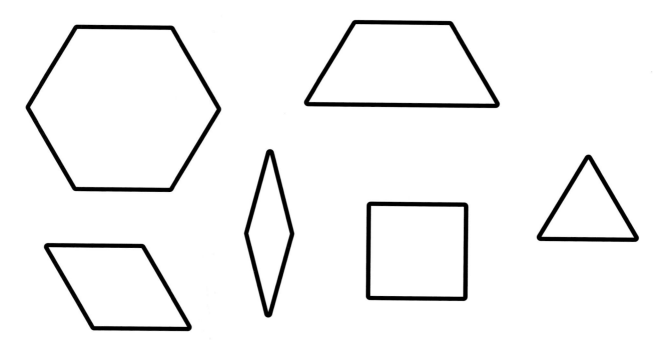

Name _____

Fill the Ship!

Fill the ship with pattern blocks.

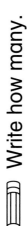 Write how many.

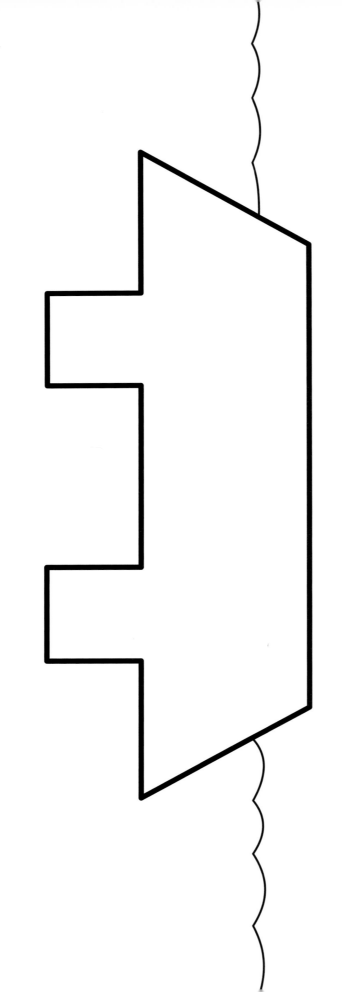

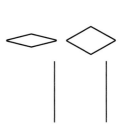

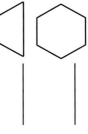

©The Education Center, Inc. • *The Mailbox*® • TEC42016 • Dec./Jan. 2004–5

Note to the teacher: Use with "Fill the Ship!" on page 256.

Science and
Social Studies Units

Home, Sweet Home

Whether you look in trees, underground, or in the ocean, you're sure to find some animals making themselves at home! Help students consider the dwellings of various critters with the following ideas. They're sure to agree that there is no place like home!

ideas contributed by Jill M. Davis
Sand Springs, OK

Tuneful Tribute

Understanding animals' need for shelter

Build on what students know about animal homes with this tuneful introduction! First, write a student-generated list of animals on the board. Then invite students to tell what they know about the homes of the listed animals. Point out that animal dwellings vary in many ways, but all animals need a place to live that provides shelter, protects them, and gives them a place to raise young. Then teach students the song below. If desired, invite youngsters to add motions by pantomiming each type of animal.

(sung to the tune of "Home on the Range")

Oh, animals have homes if they don't tend to roam,
Like an ant tucked away in its nest.
Most monkeys, you see, have their homes up in trees.
But some frogs think a pond is the best!

Homes, animals need homes—
Places where they can live, sleep, or play.
Whether lion or bat, shark, mouse, or cat,
Animals need a safe place to stay.

Above or Below?

Sorting animals by the location of their homes

Animals that live in trees or underground are the focus of this "tree-rific" project. To begin, each youngster folds a 12" x 18" sheet of white construction paper in half (to 9" x 12") and then unfolds it. He positions the paper vertically. After he traces the crease to create a ground line, he colors the bottom half of his paper brown. He draws a large, leafy tree on the upper half of his paper, extending its roots into the lower half. Next, he colors a copy of the animal cards on page 262 and then cuts them out. He places each card either on the treetop or below the ground to show where the corresponding animal is most likely to make its home. When he is satisfied with his work, he glues the cards in place. Ah, home at last!

Animal Pairs and Shelters

alligator (nest of grass and other plants)
rabbit (warren)

honeybee (hive)
sea turtle (nest in the sand)

tree squirrel (nest of leaves and sometimes other plant materials)
beaver (lodge of sticks)

hornet (nest of paper)
bat (cave)

Nests Are Best!
Identifying animal shelters

Birds aren't the only animals that build nests! Introduce students to some other nest builders with this simple activity. To begin, tell students that different types of animals use nests for a place to live or a place to raise their young. Explain that nests can be made with a wide variety of materials.

Next, write "alligator" and "rabbit" on the board and read the words aloud. Tell students that one of the animals is a nest builder and one of them is not. Then announce each animal in turn. If a student thinks the critter is a nest builder, he gives a thumbs-up sign. If he does not think the animal uses a nest for shelter, he gives a thumbs-down sign. After polling students in this manner, reveal the correct answer, sharing the information shown. Then erase the board and present a different listed pair of animals in the same manner. Students will realize that for some animals, nests are best!

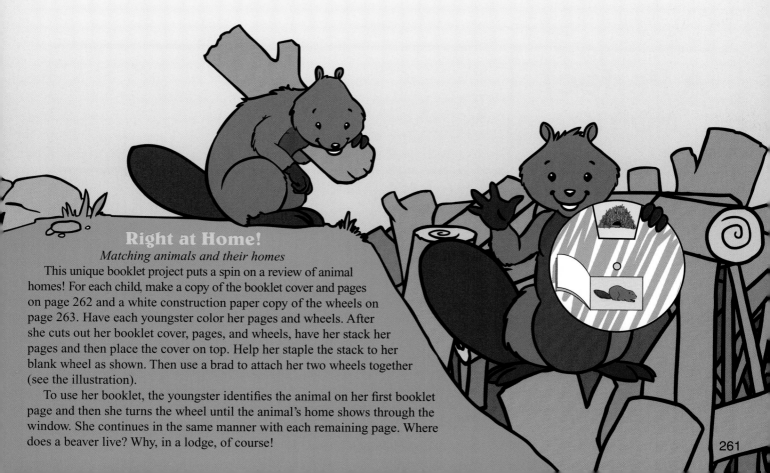

Right at Home!
Matching animals and their homes

This unique booklet project puts a spin on a review of animal homes! For each child, make a copy of the booklet cover and pages on page 262 and a white construction paper copy of the wheels on page 263. Have each youngster color her pages and wheels. After she cuts out her booklet cover, pages, and wheels, have her stack her pages and then place the cover on top. Help her staple the stack to her blank wheel as shown. Then use a brad to attach her two wheels together (see the illustration).

To use her booklet, the youngster identifies the animal on her first booklet page and then she turns the wheel until the animal's home shows through the window. She continues in the same manner with each remaining page. Where does a beaver live? Why, in a lodge, of course!

Animal Cards
Use with "Above or Below?" on page 260.

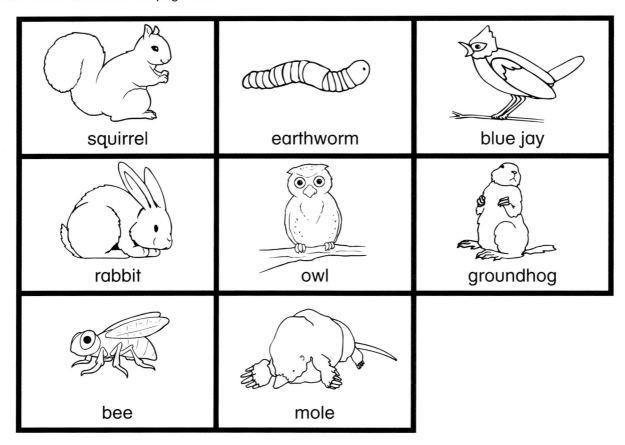

squirrel

earthworm

blue jay

rabbit

owl

groundhog

bee

mole

Booklet Cover and Pages
Use with "Right at Home!" on page 261.

A Perfect
Home

©2005 The Mailbox®

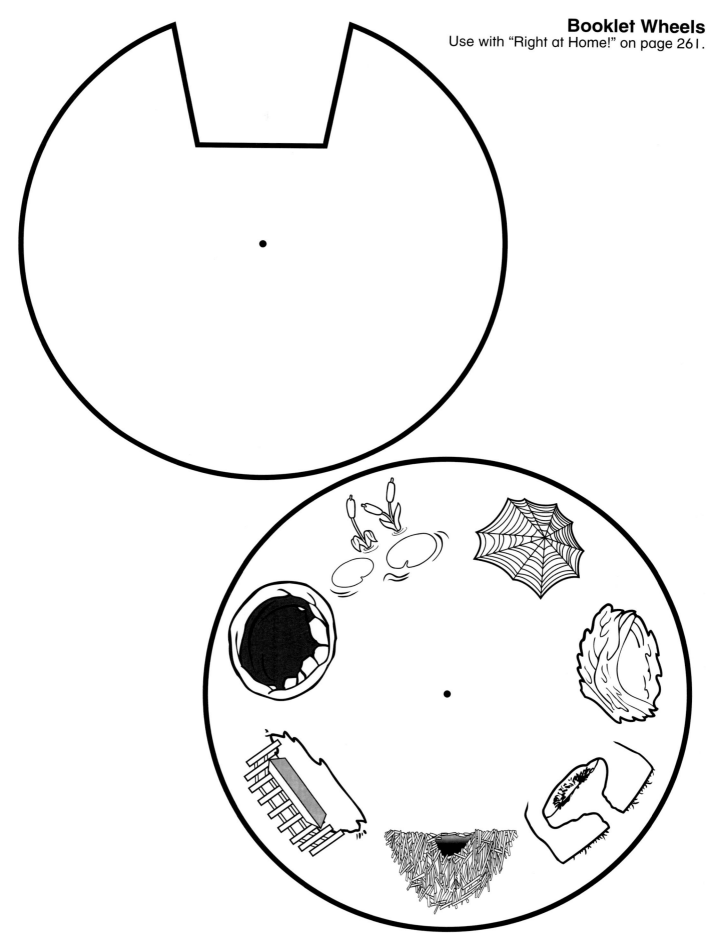

Simply

This fun-filled look at winter, spring, summer, and fall takes students all through the year!

ideas by Ada Goren, Winston-Salem, NC

Signs of the Seasons
Interpreting clues

Seasonal sights are the focus of this riddle activity! Share several magazine pictures that reflect different times of year, or read aloud a chosen book about the seasons, such as *Caps, Hats, Socks, and Mittens: A Book About the Four Seasons* by Louise Borden. Then guide students to name several sights associated with each season. Next, read aloud the first riddle shown and challenge students to guess what season it describes. After youngsters correctly guess winter, present the remaining riddles for them to solve. For a kid-pleasing extension, write a seasonal riddle (rhyming or non-rhyming) as a class, or have pairs of students create riddles for their classmates to solve.

Riddles

This season is easy to know
When you think of lots of snow. *(winter)*

Pretty flowers and buds of green
In this season are often seen. *(spring)*

This season is so sunny
That it can make your ice cream runny! *(summer)*

Leaves turn red and orange and brown
When this season comes around. *(fall)*

Spring
Summer
Fall
Winter

It's That Time of Year!
Categorizing months by seasons

Help students learn about the seasons month by month! Program a separate sentence strip for each season and month. Decorate each season strip with an appropriate symbol, such as a flower for spring and a sun for summer. Label the back of each month strip with the appropriate seasonal symbol.

At group time, post the season strips on the board to establish four column headings. On the ledge of the board, display the month strips in random order. Then tell students that fall begins in September. Have a volunteer find the September strip and post it below the correct heading. In a similar manner, have students categorize the December, June, and March strips. To categorize the remaining strips, hold up each one, in turn. Have a volunteer read the month and name the corresponding season. Invite him to flip the strip to check his response and then add it to the correct column. After all of the strips are displayed, lead students in reading each group of words. Then place all of the strips at a center for self-checking sorting practice.

Seasons!

Tree Details

Winter: Glue on cotton to resemble snow.

Spring: Color leaves. Add blossoms with a cotton swab and pink paint.

Summer: Create a leafy tree top with a cotton swab and paint.

Fall: Color green leaves. Add apples with a cotton swab and paint.

Summer   Summer

Year at a Glance
Representing seasonal changes and sights

This booklet project is a "tree-mendous" way for students to show off their knowledge of the seasons. For best results, plan for youngsters to work on their booklets over a few days. Make four copies of the booklet pages on page 266. Program each copy with a different season by labeling the boxes at the bottom. Copy the pages and booklet cover (page 266) to make a class supply.

To begin, read aloud *The Seasons of Arnold's Apple Tree* by Gail Gibbons. Then give each youngster a set of booklet pages. Have him color his trees and use provided arts-and-crafts materials to embellish them with seasonal details (see the suggestions). Ask him to add seasonal illustrations to the blank pages, providing stickers, clip art, or magazine images for this purpose if desired. Next, have each youngster personalize a booklet cover. Instruct him to cut his pages apart, stack the tree pages in random order, and create a separate stack of his illustrated pages. Staple the two stacks between his cover and a 4½" x 7" piece of construction paper as shown. Once his booklet is complete, the youngster flips the pages to match them by season. How clever!

Sights to See
Describing the seasons

Poetry is always in season with this culminating idea! Display the poem shown, omitting the words in the blanks. With student input, complete the poem with nouns or noun phrases. Then, as a class or in small groups, guide students to use the same format to pen a poem about each of the other seasons.

Next, have your young poets present the poems in a variety of ways. For example, divide students into five groups and have each group read a different line of each poem. Or have students echo you, line by line. If desired, invite each youngster to prepare a seasonal headband to wear during the poetry presentations (see the directions below). What fun!

Headband directions: Color the seasonal symbols on a copy of the booklet cover (page 266). Cut them out and glue them onto a sentence strip. Size the strip to fit and then staple the ends.

Fall is a beautiful season.
Fall is <u>pumpkins</u>
And <u>orange leaves</u>
And <u>busy squirrels</u>.
Fall is a beautiful season.

Booklet Pages
Use with "Year at a Glance" on page 265.

Booklet Cover
Use with "Year at a Glance" and "Sights to See" on page 265.

Name _____

Hooray for Presidents' Day!

The third Monday in February is cause for celebration. After all, it's a day to honor George Washington and Abraham Lincoln. Commemorate the two leaders with these positively presidential ideas!

ideas by Laurie K. Gibbons, Huntsville, AL

Legendary Leaders

What better way to begin a Presidents' Day celebration than with a musical tribute? Lead students in singing the song shown, asking them to think about who the song might describe. Then establish that the two honored men are George Washington and Abraham Lincoln. To follow up, read aloud selections such as *A. Lincoln and Me* by Louise Borden and *George Washington and the General's Dog* by Frank Murphy.

(sung to the tune of "America the Beautiful")

Presidents' Day is here again,
Reminding us of how
Two special men helped us to gain
The freedom we have now.
Those leaders of the years gone by
Were honest, fair, and wise.
They took a stand, fought for our land,
And kept freedom alive!

Presidential Patterning

Help youngsters recognize the images of Washington and Lincoln with this small-group activity. To prepare, hot-glue a quarter and a penny to each of four pieces of tagboard. Securely tape the tagboard to a tabletop at different seating places. Set out unwrapped crayons and strips of copy paper. To begin, invite up to four students to the table. Confirm that each student can identify the coin images. Then have her make crayon rubbings of the coins to create desired patterns.

Larger Than Life

It would certainly take a lot to fill George Washington's shoes! Prepare a 13-inch-long shoe cutout to represent George Washington's size 13 shoes. Place the cutout, crayons, a supply of Unifix cubes, and a supply of 12" x 18" sheets of construction paper at a center. Remind students of Washington's place in history. Then explain that Washington seems larger than life in more ways than one—he wore size 13 shoes!

To use the center, a youngster traces the shoe cutout and one of his own shoes on a sheet of paper. He labels each tracing with the corresponding name. Then he measures each length with Unifix cubes and writes the measurement. What a huge difference!

A Handy Hat

A collection of notable facts is tucked inside this stovepipe hat project! After reading aloud one or more books about Abraham Lincoln, post a student-generated list of facts about the president. Include in the list that Lincoln sometimes kept notes in his stovepipe hat. Share a picture of him wearing his hat if possible.

Next, give each youngster a hat-shaped booklet with black covers and several white pages. Have her write and illustrate a fact about Lincoln on each page, referring to the list as needed. Then ask her to use a white crayon to write a title and her name on her front cover.

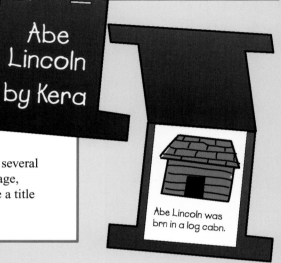

Patriotic Puppets

Review presidential facts with the help of student-made puppets! For each student, cut a slit in the top of a lidded, empty film canister. To make Washington and Lincoln puppets, each child draws facial features on two jumbo craft sticks. She draws buttons on two white strips of paper sized to fit the craft sticks and then glues the strips in place (see the illustration). To complete her Lincoln puppet, she illustrates a beard and glues two black strips of paper (coattails) to the back of the stick. Then she inserts the top of the stick into the slit of a prepared film canister. To complete her Washington puppet, she glues on two blue coattails, fastens together two cotton balls (hair) with a twist tie, and then glues the hair in place.

After students complete their puppets, announce a clue from the lists shown without identifying the corresponding president. Have each student hold up a puppet to show who the clue describes. Confirm the correct response and then continue in a similar manner with the remaining clues. He's pictured on the quarter? That must be Washington!

George Washington	Abraham Lincoln
• was the first president of the United States	• was born in a log cabin
• is called "The Father of His Country"	• wore a stovepipe hat
• is pictured on the quarter	• is pictured on the penny
• was a general	• was a lawyer

Top off your celebration with the snack idea on page 37!

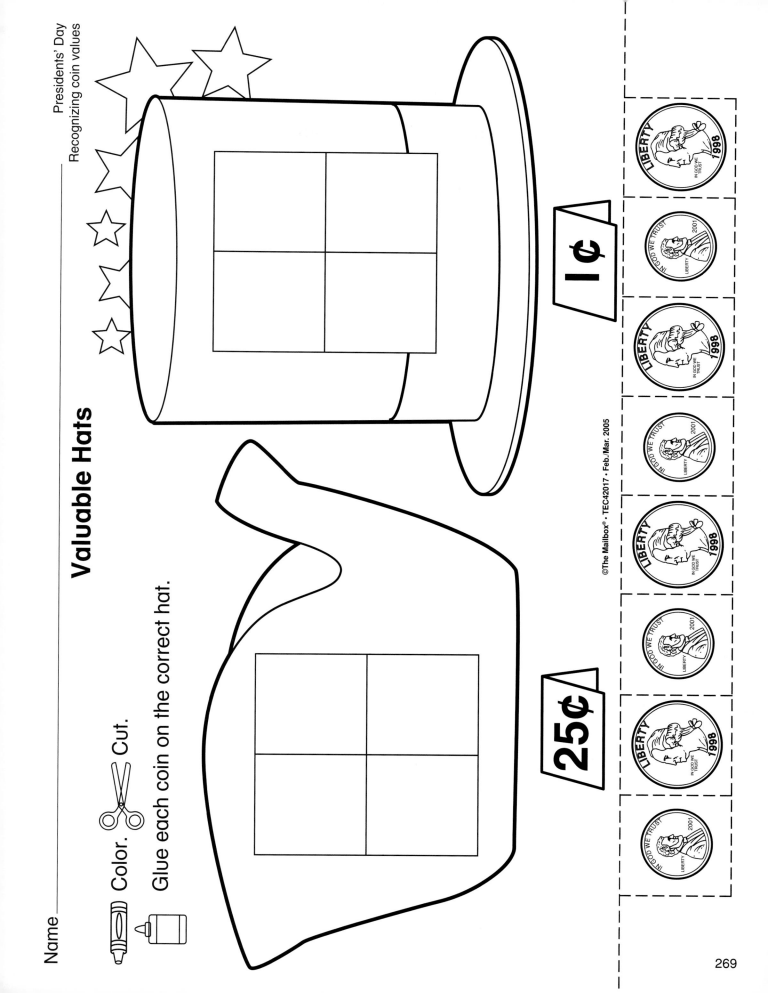

Name

Valuable Hats

Color.

Cut.

Glue each coin on the correct hat.

1¢

25¢

©The Mailbox® · TEC42017 · Feb./Mar. 2005

In the Community

With these easy-to-use ideas, your students will be eager to get right to work exploring wants, needs, goods, and services!

Cash in on this memory game to help youngsters identify three basic needs. To prepare, make two copies of the picture cards on page 272 that depict food, clothing, and shelter. Color the cards if desired. Glue each picture to a separate index card. Program each of six blank index cards with a dollar or cent sign. Tell students that the goal of the game is to purchase three different needs by pairing money cards with picture cards.

To play, two youngsters spread out the cards facedown. To take a turn, a player flips over two cards. If they show a picture and a money sign, he takes the cards. If they do not, he returns the cards to their original positions. The players alternate turns until no cards remain. Then each player tells how many different needs he purchased. Look—there's food, clothing, and shelter!

Valerie Wood Smith, Robeson Elementary Center, Birdsboro, PA

Sort It Out!
Wants and Needs

Two important social studies concepts are the focus of this pocket chart activity. Label one blank card "Wants" and one "Needs." Place the labeled cards in the top row of a pocket chart to create column headings. Color a copy of the picture cards on page 272. Cut out the cards and then glue them onto tagboard rectangles for durability.

To begin, invite students to name things they would like to have. After several students share their wishes, point out that a wish may be for a want or a need. Tell students that a need is something a person must have to survive, while a want is not necessary. Next, hold up each picture card, in turn, pausing for students to identify it as a want or a need. After a card is correctly identified, have a volunteer place it below the corresponding heading. For more picture-perfect reinforcement, provide the activity as a center-time choice.

Randi Austin, Stoutland R-2 School, Stoutland, MO

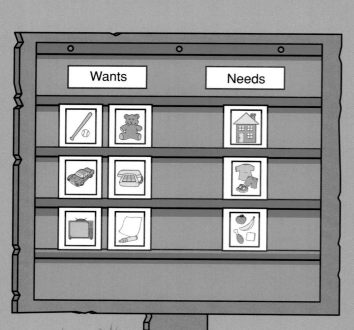

An Ode to Occupations
Goods and Services

Sing a song of services—and goods too! Lead youngsters in the song below, pausing after each verse to help them name workers who perform the corresponding type of job. Students are sure to agree that workers help communities in important ways!

(sung to the tune of "If You're Happy and You Know It")

What workers provide a service? Do you know?
What workers provide a service? Do you know?
A service is a job they do
That helps people like me and you.
What workers provide a service? Do you know?

What workers produce some goods? Do you know?
What workers produce some goods? Do you know?
Cars and shoes and chocolate cake
Are some goods that people make.
What workers produce some goods? Do you know?

adapted from an idea by Sharon L. DuCharme
Dundee Elementary School
Dundee, FL

Dear Mr. Travis,
We've been learning about goods and services. We learned that you produce goods like cookies and cakes. They are really good! Your cakes are pretty. Do you make other things too? What is your favorite thing to make?

Sincerely,
Ms. Austin's class

Community Correspondence
Goods and Services

What's one way to learn about goods and services? Ask the workers who provide them! Prompt youngsters to tell what they know about the job of a chosen worker in your community. Then compose a class letter to the worker that includes questions about the goods or services he or she provides. Now that's a "send-sational" way to connect with the community!

Randi Austin
Stoutland R-2 School
Stoutland, MO

Job Possibilities
Goods and Services

Take students on the job with this look at the future. Instruct each child to fold a sheet of drawing paper in half. Have her keep the fold at the top and ask her to write what kind of a job she would like to have when she grows up. Then instruct her to unfold her paper and write on the inside, as shown, about one or more goods or services she would provide. When her writing is complete, ask her to add illustrations. Display students' papers as desired to provide a glimpse of your youngsters at work.

Kim Minafo, Dillard Drive Elementary School, Raleigh, NC

I want to be a police officer.

I would tell kids how to be safe. That is a service.

271

Picture Cards
Use with "Necessary Things" and "Sort It Out!" on page 270.

TEACHER RESOURCE UNIT

Helping Hands

Ideas for Classroom Volunteers

Use these handy ideas to get into the swim of enlisting volunteers and making the most of their time!

Send Out a Survey!

Learn about potential volunteers as you learn about your students! Prepare a brief survey, similar to the one shown, including questions about students as well as their parents' interest in volunteering. Send a copy of the survey home with each child. When the surveys are returned, you'll not only have useful student information, but you'll also know whom to call on for a helping hand!

Lisa Kuecker
Adams Elementary
Arkansas City, KS

Simple Scheduling

Scheduling volunteers is a breeze with this calendar idea. Each month, indicate on a calendar of the upcoming month any dates that volunteers won't be needed in the classroom. Give each child a copy of the calendar to take home; also provide a note asking each parent to write her name and availability on any dates that she would like to volunteer. As the calendars are returned, use the information to establish a volunteer schedule on a master calendar. Use copies of the confirmation note on page 276 to let parents know when they are scheduled. Now that's a simple way to keep up-to-date with volunteers!

Vicki Meyer
River Ridge
Villa Hills, KY

Dear Parent,
Please complete this survey to help me get to know you and your child. Return it to school at your earliest convenience.
Thank you!
Sincerely,

Parent _____

Child _____
Child's interests:

What can you tell me about your child that may help me teach him/her this year?

If you're interested in being a volunteer, check each box that tells what you would like to do.
☐ help in the classroom on a regular basis
☐ help in the classroom occasionally
☐ chaperone field trips
☐ prepare materials at home

Do you have any hobbies that you would like to share with the class?

Additional comments:

OCTOB

S	M	T	W	T	F	S
					1	2
4	5	6 9:00 Mrs. Abee	7	8		91
10	11	12 9:00 Mrs. Abee	13	14	15	
17	18	19	20			23
26	27	28	29	30		

Volunteer Orientation

Where do classroom helpers sign in? Answer this and other questions for volunteers with an orientation letter. Prepare a letter that includes relevant information such as parking and restroom locations, sign-in procedures, and classroom routines. A few days before a volunteer's first scheduled visit, send her a copy of the letter. It will help put her at ease and ensure that everything goes smoothly!

Holly Romosier
St. Paul School
Westerville, OH

At-Home Helpers

For a parent who can't volunteer in your classroom, this alternative may be just the ticket! Place in a resealable plastic bag the supplies needed to prepare chosen teaching materials. Fill out a copy of the home volunteer form on page 276, noting any unlisted supplies on the provided lines. Then tuck the form in the bag and send the bag home with the appropriate youngster. After the parent completes the task, have him return it in the bag along with the supplies. How handy!

Julie Lewis

Michelle Woyshner
Millbridge Elementary School
Delran, NJ

Drop-Ins Welcome!

Here's a convenient way unscheduled volunteers can lend a hand without interrupting valuable teaching time. In each of several folders, place teaching materials that need to be prepared. For example, you might organize items to be traced, patterns to be cut out, or file-folder games to be assembled. Tape to the inside of each folder a form that has a space for each volunteer to sign her name, directions for the task, and any other relevant information. Place the folders in a box outside your classroom door. Designate a table in the classroom as a worktable and stock it with needed supplies. When a volunteer drops in to help, she can settle right in!

Julie Lewis
J. O. Davis Elementary
Irving, TX

Centers Made Easy

Maximize center time with the help of volunteers. At each center, place the activity instructions and materials. Also provide paper and pencils for volunteers to use in noting relevant observations. Before sending students to the centers, briefly discuss expectations for each activity and assign center responsibilities to the volunteers. Once children are involved in the activities, you'll be free to work with guided-reading groups, help children one-on-one, or circulate among the centers!

Debra Winder
Bosanquet Central
Thedford, Ontario, Canada

Confirmation Note
Use with "Simple Scheduling" on page 274.

Thanks for Offering a Helping Hand!

Dear_____,

    I am so glad that you're interested in being a classroom volunteer! I look forward to seeing you on the following date(s) and time(s):

    If any conflicts arise, please contact me as soon as possible at

            Sincerely,

Home Volunteer Form
Use with "At-Home Helpers" on page 275.

A Job for You!

Teacher: _____   Volunteer: _____

Project: _____   Return date: _____

Supplies: ☐ scissors ☐ pencil

          ☐ crayons ☐ _____

          ☐ markers ☐ _____

          ☐ ruler ☐ _____

Directions: _____

_____

_____

_____

THEMATIC UNITS

A "Bear-y" Special Welcome

Get the school year off to a "paws-itively" pleasing start with these irresistible teddy bear ideas!

ideas contributed by Lynn C. Mode
Benton Heights Elementary, Monroe, NC

🐾 Cute Correspondence 🐾

Home-school communication

Before school begins, let students know that you can "bear-ly" wait for their arrival. Here's how! Obtain a teddy bear to use as a class mascot. Plan to use the note on page 281 to tell youngsters that the fuzzy friend awaits them and to invite them to bring their own teddy bears. (Arrange to have extra stuffed animals on hand for students who do not bring any.) About a week before school starts, make a class supply of the note on colorful paper. Personalize a copy of the note for each student and then place it in a prepared envelope. Decorate the envelope with a bear sticker before mailing it. The timely correspondence is sure to set youngsters' minds at ease and build anticipation for the first day of school!

🐾 This Is the Place! 🐾

Door display

When students spot this jumbo bear, they'll know they've found the place for lots of learning fun! To create the display, cut from brown bulletin board paper a large circular shape (head) to fit above your classroom door. Use chosen arts-and-crafts materials to add two eyes, two ears, a nose, and a mouth. Next, cut a rectangle to fit along each side of the door (body) and round the ends. Cut four paper strips (arms and legs) and trim them as shown. Use a marker to add any desired details to the paws. Mount the pieces around your door to assemble the bear. Then display a welcoming message on the bear's tummy. Now that's a "grrreat" greeting!

Delena Reiter, Forest Park School, Kenosha, WI

Your students are sure to have an eye for patterns! Invite your young cubs to share their patterning know-how with the practice sheet on page 283.

 Hello!

Get-acquainted song

Once your students arrive, no doubt they'll be eager to show off their bear buddies (see "Cute Correspondence" on page 278). Use this idea to welcome both students and bears! Sit with students in a circle, inviting each youngster to hold his stuffed animal or one supplied by you. Introduce yourself and the class teddy bear. Next, lead students in the song shown, inserting the name of a youngster seated beside you. Then have students say hello to her in unison. Encourage her to tell the class something about the stuffed animal she holds. Continue around the circle in the same manner to greet each youngster. Welcome to school, everyone!

Say Hello!
(sung to the tune of "Frère Jacques")

First day of school,
First day of school,
Here we are!
Here we are!
Say hello to [child's name].
[She/he] will learn and play here.
School is fun!
School is fun!

 "Paws" for Names

Name display, phonological awareness activity

When it comes to helping students feel like part of the class, this idea is right on track! For each student, label a three-inch square and a white pawprint pattern (page 281) with his name. Within student reach, post the squares along a wall to resemble a trail. Instruct each youngster to lightly color his pawprint. Then have him find his name and tape his print atop the square. After the trail of prints is complete, invite students to sit near the display. Ask a student to point out his name and read it aloud. Then, as you repeat his name with students, lead them in clapping the number of parts (syllables). Highlight each youngster's name in this way. As students get to know their classmates, they'll increase their phonological awareness!

 Bear Pair

Puppet activity

Count on plenty of smiles and improved rhyming skills with this puppet idea. To prepare, each youngster cuts out a brown construction paper copy of the puppet pattern (page 282) along the outer edges. She folds the pattern in half. Then she trims the paper between the ears with adult assistance as needed. She tapes a craft stick inside and glues the pattern closed.

To begin, ask each student to hold her puppet. Announce the word *bear* and one other word. If the words rhyme, each student shows you the smiling side of her puppet. If they do not rhyme, she displays the frowning side. Scan students' puppets and confirm the correct response. Then continue with a desired number of rhyming and nonrhyming word pairs, including the word *bear* in each pairing.

🐾 Where's the Bear? 🐾

School tour

Help students get their bearings at school with a bear hunt—a teddy bear hunt, that is! When your students are out of the room, hide the class mascot (see "Cute Correspondence" on page 278) in the principal's office. Plan to lead students in search of the bear, stopping at several locations, such as the cafeteria and library, before concluding the search in the office. Tell the staff members at each location about your plan.

To begin, tell students with mock alarm that the bear is missing. After students search the classroom, suggest that they prepare a description of the bear and look for the mascot around the school. Write a description with students' help and then begin the search. Introduce students to the staff members you meet along the way and use the description to inquire about the bear. After tracking down the bear and returning it to the classroom, follow up with "On Location."

🐾 On Location 🐾

Pocket chart activity

Once your class mascot is back where it belongs, explore its imagined escapades with this literacy-boosting idea. Use sentence strips and a pocket chart to display the song shown. Have students recall the first place they searched; write the location on three sentence strip lengths and add them to the pocket chart. Use a pointer to direct students' attention to each word as you lead them in the song. Then invite students to suggest who or what the bear might have seen at the featured location. Use different word strips to explore the other locations in a similar manner. Wow! There's a lot to see (and do) at school.

> **Around the School**
> *(sung to the tune of*
> *"The Bear Went Over the Mountain")*
> The bear went into the [school location];
> The bear went into the [school location].
> The bear went into the [school location]
> To see what he could see.

🐾 Measure Up! 🐾

Partner math

Students buddy up to explore nonstandard measurement with this idea! On one or more classroom walls, post a few columns of pawprints (pattern on page 281) that begin at the floor and are at least as high as your tallest student. Set out a class supply of paper strips and recording sheets similar to the one shown. To begin, pair students and review strategies for working together, such as taking turns and sharing. Assign each twosome to a column of pawprints. Each student determines, with his partner's help, his height in pawprints. He writes his name on a paper strip, tapes it beside the column to indicate his height, and then completes a recording sheet. What a creative way to promote cooperation!

Mauria F. Ganther, Virginia Beach, VA

It's Going to Be a "Bear-y" Fun Year!

Dear _____ ,

   I am so glad that you are in my class! I can't wait to show you our classroom teddy bear. If you have a teddy bear or another stuffed animal, please bring it on the first day of school. I have lots of fun activities planned!

     Sincerely,

_____

Pawprint Pattern
Use with "'Paws' for Names" on page 279 and "Measure Up!" on page 280.

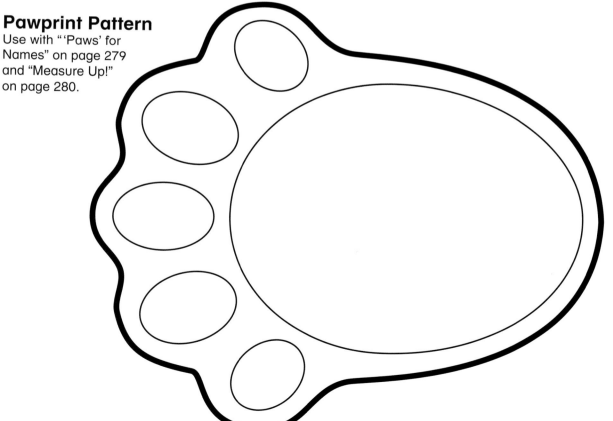

Puppet Pattern

Use with "Bear Pair" on page 279.

Name _____

Bear Buddies

Cut.  Glue to continue the pattern.

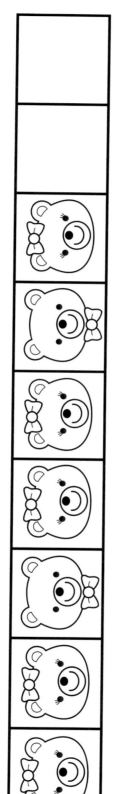

283

It's Time to Talk Turkey!

Your students are sure to have a gobblin' good time with this flock of skill-boosting ideas!

ideas by Laurie K. Gibbons, Huntsville, AL

A Wild Turkey
(sung to the tune of "Turkey in the Straw")

I'm a wild turkey, and I live in the woods.
I know how to fly like a good turkey should.
I eat in the day. I roost late at night.
And my pretty brown feathers are really quite a sight!

(Chorus)
I am a turkey. I like to gobble!
I have a beak and a bright red wattle.
I'll fan my feathers out in quite a proud display.
But I'll surely fly away before the holiday!

A Turkey Tune
Exploring rhythm and rhyme, listening for information
This catchy song not only hatches interest in turkeys, but also highlights several facts about the fine-feathered fowl! Familiarize students with the song shown. Then reinforce the factual details by sharing excerpts from a nonfiction book such as *All About Turkeys* by Jim Arnosky.

Turkeys in the Straw
Developing phonological awareness
Birds of a feather flock together, and the turkeys in this sorting activity are no exception! Use the pattern on page 287 to prepare a class supply of colorful construction paper turkeys. Label each turkey with a different turkey-related word so that there are some one-syllable words and some two-syllable words. (See the suggestions.) Place yellow shredded paper in an unlidded box to resemble straw and then tuck the turkeys among the paper. Post a large two-column chart within student reach. Label the first column "1" and the second column "2."

To begin, invite a student to remove a turkey from the straw and read it aloud. Provide assistance as needed. Lead his classmates in repeating the word as they clap the parts (syllables). Then ask the youngster to tape the turkey in the corresponding column. Have each youngster contribute to the chart in this manner. After the display is complete, encourage students to refer to it whenever they're on the hunt for turkey words!

One Syllable	Two Syllables
beak	barnyard
bird	berries
flock	dinner
hens	feather
nest	flying
nuts	gobble
seeds	stuffing
tail	turkey
toms	wattle
wing	
woods	

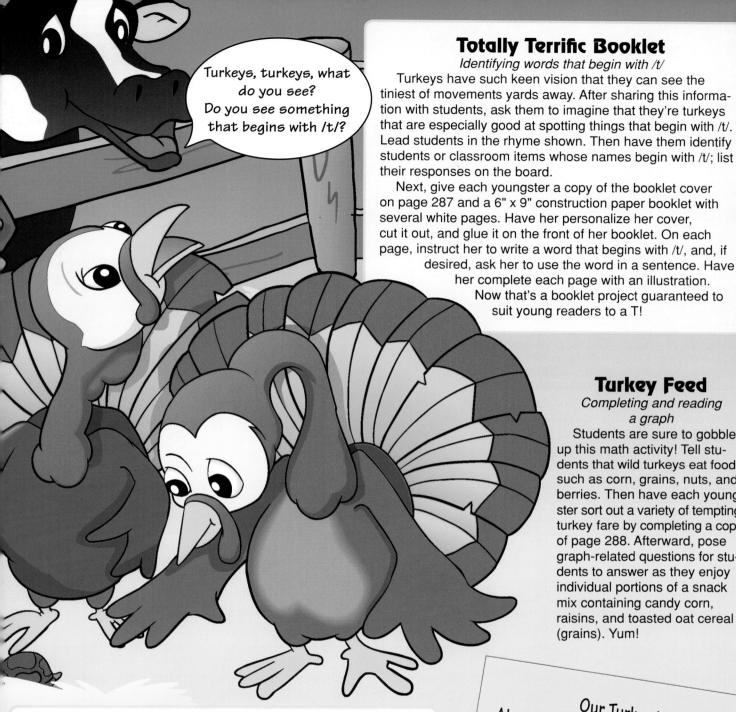

Turkeys, turkeys, what do you see?
Do you see something that begins with /t/?

Totally Terrific Booklet
Identifying words that begin with /t/

Turkeys have such keen vision that they can see the tiniest of movements yards away. After sharing this information with students, ask them to imagine that they're turkeys that are especially good at spotting things that begin with /t/. Lead students in the rhyme shown. Then have them identify students or classroom items whose names begin with /t/; list their responses on the board.

Next, give each youngster a copy of the booklet cover on page 287 and a 6" x 9" construction paper booklet with several white pages. Have her personalize her cover, cut it out, and glue it on the front of her booklet. On each page, instruct her to write a word that begins with /t/, and, if desired, ask her to use the word in a sentence. Have her complete each page with an illustration. Now that's a booklet project guaranteed to suit young readers to a T!

Turkey Feed
Completing and reading a graph

Students are sure to gobble up this math activity! Tell students that wild turkeys eat foods such as corn, grains, nuts, and berries. Then have each youngster sort out a variety of tempting turkey fare by completing a copy of page 288. Afterward, pose graph-related questions for students to answer as they enjoy individual portions of a snack mix containing candy corn, raisins, and toasted oat cereal (grains). Yum!

Where, Oh Where?
Using positional words

This crafty turkey hunt uncovers loads of opportunities to use positional words. To make a turkey, each youngster colors both sides of a wooden ice-cream spoon brown. He uses a marker to add two eyes and then glues on a construction paper beak and wattle. He glues a cupcake liner to the back of the spoon as shown.

After each youngster completes his project, have students hide their turkeys throughout the classroom. Then ask a student to use a sentence with a positional word to announce where his turkey is. As a volunteer tracks down the turkey and returns it to the owner, use the format shown to begin a list of students' hiding spots for later reading practice. Continue the search until each turkey's location is revealed. For an "egg-ceptional" follow-up, have each youngster complete a copy of page 289.

Our Turkey Hunt
Ahmed's turkey is <u>behind</u> the easel.
Olivia's turkey is <u>on</u> the bookcase.
Sasha's turkey is <u>in</u> her desk.

Turkey And...
Using describing words

Cook up a tempting exploration of describing words! Help students brainstorm a list of foods that would be tasty additions to a turkey dinner. Then guide them to name describing words for several of the foods. Next, give each youngster a white construction paper shape that resembles a covered dish, similar to the one shown. Have her illustrate a chosen food and write a descriptive caption (or dictate one for you to write). Staple students' completed work between two covers; then title the resulting class book "Turkey And…" What a tantalizing addition to your classroom library!

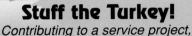

juicy blueberry pie

Stuff the Turkey!
Contributing to a service project, recording data

Promote generosity with this class project, and provide real-life math practice in the process. A few weeks before Thanksgiving, use the directions below to decorate a box so that it resembles a turkey. Display the box in an easily accessible classroom location. Nearby, post a sheet of paper that you have titled "Turkey Tally." Invite students to stuff the turkey with canned goods from home that they would like to donate to a local food bank; send home a note of explanation. Have students draw tally marks on the paper to record their contributions. As the collection grows, so will students' ability to count by fives!

Turkey Box Directions:
1. Cover a large, unlidded box with brown paper.
2. Use craft foam and chosen arts-and-crafts materials to prepare several feathers and a turkey head similar to the one shown.
3. Glue the head to the box. Glue the ends of the feathers inside the box on the opposite side (see the illustration).

Thanks!
Writing a thank-you message

What better way to show thanks than with Thanksgiving thank-you cards? Use four-inch-long pieces of tagboard to prepare several turkey head and feather templates similar to the one shown. For each youngster, fold a 9" x 12" sheet of brown construction paper in half to make a card. With the fold at the top, trim the paper as shown. Slide a half sheet of white paper inside, staple it at the fold, and trim the excess.

To complete his card, each student writes on the white paper a thank-you message for a loved one. He uses a template to prepare a construction paper head and several feathers. He adds facial details to the head and glues it in place. Then he glues his feathers to the back of his card. Finally, he fashions two feet from construction paper and glues them to his card as shown. The gobbler greeting is ready for delivery!

template

286

Turkey Pattern
Use with "Turkeys in the Straw" on page 284.

Booklet Cover
Use with "Totally Terrific Booklet" on page 285.

Turkey, Turkey, What Do You See?

Name _____

Turkey's Dinner

graph.

Turkey Feed

	0	1	2	3	4	5
berries						
corn						
nuts						

287

Write how many. _____

Circle to show which has the most.

Note to the teacher: Use with "Turkey Feed" on page 285.

Where Are the Eggs?

Read.

Draw one egg in each box to match the words.

on the leaf	**off** the leaf
above the leaf	**below** the leaf
leaves	**between** the leaves

Note to the teacher
Then help each yo...

...ter, Inc. • *The Mailbox®* • TEC42015 • Oct./Nov. 2004

...285. Tell students that wild turkeys lay their eggs in nests made of dry leaves.

Welcome to Gingerbread Town!

Use this imaginative unit to explore the whimsical world of a gingerbread town with your students. It's a fresh way to spice up social studies, math, and literacy skills!

ideas by Ada Goren, Winston-Salem, NC

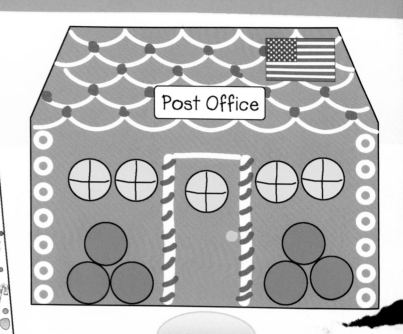

Post Office

Welcome to Gingerbread Town!
Right This Way!

Give students a hint about the upcoming activities with this idea guaranteed to pique their interest. Obtain a large piece of brown poster board or cardboard to use as a sign for your classroom door. Along the edges of the sign, mount white bulletin board trim or wavy-edged paper strips to resemble frosting. Decorate the frosting with candy-themed stickers or colorful adhesive dots. Use die-cut letters to add the message "Welcome to Gingerbread Town" and then post the sign. This way to learning fun!

Town Buildings

homes	police station
fire station	library
school	hospital
grocery store	bakery
post office	bank

Town Plans

Naming workplaces and their co...

When youngsters ask about the sign ...
"Right This Way!" on this page), announ...the together to create a gingerbread town ...uld first step is to consider what types of b... have. Post a sheet of chart paper, titl... students name buildings that are oft... each type of building, prompting stu... that relate to a variety of communit... pose relevant questions to review... places and their corresponding w... challenge, also have each youn... type of workplace on provided p... student reference, and help yo... with the following activity on p...

Creative Construction

Contributing to a model of a town

Now it's time to start building Gingerbread Town! Prepare an assortment of building-shaped templates. Set out brown paper, white crayons, hole reinforcements, adhesive dots, scissors, and other desired arts-and-crafts supplies. Read aloud the list of buildings from "Town Plans" on page 290. Then ask each youngster to tell which type of building he would like to make; encourage students to choose different types so that their gingerbread community has a variety of businesses. Write each student's name beside his choice.

Next, have each youngster use the provided materials to make a gingerbread-style building. Help him use an adhesive label to add a sign to his building. After students complete their construction, use "Everything in Place" below to incorporate the buildings into a town display.

Everything in Place

Using positional words or cardinal directions

Gingerbread Town takes shape with this class activity. In advance, draw a few roads on a large paper-covered bulletin board or wall space within student reach. Use markers or construction paper cutouts to incorporate trees, a lake, or other scenic details. For added fun, give selected locations thematic names such as Candy Cane Forest or Lollipop Lake. To begin, have each youngster sit near the display and hold the building that she prepared earlier (see "Creative Construction" on this page). Then give each student, in turn, a direction with a positional word or a cardinal direction to tell where she should post her building. For example, you might tell her to put her building *next* to the forest or *south* of the hospital. Once all of the buildings are in place, invite students to admire their too-cute town!

This worker sells goods. He uses mixing bowls and spoons.

Who's Who?

Identifying community helpers and their jobs

Your students may have noticed that Gingerbread Town is missing some things—or rather, some people! Use this activity to introduce students to several of the community helpers. In advance, copy the gingerbread workers on pages 294 and 295 onto construction paper. Color them as desired and cut them out. Without revealing the workers to students, describe each one, in turn, by telling about its corresponding job. After students correctly identify a worker, invite a volunteer to add it to the display. **To adapt the activity for more advanced students,** also invite students to present clues about different types of community helpers and challenge their classmates to identify them. Wow! Gingerbread Town sure is busy!

291

A Trip to the TOWN

Writing a story

An imaginary trip is the focus of this sweet writing activity. Ask students to pretend that they just returned from Gingerbread Town. Prompt them to consider what they might have seen and done during their visit. Then have each youngster write and illustrate a brief story about his trip.

Next, staple each youngster's work into a construction paper folder. Instruct him to add a relevant cover illustration; or take a photo of him near the sign you prepared earlier (see "Right This Way!" on page 290) and then have him tape the snapshot on the front cover of his folder. Ask him to title his booklet and sign his name. Then arrange for him to share his tantalizing tale in a small group.

My Trip to Gingerbread Town by A.J.

Welcome to Gingerbread Town!

Five red gumdrops and seven green gumdrops make 12 gumdrops in all.

Grocery Store

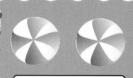

Math Around Town

Solving word problems

Problem-solving skills can be handy all around Gingerbread Town! For each student, prepare a house-shaped math journal that has a construction paper cover and several blank pages. Ask each youngster to decorate her front cover to resemble a gingerbread house. On each of several days, present a word problem that features a different place. For example, you might pose a grocery store problem that requires students to determine the total number of candies purchased. Or you might ask students to determine how many cookies are left at the bakery after several are sold. Have each youngster solve the problem in her journal. After each student has an answer, confirm the correct solution. What a simple way to put math skills on the map!

Good Enough to Eat!

Displaying and interpreting data

Surely all this talk about gingerbread has your youngsters thinking about snacktime! Serve up a delectable treat along with a helping of data analysis. Prepare two charts—one for predictions and one for results—as shown. Use packaged gingerbread mix to make the snack with students or bring in prepared gingerbread. Plan to have whipped topping available.

To begin, post the first chart. Then have each youngster place a personalized sticky note on it to show his taste-test prediction. Next, invite each student to sample the gingerbread. Display the second chart and ask each student to record his response with a personalized sticky note. After the charts are complete, guide students to compare the two sets of data.

Will You Like It?

Yes   No

Did You Like It?

Yes   No

Sweet centers

Expand your gingerbread theme with these tempting ideas!

A Full Cookie Sheet

Estimating

How many cookies will a jumbo cookie sheet hold? That's what students ponder at this mouthwatering estimation station. Arrange large pieces of aluminum foil on a wall or bulletin board to resemble a jumbo cookie sheet. Prepare a supply of identical gingerbread men. Post one gingerbread man beside the cookie sheet and put aside the remaining gingerbread men. Set out paper for student estimates and a plastic mixing bowl. When a student visits the center, she studies the display and estimates how many cookies will fit on the cookie sheet without overlapping. She writes her estimate and then deposits it in the bowl.

After each youngster has made an estimate, fill the cookie sheet by taping on a number of the gingerbread men that you set aside. Lead students in counting the cookies; then help them categorize their estimates on a chart similar to the one shown.

Too Few	Just Right	Too Many
10	16	50
12	16	22
12		

Gingerbread Play Dough Recipe

1 c. flour
½ c. salt
1½ tsp. each of ground cloves, allspice, ginger, and cinnamon
1 tbsp. vegetable oil
½ c. water

Mix the ingredients in a bowl. Knead until smooth. Store in an airtight container; refrigerate until ready to use.

50¢

Busy Bakers

Participating in dramatic play

Tantalize students' senses and spark their imaginations with a Gingerbread Town bakery! To prepare gingerbread-scented dough, knead a small amount of gingerbread mix into some play dough or use the recipe shown. (Caution students not to eat the dough.) Provide rolling pins, cookie cutters, cookie sheets, and spatulas. Also set out materials for making signs. Then let the faux baking begin!

Batches of Words

Sorting by word families

This activity is a reading treat! Choose two or three word families to reinforce. For each word family, label several gingerbread man cutouts with different words. Place the cutouts in a cookie tin. Label a separate paper plate or plastic seasonal plate for each word family. Set the plates and tin at a center stocked with paper. A student sorts the cookies on the appropriate plates and then writes each group of words on her paper.

Gingerbread Workers
Use with "Who's Who?" on page 291.

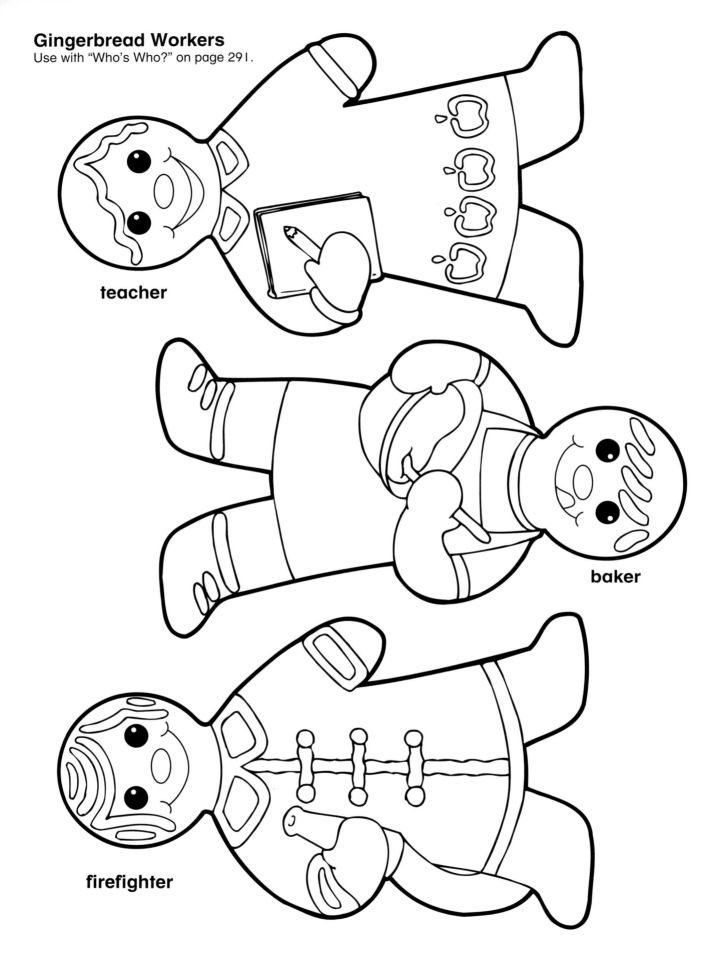

teacher

baker

firefighter

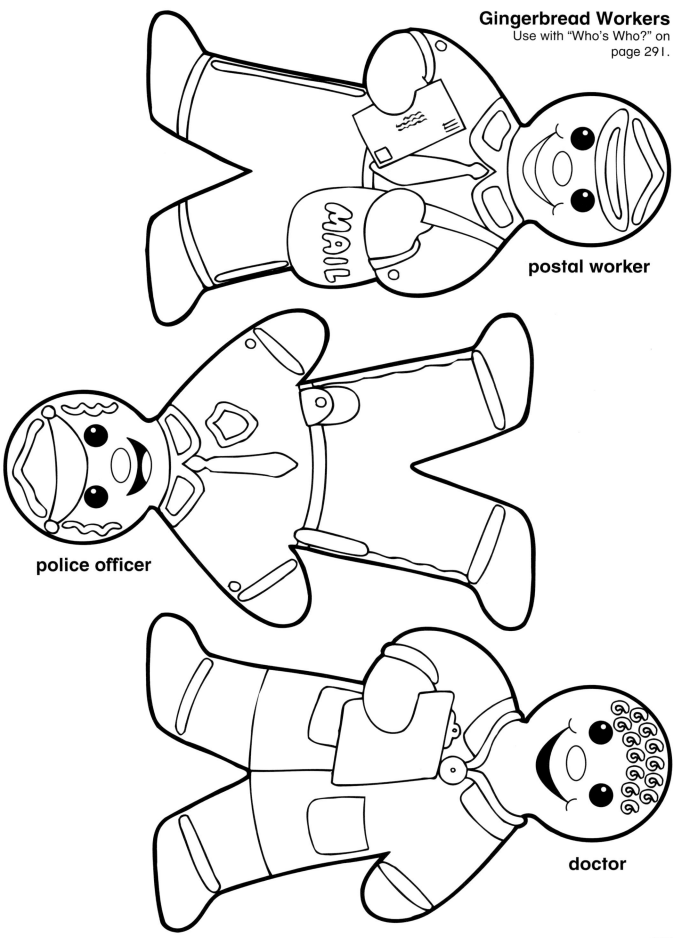

postal worker

police officer

doctor

Crazy for Kites

There's something special about high-flying toys with tails! So why not use the topic of kites to make skills practice fun? Try the kite ideas that follow, and watch your students' learning soar!

ideas by Ada Goren, Winston-Salem, NC

All Kinds of Kites!
Writing descriptions, making comparisons

Breeze into the topic of kites with this descriptive-writing activity! Make a class supply of the kite cards on page 299 and then cut the cards apart. Give each child a card and identify the type of kite that is pictured on it. Encourage students to tell what they notice about their kites, including the shapes and whether they have bows. Next, ask each youngster to color her kite as desired and then describe it on provided paper. Help her mount her writing and kite on construction paper. Then collect students' completed work. To follow up, display two work samples at a time and have students tell how the kites are alike or different.

For an easier activity, color an enlarged copy of each kite card and cut it out. On each of several days, display a different pair of cards for students to compare.

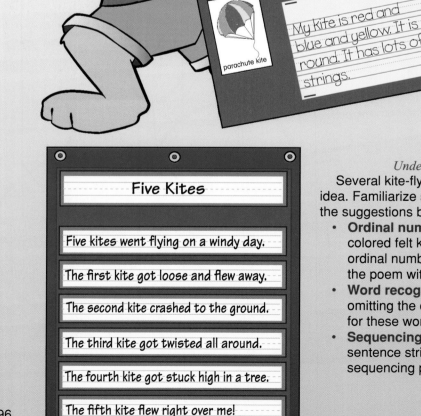

parachute kite

My kite is red and blue and yellow. It is round. It has lots of strings.

Orderly Flights?
Understanding and reading ordinal numbers

Several kite-flying attempts are the topic of this easy-to-adapt idea. Familiarize students with the poem shown. Then try one of the suggestions below.

- **Ordinal numbers:** On a flannelboard, arrange five different-colored felt kites in a row. Ask students several relevant ordinal number questions. Then have volunteers dramatize the poem with the kites.
- **Word recognition:** Display the poem in a pocket chart, omitting the ordinal number words. Prepare separate cards for these words and ask students to set them in place.
- **Sequencing:** Write each line of the poem on a separate sentence strip and then place the strips at a center for sequencing practice.

Five Kites

Five kites went flying on a windy day.

The first kite got loose and flew away.

The second kite crashed to the ground.

The third kite got twisted all around.

The fourth kite got stuck high in a tree.

The fifth kite flew right over me!

Jumbled Bows
Reviewing phonics

Reinforce letters or rimes with an intriguing kite mix-up! Program each of several construction paper kite shapes with a different letter or rime. Tape a length of string to each kite and prepare one bow per kite (pattern on page 300). To reinforce letter-sound relationships, glue appropriate clip art to each bow. To reinforce rimes, label the bows with words that include the selected rimes. Next, adhere a piece of magnetic tape to the back of each bow. Display the kites on a magnetic board and place each bow on the string of a kite that does not have the matching letter or rime. Then have students unscramble the bows.

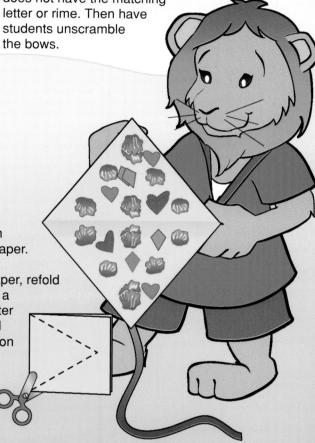

Two Halves
Understanding symmetry

What better tool for introducing symmetry to students than kites? Have each child fold a sheet of construction paper in half. Instruct him to cut a large triangle from his paper, as shown, and then unfold his paper. Prompt him to notice that the resulting kite shape is symmetrical.

Next, ask him to place a few drops of paint on the top half of his paper, refold his paper, and then gently press it. Have him unfold his paper to reveal a symmetrical paint design. For additional decoration, invite the youngster to cut small shapes from folded scraps of paper to create symmetrical figures. After he glues the shapes on his kite, have him tape on a ribbon tail. Up, up, and away!

How Puzzling!
Sorting word families

Students piece together word families at this center. Prepare three identical diamond kite shapes. Trace each kite on a separate sheet of tagboard to make workmats. Divide the tracing into four sections as shown. Next, divide one kite into four sections and write a different word from the same word family on each section. Program the remaining kites with different word families. Cut apart all of the kite sections and scramble them. Place the kite sections and workmats at a center. A student sorts the sections by word families and then reassembles the kites on the workmats.

It's a String Thing!

Estimating and measuring length

Whether your students use standard or nonstandard units of measure, they'll be eager to size up kites with this idea. Letter four construction paper kite shapes from *A* to *D* and tape a string to each one. Trim the strings so that they are different whole-inch lengths, and then place the kites on a table with copies of the recording sheet on page 300. Also provide a ruler or nonstandard units of measure such as cubes or counters. Show students how to straighten the strings for accurate measuring.

To complete the activity, a child writes his estimate for the length of the first string on his recording sheet. He determines the length to the closest unit of measure and records it. Then he sizes up the remaining strings in the same manner.

Contraction Kites

Reading and writing contractions

Give students' word skills a lift! Display on a wall a construction paper kite that you have programmed with a chosen contraction. Post a cloud shape within student reach. Have students name the contraction and the two corresponding words. Then write the two words on separate bows (pattern on page 300 and tape them to the tail. Next, ask students to use the contraction in a sentence. After you write the sentence on the cloud, have a volunteer underline the contraction. As students learn more contractions, prepare additional kites and clouds. What a high-flying word reference!

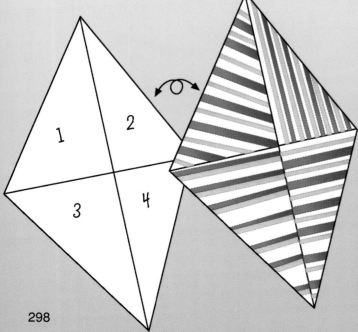

Same but Different

Following directions

This cooperative group activity has interesting results! For each student, divide an 8" x 11" white diamond kite shape into four numbered sections as shown. Arrange for students to work in groups of four. Explain that each group will decorate a kite for each group member. In each group, one student cuts apart her kite sections. She keeps one section and gives one section to each group member. Then she announces a design for her kite, such as orange and blue stripes. Each student decorates the blank side of her section accordingly.

Next, help the youngsters turn the sections facedown, reassemble the kite, and then tape the pieces together. Prompt students to compare and contrast the decorated sections. Then have them prepare a kite for each remaining group member.

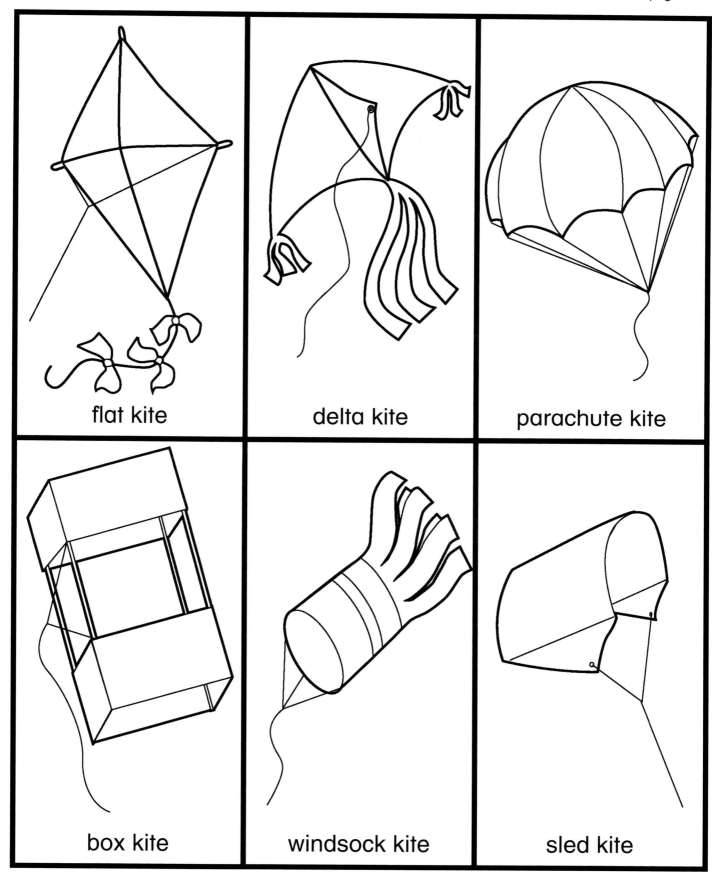

flat kite

delta kite

parachute kite

box kite

windsock kite

sled kite

Kite Bow Pattern
Use with "Jumbled Bows" on page 297 and "Contraction Kites" on page 298.

Name _____

Kites
Recording sheet

How Long Are the Strings?

Kites	I think…	I measured…
A		
B		
C		
D		

Note to the teacher: Use with "It's a String Thing!" on page 298.

In the Clouds

Read the word bank.
Write each word below -ill or -ip.

Word Bank

bill	dip	hip	fill
lip	hill	pill	sip
	will	rip	

-ill	-ip
1. _____	1. _____
2. _____	2. _____
3. _____	3. _____
4. _____	4. _____
5. _____	5. _____

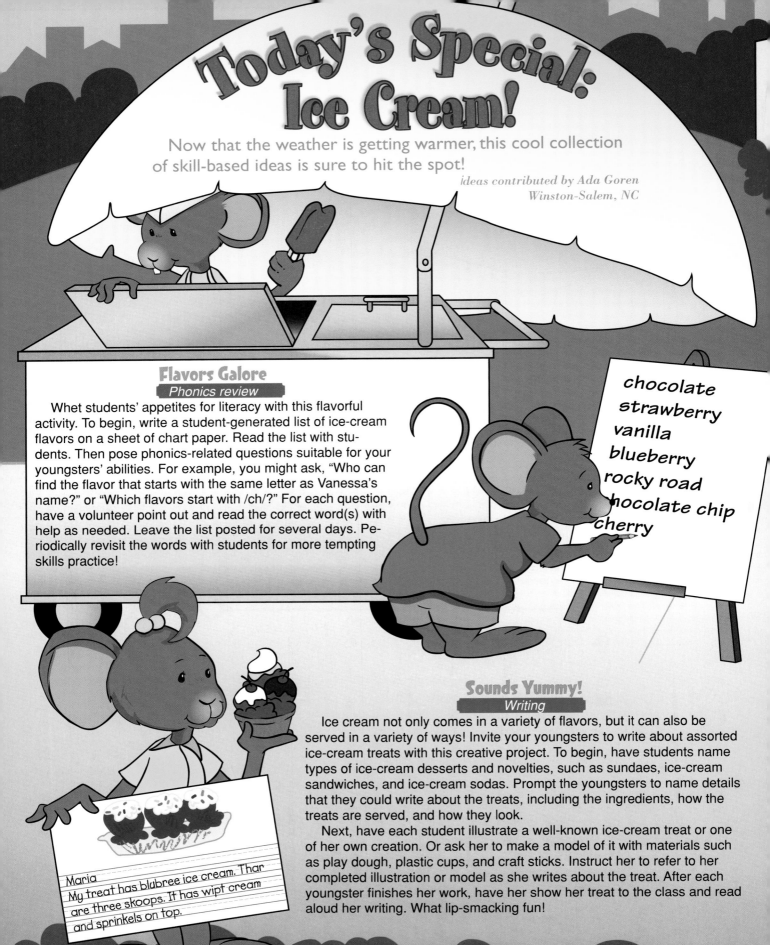

Today's Special: Ice Cream!

Now that the weather is getting warmer, this cool collection of skill-based ideas is sure to hit the spot!

ideas contributed by Ada Goren
Winston-Salem, NC

Flavors Galore
Phonics review

Whet students' appetites for literacy with this flavorful activity. To begin, write a student-generated list of ice-cream flavors on a sheet of chart paper. Read the list with students. Then pose phonics-related questions suitable for your youngsters' abilities. For example, you might ask, "Who can find the flavor that starts with the same letter as Vanessa's name?" or "Which flavors start with /ch/?" For each question, have a volunteer point out and read the correct word(s) with help as needed. Leave the list posted for several days. Periodically revisit the words with students for more tempting skills practice!

chocolate
strawberry
vanilla
blueberry
rocky road
chocolate chip
cherry

Sounds Yummy!
Writing

Ice cream not only comes in a variety of flavors, but it can also be served in a variety of ways! Invite your youngsters to write about assorted ice-cream treats with this creative project. To begin, have students name types of ice-cream desserts and novelties, such as sundaes, ice-cream sandwiches, and ice-cream sodas. Prompt the youngsters to name details that they could write about the treats, including the ingredients, how the treats are served, and how they look.

Next, have each student illustrate a well-known ice-cream treat or one of her own creation. Or ask her to make a model of it with materials such as play dough, plastic cups, and craft sticks. Instruct her to refer to her completed illustration or model as she writes about the treat. After each youngster finishes her work, have her show her treat to the class and read aloud her writing. What lip-smacking fun!

Maria
My treat has blubree ice cream. Thar are three skoops. It has wipt cream and sprinkels on top.

302

vanilla
10

chocolate
5

strawberry
3

butter pecan
0

Scoop Survey
Data collection

The most popular flavor rises to the top with this "scooper" class activity! From construction paper, cut four large ice-cream scoops and one ice-cream cone. Label each scoop with a different flavor and then display each scoop on a different classroom wall. Next, have each student stand near the flavor that she likes the most. After you label each scoop with the corresponding number of students, post the ice-cream cone on a wall. With students' help, arrange the scoops on the cone in number order so that the greatest number is at the top (place any scoops with identical numbers one after another). Then guide students to read and interpret the mouthwatering data!

Cool Measures
Capacity

Math is useful for all sorts of tasks, including sizing up portions of ice cream! Set out several different-size plastic bowls and ice-cream containers. Label them with alphabet letters for easy identification. Also provide an ice-cream scoop, some measuring cups, and a large container of rice (or something else suitable for measuring).

Arrange for small groups of students to explore the materials. Which container holds the most? The least? How many scoops fit in each container? How many cups? Encourage youngsters to illustrate and label their observations on provided paper. For more advanced students, have youngsters estimate and then measure the number of scoops (cups) each container can hold.

Sundae Menu
Problem solving

Here's a deliciously fun way to use the make-a-list strategy. Make two white construction paper copies of the patterns on page 305. Color each ice-cream scoop and topping to resemble a different flavor. Color one dish as desired and plan to discard the second dish. Cut out the patterns. Then prepare them for flannelboard use or adhere a small piece of magnetic tape to the back of each pattern.

To begin, randomly display the patterns and identify each flavor and topping choice. Wonder aloud how many different sundaes can be made if each sundae has one scoop of ice cream and one topping. Then help students determine the answer by creating sundaes with the patterns; briefly list the ingredients for each sundae. Wow! There are four different sundaes on the menu!

Beth Marquardt, St. Paul's School of Early Learning, Muskego, WI

vanilla, hot fudge
vanilla, strawberries
mint, hot fudge
mint, strawberries

Chilly Changes
Solids and liquids

There's no tastier way to explore changes in matter than by making frozen treats! Explain to students that ice cream begins as a *liquid*. Point out that liquids have no shape of their own. Ask students to tell how ice cream served on an ice-cream cone is different. Guide them to realize that it is a *solid,* but that if air warms it, it will become a liquid again. Then use the recipe shown to help students investigate some chilly changes.

Creamy Pops
(makes 8)

Ingredients:
14 oz. can sweetened condensed milk
1 c. milk
¾ c. orange juice
2 drops yellow food coloring
1 drop red food coloring

Directions: Mix the ingredients in a large bowl. Evenly divide the mixture by partially filling eight five-ounce paper cups. Cover each cup with foil. Then slit the top of each foil-covered cup with a knife. Poke a wooden stick through the slit and into the mixture to serve as a handle. Freeze the pops for about four hours or until firm.

From the Farm to the Store

A farmer milks the cows. 1

MILK

A truck takes the milk to a factory. 2

The milk and some sugar go in a vat. 3

Machines turn it into ice cream. Then fruit or nuts may get mixed in. 4

Some ice cream goes in buckets. It gets frozen. 5

PAT'S SHOP

A truck takes the ice cream to a store. 6

From the Farm to the Store
Informational text

This "dairy" cute booklet begins at the farm and ends at the store! Read aloud a factual book about making ice cream, such as *From Cow to Ice Cream* by Bertram T. Knight. Then give each student two white construction paper copies of the booklet cover on page 306 and one copy of each booklet page on pages 306 and 307. After you read the booklet pages with students, have each youngster cut out his covers and pages. Guide students to correctly sequence and number their pages. Then invite them to color their pages.

Next, ask each student to title one booklet cover and illustrate it to resemble a barn. Instruct him to illustrate the second cover to resemble a store. To assemble his booklet, have him stack his pages in order. Then ask him to sandwich the pages between his covers (with both cover illustrations facing out). Help him staple the stack to make a booklet as shown. So that's how we get ice cream!

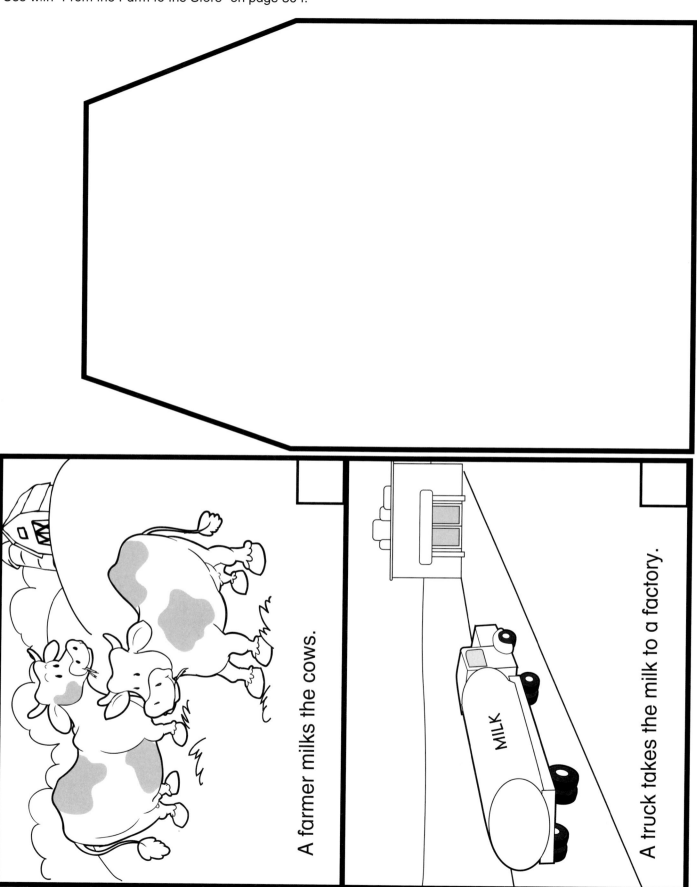

A farmer milks the cows.

A truck takes the milk to a factory.

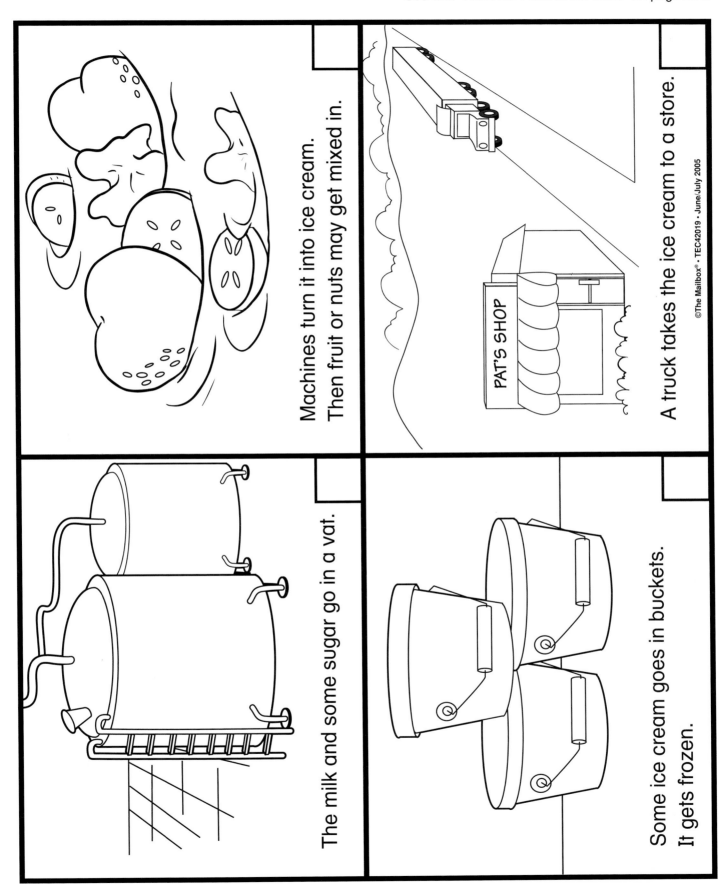

Machines turn it into ice cream.
Then fruit or nuts may get mixed in.

A truck takes the ice cream to a store.

PAT'S SHOP

©The Mailbox® • TEC42019 • June/July 2005

The milk and some sugar go in a vat.

Some ice cream goes in buckets.
It gets frozen.

IN THE GARDEN

Cultivate a variety of skills with this patch of fresh ideas and reproducibles!

ideas contributed by Beth Marquardt
St. Paul's School of Early Learning, Muskego, WI

STORY OF A SEED
Understanding how plants change as they grow

Once a seed is planted, a lot can happen to it! Have students explore the sequence of events from seed to flower with this easy-to-adapt idea. Make an enlarged copy of the cards on page 311. Color the cards and cut them out. Then teach students the song shown, displaying each card during the corresponding verse.

For more advanced students, give each youngster a copy of page 311 after he is familiar with the song. Have him color his picture cards and then cut out the cards and sentence strips. Next, guide the youngster to glue each card and the corresponding sentence on a separate piece of construction paper. Ask him to sequence the prepared cards and then read them aloud. Have him store his cards in a large resealable plastic bag for take-home sequencing and reading practice.

From Seed to Flower

(sung to the tune of "If You're Happy and You Know It")

It's time to plant a little seed in the ground.
It's time to plant a little seed in the ground.
Put a little seed in the ground;
Pat the dirt down all around.
It's time to plant a little seed in the ground.

A seed is planted in the ground.

When the seed begins to grow, it's called a sprout.
When the seed begins to grow, it's called a sprout.
It will need water and some sun—
The growing won't be done.
When the seed begins to grow, it's called a sprout.

It rains. The seed begins to grow.

From the little sprout will come a helpful stem.
From the little sprout will come a helpful stem.
Then some leaves will start to grow,
Getting water from below.
From the little sprout will come a helpful stem.

A stem grows. Some leaves grow.

Then, finally, a flower will appear.
Then, finally, a flower will appear.
With colors nice and bright,
It will be a pretty sight!
Then, finally, a flower will appear.

Then a pretty flower grows!

TAKE A PEEK!
Identifying parts of plants

Students take a close look at plant parts with this supersimple project! Give each student a copy of page 312. Invite youngsters to tell what they know about the featured plant parts. Add to the discussion as needed to familiarize students with some of the functions of the plant parts, such as the ones listed on this page.

Next, have each youngster color her plant card and complete the words on her cover sheet. After she cuts out the card and cover sheet, have her carefully cut the cover sheet sections just to the vertical line. Then help her staple her cover sheet to her plant card as shown. To review the parts of plants, the youngster reads a word and then lifts the corresponding flap to check that she correctly identified the word. **For more advanced students,** have each youngster write a function of each plant part on the back of its flap.

flower: makes seeds
leaves: make food
stem: helps hold up the plant
roots: hold the plant in the soil

GROWING WRITERS
Journal writing

This adorable journal project is sure to help students' writing skills blossom! For each student, staple several sheets of writing paper into a 9" x 12" construction paper folder to make a journal. Instruct each youngster to write his name on his front cover. Over several days, ask students to respond to provided journal prompts (see the suggestions). After a student's journal is complete, have him decorate it to resemble a watering can by following the directions below.

Decorating Directions:
1. Draw a handle on a 6" x 9" construction paper rectangle. Cut it out.
2. Glue the handle to the back of the journal (see the illustration).
3. Glue a 2" x 9" construction paper strip to the back of the journal to resemble a spout.
4. Fashion a spout tip from construction paper and then glue it in place.
5. Add desired decorations.

Journal Prompts
The Best Garden Ever!
If I could grow anything in a garden, I would grow…
One day, I went to my garden and saw…
If a flower could talk, what would it say?
The Lonely Flower

PICK SOME MATH!
Adding or subtracting

Numbers seem to grow at this center! To prepare, secure a die-cut flower or the front panel of a seed packet to each of several jumbo craft sticks as shown. Near the bottom of each stick, write a number appropriate for your youngsters' addition or subtraction skills. Stand the sticks in blocks of floral foam so that the numbers are concealed. Add a label similar to the one shown to identify the activity as addition or subtraction practice. Place the prepared foam at a center stocked with paper.

Each partner, in turn, takes a stick and then announces its number. She uses her number and her partner's number to write either an addition or subtraction sentence. Then she returns her stick to the foam. The partners pick a new pair of numbers for more number-sentence fun!

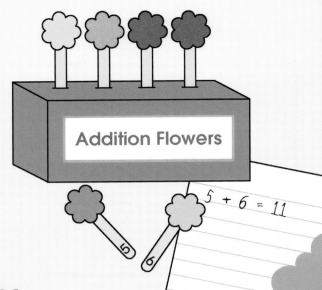

Addition Flowers

$5 + 6 = 11$

FAVORITE FLOWERS
Graphing

Give graphing a "seed-sational" twist! Gather three or four empty seed packets for different types of flowers. Cut the front panel from each packet and discard the rest. Title a sheet of chart paper "Which Flower Do You Like the Most?" Then prepare a graph below the title, using the panels from the seed packets as column headings. After each student contributes to the graph, prompt a class discussion to help youngsters interpret the results.

Sherri D. Ault, Garfield Elementary, Monmouth, IL

FACT-FILLED POSIES
Reviewing plant facts

This display of beautiful blooms not only brightens a classroom, but also showcases what students know about plants. For each student, prepare two six-inch white circles and cut a large blossom from a 12" x 18" sheet of construction paper. Have each youngster write a chosen plant fact on a circle. Then ask him to glue the circle in the center of his blossom.

Next, set out shallow containers of colorful paint. Have each youngster use the paint to make fingerprints all over a blank circle (flower center). As the paint dries, ask the youngster to add a construction paper stem and leaves to his flower. Then help him staple his painted circle atop his writing as shown. Post students' completed flowers on a hallway wall. How pretty!

Plant water grow.

jennifer tipton cappoen

A stem grows. Some leaves grow.

A seed is planted in the ground.

Then a pretty flower grows!

It rains. The seed begins to grow.

Plant Card and Cover Sheet
Use with "Take a Peek!" on page 309.

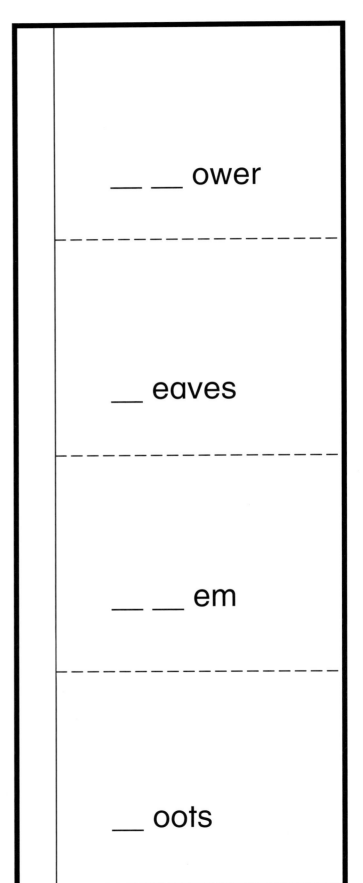

__ __ ower

__ eaves

__ __ em

__ oots

Index